PIMLI

854

THE KING'S GLASS

Carola Hicks, an acclaimed art historian and witty, perceptive writer, died in 2010, in the last stages of completing her final book, *Girl in a Green Gown*. Born in Sussex, Carola studied archaeology at Edinburgh University, and was an actress, journalist and House of Commons Researcher, before taking up an academic career. For several years she was curator of the Stained Glass Museum at Ely Cathedral, and then became a Fellow and Director of Studies in art history at Newnham College, Cambridge. Her books include *Animals in Early Medieval Art, Improper Pursuits: The Scandalous Life of Lady Di Beauclerk* and three fine 'biographies' of works of art: *The Bayeux Tapestry: The Life Story of a Masterpiece, The King's Glass: A Story of Tudor Power and Secret Art* and *Girl in a Green Gown: The History and Mystery of the Arnolfini Portrait*.

ALSO BY CAROLA HICKS

THE KING'S GLASS

A Story of Tudor Power and Secret Art

CAROLA HICKS

PIMLICO

Published by Pimlico 2012

2 4 6 8 10 9 7 5 3 1

Copyright © Carola Hicks 2007

Carola Hicks has asserted her right under the Copyright, Designs
and Patents Act 1988 to be identified as the author of this work

First published in Great Britain in 2007 by
Chatto & Windus

Pimlico
Random House, 20 Vauxhall Bridge Road,
London SW1V 2SA

www.vintage-books.co.uk

Addresses for companies within The Random House Group Limited can be found at:
www.randomhouse.co.uk/offices.htm

The Random House Group Limited Reg. No. 954009

A CIP catalogue record for this book
is available from the British Library

ISBN 9781845951870

The Random House Group Limited supports The Forest Stewardship Council (FSC®), the
leading international forest certification organisation. Our books carrying the FSC label are
printed on FSC® certified paper. FSC is the only forest certification scheme endorsed by
the leading environmental organisations, including Greenpeace. Our paper procurement
policy can be found at www.randomhouse.co.uk/environment

Printed in Great Britain by Clays Ltd, St Ives plc

Contents

List of Illustrations

All the illustrations, unless otherwise specified, are reproduced by kind permission of the Provost and Fellows of King's College, Cambridge.

Acknowledgements

It is impossible to see enough of King's College Chapel and its windows: every visit seemed to reveal something new in the glass. Writing this book has increased even further my admiration and respect for the late Hilary Wayment, who knew more about the windows than anyone and devoted over thirty years to their study. It also revived happy memories of the late Dennis King, eminent Norwich master glazier, who conserved the glass for many years. I am most grateful to King's College, and particularly the Archivist, Dr Patricia McGuire, and the Assistant Librarian, Mrs Wai Kirkpatrick for their kind assistance. I should also like to thank the Honorary Librarian of the Worshipful Company of Glaziers and Painters of Glass, and the staff of the Library of the Society of Antiquaries of London, the Guildhall Library, Cambridge University Library and Newnham College Library. I have received additional help, advice and information from Dr Frank Woodman, Alison Heald of Historic Royal Palaces, Anne Jones, Leonie Seliger, Liz and Chris Walker and Keith Barley.

I am grateful to my agent, Clare Alexander, for her continuing support, and to my husband Gary for reading and commenting on the text. Thanks to everyone at Chatto & Windus for helping to create this book, and especially to my editor, Jenny Uglow, who brought order and lucidity to the windows' tangled and absorbing tale.

Prologue

Today, the chapel of King's College, Cambridge, is inseparably linked for many with the celebration of Christmas. Its Festival of Nine Lessons and Carols is beamed around the world, letting millions watch white-surpliced choristers process through the majestic space to take their places in the flickering candlelight. High above their heads are the chapel's windows, great shadowy jewels on this winter evening, when the focus is on the eager young faces and the solo treble of 'Once in Royal David's City'. On a summer's day, however, the windows blaze into life, walls of floating light and colour that sparkle and ripple to the changing rhythm of the clouds and sun, 'flecking the vast interior with glory', according to one former King's undergraduate, E. M. Forster. And he marvelled at how 'the painted figures sprawl and swirl', enacting the story of Christ's life, and death and resurrection in a series of vibrant scenes that were integral to the chapel's function of prayer, music and teaching.

In the summer you may have to fight your way through crowds of tourists but it is always possible to see the glass because it is set so high in the walls. Many visitors may have little idea of the windows' erratic history, the triumphant culmination of a long-drawn-out building project completed despite wars, the death of kings and extreme religious conflict.

They will recognise some scenes, like the Nativity and the Crucifixion, but may be less familiar with the way the glass links the Old and New Testaments, making the deliberate connections expounded by medieval theologians. Nor may they immediately identify all the symbols that associate the windows so firmly with the Tudor dynasty.

This book tells the untold story of the chapel's stained glass windows and the people who created them, the innovative immigrant artists and craftsmen who worked for the Tudor kings in a turbulent era when foreigners were suspect. For the windows were a royal project, made under the direct supervision of the king's glaziers at a time of drastic political and religious change. In King's College Chapel, art and history come together to commemorate for ever the kings whose wealth and power were reflected in the glass.

Masterpieces can bloom in unexpected places: medieval Cambridge, on the edge of the awful fens, was an unprepossessing spot. Yet out of its mists and marshes, stench and squalor, rose the chapel whose walls of glass and soaring vault would make the town famous.

The fens were the damp, northern equivalent of a desert, its oases the islands that rose out of the flooded landscape and attracted the solitaries, hermits and monks who wanted to escape the real world, like St Guthlac, who dwelled amongst 'immense marshes, now a black pool of water, now foul running streams, overhung by fog, studded by many islands and reeds and hillocks and thickets, traversed by the windings of tortuous streams all the way to the North Sea'. Yet paradoxically these isolated spots saw the birth of the monastic communities that helped turn Cambridge into a centre of learning.

Around the scholars lived sullen, stunted locals (many web-footed, rumour had it) who tucked moles' feet into their tattered clothing to ward off rheumatism, and numbed themselves against the weather with opium made from the local poppy. They stocked the market and fed the colleges from the packed watery larder of the fen. The most popular local delicacy was eels, while pike, tench and bream were prized items offered to visiting royals and dignitaries. Fish traps and bird snares were made from the local willows, and hunters lurked in sedge and reed to catch bustards and bitterns, cranes and ducks. Ordinary people were only permitted to kill enough for their own consumption but the game somehow made its way to the tables of important visitors and their hosts, the privileged, sedentary members of the colleges, who worked with their minds and not their aching bodies.

The town depended on other products of the fen too — reeds for thatching roofs, hay or sedge mixed with clay for cottage walls. The locals sustained the growing population of the university as builders and servants, food providers and landlords. But the fenmen regarded the brain-workers as incomers and oppressors. Town hated gown, always had and always would.

The origins of that antagonism went back to the thirteenth century, when the king first awarded special privileges to protect the handful of fledgling institutions from exploitation by greedy townspeople. Members of the university and occupants of its hostels and embryonic colleges steadily gained immunity from the civil justice administered by the mayor and his burgesses, and became answerable only to the ecclesiastical courts because all of them were ordained in or studying for the Church. Brooding resentment too easily turned into physical violence. The most memorable riot was that of 1381, the year of the Peasants' Revolt, when angry townspeople broke into hostels and colleges, then looted the university chest to seized the hated deeds and charters of privilege which they triumphantly (though naively) burned in the marketplace. The university took its revenge by having one prominent burgess hanged and the others imprisoned.

In theory just a couple of days' journey from London, Cambridge was a distant little town with a dreadful climate. In autumn, eerie fogs rolled up from the surrounding bog and fen, in winter and spring, cutting winds blew straight off the Russian steppes, in summer the moist air brought disease in the form of a local, virulent variant of the recurrent plagues that broke out in all cramped, insanitary towns. The 'Cambridge Fever' struck almost every year and was a pestilence so contagious that an outbreak often postponed the start of the autumn term. Many believed it was carried by the noxious miasma floating in the air, but it was more likely caused by the polluted water of the stagnant King's Ditch that surrounded the town. 'Cambridge, by reason of the neighbouring fen, is much exposed to fever, as I have experienced more frequently than I could wish' wrote one disgruntled scholar in 1550. This contagion was subtly different from the national ailment, the *Sudor anglicus*, the English sweating sickness (so sudden in its attack that you could be 'merry at dinner and dead at supper').

The Dutch theologian Desiderius Erasmus, who lived in Cambridge from 1511 to 1514, blamed all the infections on the filthy habits of the locals:

> *Englishmen never consider the aspect of their doors and windows, their chambers are built in such a way as to admit of no ventilation . . . the floors are covered with rushes, occasionally removed but so imperfectly that the bottom layer is left undisturbed, sometimes for twenty years, harbouring expectorations, vomitings, the leakage of dogs and men, ale-droppings, scraps of fish and other abominations not fit to mention.*

Although the colleges always laid down fresh rushes for their visitors, they did not necessarily remove the layers beneath. Erasmus was charmed yet also repelled by Cambridge, endlessly trying to weigh up whether the stimulating intellectual companionship could compensate for the awfulness of the place and the terrible weather. As for the town's dirt, he demanded 'policemen who should have the charge of seeing that the streets were kept clean from filth'.

In comparison with many other medieval towns, Cambridge had low standards. In the fourteenth century, one Chancellor was so disgusted that he complained repeatedly to Parliament how the mayor and bailiffs neglected their official duties of cleaning and maintaining the streets. The pigs that freely roamed the town caused the worst problems. Officials passed a measure in 1445 that was intended (like modern parking controls) to ban them between the hours of 7 a.m. and 6 p.m. Any pig wandering the streets within this period was liable to be slaughtered, and its owner entitled to buy back the carcass for fourpence, or a penny per leg. Dung was another hazard, although it bothered Cambridge folk less than others. The noxious rubbish heaps outside Coventry's houses were cleared every twenty-four hours, those of Southampton every two days, and Leicester three days, but Cambridge permitted its stinking piles to accumulate for a week before removing them.

In the heart of this teeming, reeking, unhealthy community, labourers added to the chaos and the noise when they began to dig foundation trenches for the chapel that was to be the greatest in England. No one could have imagined that it would take almost a hundred years for all the windows to be installed.

Chapter One: The Warring Kings

THE WINDOWS' CHEQUERED history started with the Wars of the Roses,* the dynastic struggle whose roots lay in the 'Lancastrian' Henry IV's unlawful deposition of his cousin, Richard II, in 1399. Two generations later, the increasingly bloodthirsty conflict destroyed Henry VI before he had time to complete the chapel of the King's College.

From Tudor times, posterity was kind to Henry VI, whose responsibility for civil war, the loss of English territories in France and the country's grave economic decline were offset by emphasis on his spirituality and on his charity in founding a school at Eton and a college in Cambridge to educate poor boys. This was not how his contemporaries saw it. It was only after his inglorious death – no honourable defeat in battle but murdered as a prisoner in the Tower of London at the command of his usurper, the Yorkist Edward IV – that his saintly reputation emerged.

Henry VI succeeded to the throne at the age of nine months, after his father Henry V's premature death in 1422. There was not even enough time to appoint an official regent, so the infant king ruled immediately through his council, under the protection and guidance of his powerful uncles and

* The conflict did not receive this name till late in the sixteenth century.

great-uncle. To celebrate the opening of Parliament of 1425, when he was three and a half, he had to march in procession down the long nave of St Paul's Cathedral, then ride in state through the City. Inevitably, he acquired the sense of a divine right to rule, confirmed through the rituals of his coronation in Westminster Abbey, in 1429, where the Archbishop of Canterbury anointed him with oil from the legendary golden flask shaped like an eagle that the Virgin herself had presented to St Thomas à Becket. He was just eight, and people noted how the traditional crown of Edward the Confessor seemed too heavy for his youthful head. It would have been dangerous to regard this as an omen.

He was doubly sanctified by a second coronation in Paris, because he had also inherited from Henry V the crown of France. This coronation took place a few days after his tenth birthday. Henry's time in France reinforced his sense of being sanctioned by God, twice-anointed and ruling two kingdoms. He had gained a wealth of new impressions, the graceful cathedrals of northern France, the royal abbey of Saint-Denis that outdid Westminster, and the dazzling glory of the royal family's private chapel in the palace, the Sainte Chapelle. This had been built by his own ancestor, the saint-king Louis IX (from whom he was doubly descended through his father and through his mother) to house the most sacred relics in the world, the Crown of Thorns and a fragment of the True Cross, which Louis had acquired, at vast expense, from the Emperor of Byzantium. There were other Crucifixion relics too, and Christ's foreskin, an object much prized by pregnant women, and loaned to his own mother in England to keep her safe at the time of his birth. Louis intended the whole building to be a glorious shrine for these treasures.

Entering the chapel was like stepping into a giant jewellery box, with dizzying slender stonework framing tiers of stained glass windows whose myriad panels glowed like gems and were reflected in the glittering wall surfaces of gilding and mosaic. For an impressionable adolescent with a sense of divine mission, the experience must have been a culmination of sensual ecstasy. Commissioning a building like that would make him a saint too.

As the boy king grew up, some of his court realised that he found it difficult to reconcile his sense of majesty with the patience to acquire the necessary skills of kingship. However, at fourteen, following the unexpected death of his loyal uncle and virtual regent, the Duke of Bedford, he began to take part in the decision-making process and, when it deemed him sufficiently experienced, the old ruling council dissolved itself. In November 1437, it transferred all its powers to the king. He was not quite sixteen.

As well as the crown of France, Henry may have inherited an additional legacy from his maternal grandfather, Charles VI of France, known as Charles the Mad, whose manic behaviour had created the power vacuum that resulted in the English triumph at Agincourt in 1415. It was not a good precedent. As a young man, Henry displayed no overt signs of madness but was growing increasingly unstable. Some daring critics described him as childish, or even foolish, though these were treasonable views. Initially content in his marriage to the French princess Margaret of Anjou in 1445, he seemed, however, incapable of producing an heir, which was the ultimate mark of failure for a king and a dynasty. But there had been a pleasing family expansion in 1437 when he met for the first time his two half-brothers. His mother, Henry V's widow, had been so discreet about her relationship with the Welsh adventurer Owen Tudor that she had not told Henry VI about her second marriage or the existence of his half-siblings until she was close to death. But the young king eagerly embraced his new family responsibilities, allegedly taking care of 'his two half-brothers, the Lords Jasper and Edmund, providing for them most strict and safe guardianship, putting them under the care of virtuous and worthy priests, both for teaching and for right living and conversation, lest the untamed practices of youth should grow rank if they lacked any to prune them'. Such emphasis on the king's sense of duty was a flattering Tudor gloss.

Henry's manifestations of obsessive behaviour and irrational changes of mind, reported during the 1440s, can probably be interpreted as the first symptoms of the mental illness that would manifest itself a few years later. At the start of that decade, however, the king's passion for architecture gave him a reputation for piety which, for the moment, helped keep him safe on the throne. In August 1440, to mark his accession to power, he decided to honour God and his birthplace, Windsor Castle, by converting the parish church in the adjacent village of Eton into something that resembled the Sainte Chapelle, as the focal point of a new school for poor scholars.

At the same time, he decided to found a college in Cambridge, joining the ranks of other royal and aristocratic patrons who supported the university. In September 1440, Henry started buying up parcels of land in the centre of the town, and by February 1441, preparations for what he proposed to call the Royal College of St Nicholas were well under way. The name commemorated Henry as much as the popular patron saint of children, captives and sailors, because the feast day of St Nicholas, 6 December, was also the king's birthday.

In the early spring of 1441, Henry laid the foundation stone for his building works at Eton, then on 1 April travelled to Cambridge where, on the following day, Passion Sunday, he laid the foundation stone for his new college there. A contemporary verse described him as 'kneeling on his knee' in what is now the south turret of the gatehouse that leads to the Old Schools courtyard.

His plans were relatively modest: the new college would consist of twelve Fellows and scholars led by a rector, a fairly standard community for the time, and its purpose was to train priests, confound heresy and honour the Church. They would live in purpose-built collegiate accommodation in the traditional Cambridge arrangement of ranges of Fellows' rooms and a communal dining hall set around a rectangular courtyard approached by a defensive gateway. This complex, later called the Old Court, lay next to another courtyard, then just half-built, that would accommodate the university's various teaching departments, known as the Schools. Henry's initial plan did not include a chapel, because most colleges worshipped in one of the local parish churches; that of St John Zachary was close to the college.

Henry was only nineteen but had instigated two important projects intended to blend educational mission with architectural distinction. This would outdo his uncle, the duke of Gloucester, who gave his library to Oxford, and would draw attention to the smaller university the duke had ignored. Perhaps he already found that immersing himself in building plans, right down to the detailed specifications of dimensions and layout, was far more satisfying than dealing with the problems of Normandy (where French revolt was imminent) or having to endure the constantly undermining presence of his powerful uncles.

Even if the enthusiastic young king preferred creating beautiful buildings for posterity to coping with the real world, it was unfortunate that he came across a new model that inspired him to make radical alterations to both foundations after the builders had started. At Winchester in August 1441, he visited the respected school that the Bishop of Winchester, William of Wykeham, had founded some fifty years earlier, and realised that it was formally linked with the college the bishop had founded at Oxford. Called by the 1440s 'the New College', its original name, the College of St Mary of Winchester, spelled out the connection. So Henry decided to associate his school and college too, and announced that students from Eton would proceed to what Henry now renamed the Royal College of the Blessed Mary and St Nicholas in Cambridge.

His foundations were smaller than Wykeham's, who knew about buildings because he had served as clerk and surveyor of royal castles and manors under Edward III before promotion to the bishopric. He had designed his Oxford college around a whole quadrangle, the first time anyone had used such a plan, its north range formed by a hall joined to a chapel whose lofty walls and large windows were supported by tall external buttresses which ended in pinnacles. Another ostentatious feature was a cloister with a large bell tower.

Anxious to emulate Wykeham's achievement, Henry reviewed his own projects, and revised the statutes of the Cambridge college to increase student numbers to the scale of his rival: instead of twelve Fellows and scholars, it would house seventy, supported by six clerks, ten secular priests and sixteen choristers. Instead of being called Rector, the college's head would become its Provost, as at Eton. In August 1443, Henry bought up more land to the south of Old Court, even though this meant demolishing a dense network of houses and streets, just like in Oxford. Further proof that he was copying Wykeham came when Henry decided that his college must have its own chapel too. He planned to lay the foundation stone himself, as he had done in Old Court: 'for the great devotion and desire we have that it should be devoutly and solemnly done, we had disposed us to be there in our own person'. But unfortunately, owing to an outbreak of the Cambridge Fever, he had to delegate the task to the Marquis of Suffolk, who performed the ceremony on 29 September 1444.

But Henry kept changing his mind. As domestic and foreign problems worsened, he escaped from events beyond his control by spending more time and resources on his pet projects. For Cambridge, he dreamed up a radically different architectural scheme to outdo Wykeham. His college would have the largest courtyard, the longest ranges, the tallest tower and the finest chapel. No matter that work was already well advanced on the previous chapel. Three years after it was started, he envisaged another, twice the size, which, like that of the New College, would occupy the north side of a huge quadrangle. More space for accommodation was also essential, according to the Provost and scholars, who, 'considering their own numbers and those of others daily flocking together', were complaining about having to fit far too many people into the cramped accommodation of the Old Court, itself still under construction. So Henry began to draft a manifesto that would serve as a building brief for his master masons, and prove that he was a greater architect than William of Wykeham.

The first phase was the Mark Two chapel. Starting another building 20 metres (66 feet) south of one that was regarded as obsolete before it was even finished must have seemed like madness to those around the king and to the baffled townspeople. It added insult to injury that the former 'new' chapel occupied the site of the ancient parish church of St John Zachary that Henry had just demolished.

In March 1448, he issued the 'final' (only, for Henry, nothing was ever final) version of his grandiose plans in an eccentric and defensive document that he called his 'Will and Intent' – not in the sense of a last testament, for he was still only twenty-seven, but as a command: this was the king's will, and he intended it to be obeyed. It was extraordinarily specific, and proved how the king had been obsessed for the last few years with plans, designs and measurements. Perhaps he believed he had found his true vocation as an architect. But he also stressed that his real intention was to honour God.

He laid down the exact size, shape and decoration of the new chapel. It would consist of an antechapel and a choir of approximately equal lengths, with no aisles but a series of side chapels off the antechapel. The choir would contain thirty-five stalls on either side for the seventy Fellows and scholars. His calculations included the numbers and shapes of all the windows: 'In the east end of the said church shall be a window with eleven daies* and in the west end a window of nine daies and between every buttress a window of five daies.' As the ultimate status symbol, the entire chapel was to be vaulted in stone, an ambitious feature which would rank it with the greatest of Gothic cathedrals. The materials used must be of the highest quality, including the 'most substantial and best abiding stuff of stone, lead, glass and iron'. However, the internal decoration should be simple and restrained. This chapel would form the north range of a giant quadrangle of two-storeyed accommodation, with towers at the remaining corners and a handsome gatehouse in the middle of the east range. On the newly cleared land between the west end of the chapel and the river there would be a free-standing cloister with an elaborate bell tower 36.5 metres (120 feet) high, taller than the one at New College.

Henry had clearly given some thought to the long-term funding of the project. The Will and Intent promised an annual income of £1,000 from the royal revenues for the next twenty years. He added that £200 should be spent 'to stuff [the chapel] with jewels for the service of God', laid down the wages of the master craftsmen, and concluded by urging his executors, heirs and successors to be faithful to his desires and obey his plans down to the last detail.

Henry laid the foundation stone at the east end of the new chapel in

---

* By which he meant the individual openings in a window, called 'lights'.

1449.* Putting up one chapel after another at Cambridge, as well as making radical alterations at Eton, was further ammunition for those who were beginning to doubt Henry's competence, or even sanity. And his successful attempts to persuade the Pope to grant bulls exempting his college from normal university controls did not make it popular either. In the troubled Parliament of 1451, which tried to set limits to the king's expenditure as one response to the growing civil unrest, the Commons dared to criticise the way he was diverting extra money into his twin projects as extravagant and reckless (in their words, 'overchargefull and noyous'). Contemporary opinion had little impact on the king, but the building works slowed down and suffered cutbacks when the promised annual grants of £1,000 kept failing to materialise. Meanwhile, the country suffered the humiliation of losing its remaining French territories and began to drift towards civil war. Sceptics were vindicated when the king suffered a complete mental breakdown in the summer of 1453.

Henry VI remained in what contemporaries described as a state of total withdrawal for a year and a half. (A modern psychiatrist might diagnose manic depression or schizophrenia.) During this period, his council took the opportunity of reducing royal resources, at a time when the King's College was already so unpopular in Cambridge that the townspeople attacked it and physically tried to prevent its scholars from taking their degrees. This deep resentment resulted not just from its exemptions from local jurisdiction that Henry had negotiated with the Pope, but from the huge site's harmful impact on the town.

In 1455, Henry appeared to recover a little, but it was too late: the damage had been done, both for those who still supported him and those who schemed to replace him. He became an uneasy puppet, barely capable of going through the motions of kingship, tugged between his unpopular French wife and the Yorkist faction, who backed Edward, Earl of March, son of Richard, Duke of York, to replace Henry. The king's only comfort

---

* It has been part of the chapel's canonical history that this took place in 1446. But this arises from the misdating of a letter.

lay in the realms of piety and contemplation. He was reputed to wear a hair-shirt as a warning against pride on the ceremonial occasions when he had to wear the crown, and he spent an increasing amount of time in religious houses, where people commented how much he slept. Yet he had not forgotten his Cambridge college, which might have seemed to him the only good thing left in his life. In 1459, for example, he tried to get work restarted by donating £100 and a set of bells, and the college purchased more building stone. But in 1461, Henry's deposition by the Yorkists put the whole project into question.

The new king, Edward IV, was obviously reluctant to support building schemes so closely associated with the man he had just overthrown. He tried to cut off what little income remained by ordering the revenues destined for the King's College to be diverted to the Exchequer, and it was rumoured that Provost and Fellows were so impoverished that they were reduced to pawning the college plate. Edward preferred to mark his own reign by diverting craftsmen from Eton to rebuild St George's Chapel at Windsor to provide better accommodation for the Garter Knights and a home for his own tomb, in proximity to them for eternity.

Edward made his first official visit to Cambridge in 1462. He could not have failed to notice the King's College – the half-built courtyard ranges of Old Court adjacent to the Schools, the brand new 'old' chapel to the south, and beyond that the gigantic monument to his predecessor's folly, the partially built walls of a much greater chapel. Although the first five bays at the eastern end, their buttresses and side chapels were quite well advanced, the remaining seven bays existed only as foundations.

The Provost and Fellows struggled to keep the work going but it was a slow business, their general depressed state indicated by low student numbers, which had fallen to twenty-three in 1465. But after Edward's wife, Elizabeth Woodville, took over the patronage of the Queens' College (previously supported by Henry's wife, Margaret of Anjou), the king came to realise the benefits of associating the Yorkist dynasty with virtuous educational and religious schemes. Another factor may have been the need to reclaim popularity after his temporary deposition in 1470, when Warwick the Kingmaker put Henry VI back on the throne for six months. By then, the wretched Henry was just 'a stuffed woolsack lifted by its ears, a shadow on the wall, bandied about as in a game of blind man's buff', as one contemporary put it. He was obviously incapable of doing anything more for the college he had founded.

Edward soon fought his throne back, and insured himself against further threats by ordering Henry's death. He visited Cambridge in 1476 and stayed at the King's Hall (a college that Edward III founded to train administrators for the royal household) which had a conveniently self-contained royal suite with its own kitchen and wine-cellar, and was located just to the north of Old Court. Now Edward made a serious commitment to Henry's college when he appointed his former chaplain, Walter Field, to the provostship and guaranteed enough money for work to resume on the chapel. With the prospect of regular royal grants, the masons worked hard to complete the six eastern bays, with the aim of roofing the choir so that the eastern half of the building could come into use. During the early 1480s, the walls rose higher and higher, tall enough for the stonework of the huge window openings to be put into place. In 1482, Edward celebrated Whitsunday in Cambridge, and inspected progress. He attended mass in the old chapel, where he sat in a 'closet' that local carpenters had built specially for the occasion. In the new chapel, the choir bays were almost complete, and would soon be ready for a temporary timber roof: Henry's stone vault would have to wait until the antechapel walls were up as well.

The sudden death of Edward in May 1483, the once golden young man now a bloated, discredited figure, did not upset the chapel's momentum despite the succession crisis when his brother Richard made himself king, usurping Edward's son and rightful heir. The boy's sinister disappearance from the Tower of London, together with his younger brother, would help cause Richard's downfall and breed future claimants to the throne. But King Richard III enthusiastically pushed Henry's Cambridge project forward. In preparation for his first royal visit in October 1483, the Schools were repaired and a welcome procession organised. Richard contributed 20 marks to another building scheme almost opposite the new chapel, the extension of Great St Mary's Church, for long the base for university services and functions, but now far too small. His generosity earned him the promise of an annual service to commemorate the souls of himself and his queen.

He returned to Cambridge in March 1484 and stayed at the King's College, accompanied by his son Edward and his wife, Anne, who was taking her brief turn as patroness of the Queens' College but died a few months later. The town expended the lavish sum of £6 5s on the gift of fish for the king, and the Archbishop of York, as university Chancellor, gave public thanks for the many benefits this most renowned prince had conferred, decreeing an annual mass to be said during the king's lifetime and a requiem mass and obsequies after his death. He gratefully acknowledged Richard's support for the university and his 'devout intention, founding and erecting the buildings of the King's College, the unparalleled ornament of all England'. Attributing the foundation of the college to Richard did seem to be ignoring the facts, but was clearly a mark of Henry VI's political obliteration. (Richard's own oblivion was signalled just two years later when the town accounts hastily referred to 'the Lord Richard III late in fact and not in right, King of England'.)

By early August 1484, the stonework of the great east window was finished and Richard announced his intention of getting the choir in use as soon as possible. He instructed the master craftsmen 'to take stone-cutters, smiths, carpenters, masons, glaziers and other workmen' and purchase all supplies and equipment required. The specific mentions of glass, lead and iron confirmed that it was time to glaze the eastern windows, which would not have been feasible until the temporary roof was up and the scaffolding still available. The royal glazier dined in college that same August, and another London glazier, John Thrower, was recorded as working on the chapel at that time.

Early in 1485, Richard gave a further £360 to Provost Field, 'towards the building of the church within the King's College', and he visited the town again in March (when the university paid his minstrels the fee of 6s 8d, plus a kind 2s 8d for wine). It really looked as if the chapel would soon be functioning, given a committed patron, craftsmen standing by, and all necessary supplies ordered. But six months later, Richard III was killed at the Battle of Bosworth. The project once again ground to a halt.

Chapter Two: 'My Beloved Mother'

AMONG THE HUNDREDS of Tudor symbols in the chapel's glass, the second most recurrent is a squat green tree springing from a little trunk. There are over seventy examples of this motif, three appearing in the top of each of the twenty-four great windows. It has several variant forms: it may be large or small, surmounted by a crown or held up by an angel, it may have red or white berries, or the leafy details may be picked out in black paint. Always prominent, despite the great height, through its strong colour and readily identifiable form, this was the symbol of Henry VII's victory over Richard III at Bosworth Field. The green plant was the hawthorn bush from which the slain king's crown was retrieved and presented to Henry. This striking yet simple image in the glass was shorthand for a whole history that encompassed the end of the Yorkists and the triumph of the first Tudor, whose victory in the battle so literally gained him the English crown.

Henry's true claim was through birth, for he was the Lancastrian heir to the throne. This was through his mother, Margaret Beaufort, great-granddaughter of John of Gaunt, Duke of Lancaster and third son of Edward III. In 1453, when she was ten, Henry VI had made the orphaned Margaret the ward of his half-brothers, Edmund and Jasper Tudor. In the following year, Edmund, in high favour with the king (who then had no heir of his own), was allowed to marry his wealthy ward Margaret Beaufort. She was twelve and he was twenty-six. He proceeded to consummate the marriage immediately, because the birth of an heir would give him control of her estates. However, he had no direct route to the throne because Henry and his wife had at last produced a son. Margaret conceived rapidly, yet was a widow before she was even a mother. Edmund died when she was six months pregnant, and she gave birth to the future Henry VII when she was thirteen and a half. Undoubtedly, these brutal experiences bred the survival instincts that helped her to turn herself into the most influential woman in the country.

She saw little of her son while he was being brought up, as befitted a young nobleman, in a separate aristocratic household. After Edward IV overthrew Henry VI in 1461, Margaret's dangerous Lancastrian heritage was partly neutralised when her second husband backed the new regime. She kept a low profile, tactfully staying away from court and developing the interests in education that would lead her to Cambridge. After the extraordinary events of 1470–1, when Henry VI was briefly reinstated, then put to death after Edward IV resumed power, she had to be even more cautious because her son, as the main Lancastrian claimant, was a threat to the king. Margaret made him flee the country under the protection of his attainted uncle Jasper Tudor. Her situation worsened in October 1471 when her husband died and Margaret sought genuine refuge in her alternative role as a pious educationalist. Piety may have been safer than politics, but she acquired a genuine passion for the reform of learning, which helped to transform Cambridge University – and would lead to the resumption of work on King's College Chapel.

In 1472 she took a new husband, Thomas, Lord Stanley, deliberately associating herself with the Yorkist court since Stanley was a loyal servant of Edward IV. Now she campaigned to reinstate her son. Edward's sudden death in 1483, followed by Richard III's dubious usurpation, strengthened Henry Tudor's claim to the throne and Margaret began to intrigue and intervene on his behalf, forming an alliance in 1484 with her former enemy,

Edward IV's widow, to work for the marriage of Edward's eldest daughter Elizabeth to Margaret's son, the ultimate, brilliant reconciliation between the houses of York and Lancaster. This alliance proved fatal for Richard III, and Margaret's husband, Lord Stanley, tipped the balance at the Battle of Bosworth by changing sides from Richard to Henry. Stanley was even reported to be the man who placed the crown rescued from the hawthorn bush on Henry's head.

Margaret had not seen her son for fourteen years. Yet their relationship became the closest in both their lives. Their letters suggest an intimacy that went far beyond the standard compliments of day. He wrote to her: 'I should be as glad to please you as your heart can desire it; and I know well that I am as much bounden to do so as any creature living, for the great and singular motherly love that it hath pleased you at all times to bear towards me.' She responded equally, beginning her letters with tender phrases like 'My dearest and only desired joy in this world', or 'My own sweet and most dear king and all my worldly joy'. In a letter written on his birthday, 28 January 1501, she finished: 'At Calais town, this day of St Anne's, that I did bring into this world my good and gracious prince, king and only beloved son. By your humble servant, bedeswoman and mother.'

Surviving images of Margaret are consummate projections of a pious, learned woman that make her look like a nun. Holding a book of hours or kneeling in prayer at an altar, she wears a severe black gown and a stark white headdress whose angular coif conceals her hair and forehead, while a widow's wimple covers her chin and neck. Yet her official designation was the King's Mother, a unique title, and she spent much time at court, where, it was noted, her influence and power were far greater than those of the queen.

Her favourite residence was Collyweston in Northamptonshire, a manor house which she extended over the years and turned into a real Tudor palace, with chapel, grand gardens and an extensive hunting park for the king's pleasure. Margaret did not, however, share this residence with her husband, from whom she amicably separated in 1499, an unusual act for a woman at this time. It was possibly a political decision to detach herself from a family whose loyalty Henry was beginning to suspect; it also proved her desire for independence. This freedom enabled her to lavish her time, money and energy on the University of Cambridge.

At the end of the fifteenth century, Oxford and Cambridge still lacked the glamour and reputation of the great continental centres of learning at Louvain and Paris, Bologna and Padua. Oxford, however, was the larger university and its pioneering college founders had encouraged modern studies that reflected some of the humanistic scholarship of the Italian renaissance. But Cambridge, where there was such a dearth of Latin speakers in 1491 that the university had to hire an Italian to help compose speeches and draft letters (his fee was 20 pence per letter), still needed the support of enlightened patrons like the King's Mother.

Margaret had already made her presence felt in the town in 1489, when she gave a buck to be roasted at a feast, and the burgesses of Cambridge responded by presenting her with 6 pounds (2½ kg) of comfits (a tooth-rotting confection of nuts and spices coated with sugar, a standard gift for special visitors), a flagon of the sweet, aromatic wine called hippocras, and three local pike. By 1501, she was a figure of enormous influence and a subtle negotiator in the constant disputes between the university and the civic authorities, intervening by a regular stream of letters, and sometimes even summoning the proctors to Collyweston.

Thanks, in part, to her impact, the intellectual tide was starting to turn. John Doget, Provost of King's College from 1499 to 1501, had studied in Padua and Bologna and wrote a commentary on Plato that showed his knowledge of classical texts and their renaissance interpretations. He was succeeded by John Argentein, a former Eton and King's scholar who had specialised in medicine and astronomy, then extended his studies at Padua University. A worldly scientist, he served at the court of Edward IV, was doctor to the uncrowned Edward V during his fatal stay in the Tower, then physician to Richard III. Argentein made an astonishingly smooth transition to the Tudor regime, rapidly appointed royal physician to the queen and the infant Prince of Wales. The provostship of King's was a suitable reward for his versatile roles as courtier, doctor and humanist theologian. (He provided a Latin glossary of 'difficult Hebrew words' translated into Greek in the New Testament.)

Persuading her son to become involved in Cambridge by supporting a college of his own – especially the one that Henry VI had founded – would prove him to be a forward-looking king who encouraged the new learning, a triumph of maternal influence that also complimented the whole Tudor dynasty. Instrumental in Margaret's scheme was Bishop John Fisher, her long-standing confessor and spiritual adviser. Impressed on their first meeting over university business in 1495 by his direct nature and formidable scholarship, she plucked him from an obscure but honourable career as a Fellow of tiny Michaelhouse to become her personal chaplain and a member of her extensive household. 'She ceased not till she had procured him out of the university to her service', as his first biographer put it. In touch with a whole circle of university men and keen to improve the general standards of teaching and preaching, in 1503 she established the first salaried university professorships at Cambridge, and at Oxford too, and funded daily lectures in theology. But when Margaret's man Fisher, now the university's Vice-Chancellor, was appointed Cambridge's first divinity professor, this was not just the university keeping in with its royal patron, but a genuine response to his scholarship and integrity.

Fisher's reputation rose even higher when the king made him Bishop of Rochester in 1504. On this occasion, Henry told his mother, who had been clearly pressing for the appointment, that it was on the grounds of ability rather than special pleading that he had promoted 'your confessor to a Bishopric . . . for none other cause than the great and singular virtue that I know and see in him, as well as in cunning [knowledge] and natural wisdom and specially for his good and virtuous living and conversation'. Fisher was equally anxious to stress that he had gained the post not through pressure from the King's Mother but through the recommendation on merit from his own powerful patron Richard Foxe, Bishop of Winchester and Lord Privy Seal.

Margaret's next benefaction to Cambridge was the foundation of a college. The first that attracted her interest was the Queens' College, where she became patron after the death of her daughter-in-law, Queen Elizabeth, in 1503. But this was already a thriving institution which did not need much more from her than the use of her name. Her appetite for sponsoring education was now so whetted that she decided to take over a failing institution that was in genuine need of assistance from someone who would encourage the latest forms of learning.

The one that caught her eye was already associated with Henry VI, so her involvement would be an effective way of linking Lancaster and Tudor. God's House had been founded in 1442 to train teachers of grammar. It had originally been located on Milne Street, but when Henry VI cleared the site for King's College, he moved it out beyond one of the town gates, and provided new endowments. After his fall, it struggled to survive until Bishop Fisher, a good friend of the master, John Syclyng, drew it to the attention of his own keen patron, the King's Mother.

Margaret declared herself 'heir to all King Henry's godly intentions' when, in 1505, Henry Tudor acknowledged the 'sincere love which she bears to Henry VI' and granted her letters patent to change the college's statutes. Even its new motto, *Souvent me souvient* ('Keep remembering me'), echoed that of Henry VI's day, *N'oubliez-pas* ('Do not forget'). Founding what she renamed Christ's College was an enthralling activity which exercised Margaret's considerable talents for organisation. To oversee the day-to-day planning, she installed Fisher as President of the Queens' College (having forced the previous incumbent to resign) so that he could keep an eye on progress. With Fisher's guidance, she took a direct role in drawing up the statutes, and handed over generous sums of money for rebuilding. Margaret may have once harboured secret plans to associate herself with the even more ambitious scheme of completing King's College chapel, but with true maternal generosity, she let her son take the credit.

Just as the Yorkist Edward IV had needed some time to see the point of committing himself to the college founded by a Lancastrian king, so Henry Tudor seemed initially content to ignore the half-built chapel that his rivals had adopted. It took twenty years to persuade him that his own family would benefit from his support of the King's College. He had not previously shown any particular interest in Henry VI's foundation, despite having seen the unfinished chapel several times. He first visited Cambridge in the spring of 1486 at the start of the triumphant national itinerary that followed his coronation and returned the following year to boost morale by touring eastern England in the face of a threatened invasion from Flanders. There were further visits in 1489 and 1498. Perhaps his mother's emphasis on the family connections for her own foundation finally made Henry realise the benefits of publicly associating himself with a Cambridge college. In 1506 he returned, and this time committed himself to King's College Chapel.

Chapter Three: A Royal Visit

FILLING THE CHAPEL with Tudor symbols recorded the dynasty. The most frequent symbol in the windows was the red rose that represented the house of Lancaster and so recalled Henry Tudor's royal heritage. Studded like rubies against a background of strong blue glass, the red roses contrasted with the adjacent green of the hawthorn bush or the gold of the surmounting crowns. The design was simple and uncluttered – an inner core of white, encircled by five red outer petals. The bloom swayed on a stem of green or white, sometimes with leaves or buds sprouting from it. The proper Tudor rose combined red and white petals to symbolise the union of Lancaster and York, but that version was far less frequent in the chapel, where there were only thirteen examples compared to an overwhelming total of ninety-four red Lancastrian ones. The message was that Henry was king by descent, not by marriage into the Yorkist family whose badge was a white rose.

In April 1506, Henry VII celebrated St George's Day at Cambridge. Honouring England's patron saint was a major event in the immutable cycle of court rituals that let the king combine festivity and ceremonial, worship and ostentation. And this was the most important of all, the high day of the year, the saint's day that recalled the glorious martyrdom of the country's protector, long celebrated by Henry's eminent predecessors. Richard I had placed his crusading army under the saint's care, Edward III clad his soldiers with the saint's emblem of a red cross on a white ground to frighten the French, and Henry V, crying 'God for Harry, England and St George', won his victory at Agincourt against all the odds, direct proof of the saint's miraculous intervention. After that great day, the Archbishop of Canterbury decreed that 23 April must be commemorated for ever as joyfully as the feast of Christ's Nativity. Henry Tudor did his duty by contributing handsomely towards completing the reconstruction of the Windsor chapel that Edward III had dedicated to St George as the meeting place for his new chivalric order, the Knights of the Garter.

Indeed it was only because the building works at Windsor had made that chapel unusable (they were just finishing the roof) that Henry decided to spend this St George's Day in Cambridge. He knew it as a convenient halt on the pilgrimage route to England's most popular shrine. The chapel of Our Lady at Walsingham commemorated a miraculous apparition of the Virgin Mary, and its healing spring, holy well, glittering inner sanctum, potent, bejewelled image of Mary herself, and relics of the highest authenticity, such as the phial of the Virgin's milk and the finger of St Peter, were magnets for the devout, the guilty or simply the curious. A pilgrimage here was a valid substitute for visiting Compostela, Rome or Jerusalem. Henry had prayed there often, especially during the anxious 1490s when one of the pretend Princes in the Tower, Perkin Warbeck, alleged Duke of York, threatened his throne by claiming to be the true king. Saying prayers at such a shrine was also a form of insurance against spending too much time suffering in Purgatory while awaiting the Last Judgement, which would send you to Heaven or to Hell for eternity. It was no different for king or humblest subject, yet the volume of prayers said over a lifetime, combined with those that others offered after your death, might lop off some of those interim torments. Theologians claimed that Purgatory lasted for around 9,000 years so anything to shorten that was much to be desired.

Coming to Cambridge thus allowed Henry to combine an official function with the care of his soul, saving time for this workaholic monarch. Furthermore – and this might have been the most important reason to him – it pleased his mother, who was by then deeply involved in university matters. Finally, he was aware of this unfinished building that loomed embarrassingly between the monarch and the loyal citizens of the little town. And loom it did literally, in the shape of the huge, cliff-like, half-finished structure that Henry VI had intended, over fifty years ago, to be the finest building of the day and the greatest memorial to his piety. But he had been broken on the wheel of fate, and his vainglorious incomplete scheme now scarred the centre of the town. Younger residents, like the students and clerks who thronged the lanes that snaked through their dense terrain of colleges, halls and hostels, only knew the vast patch of barren ground and the jagged walls. The whole site was fenced off to protect the mounds of stone that weathered away year by year, as each winter frost cut new cracks, while the roots of ivy, moss and willow herb burrowed further into the pitted surfaces. Derelict workmen's huts mouldered away, their roof beams rotted or plundered. The once neat foundation trenches had fallen in, tunnelled by rodents, and were now full of loose earth and rubble. Over this wasteland towered severed walls of dizzying, almost unimaginable height, surely the work of giants. The window spaces were great empty sockets where the wind howled through. Birds perched on the carved stonework, splattering it with their droppings.

Older citizens resentfully recalled how the heart of their town had been ruthlessly ripped out. Most inconsiderate of all, the ruin had blocked the thoroughfare giving access to the riverside wharves that maintained trade and supplied food in a region notorious for impassable winter roads. Such mundane needs counted for nothing when weighed against a fanatic's ambition to build a college and a chapel that would make the world wonder. But then Henry VI was deposed and his Yorkist successors failed to complete the project. So the eyesore became part of the townscape where, after all, new works were always beginning, with scaffolding, masons' huts and mounds of stone and timber everywhere. The only difference was that the other buildings were eventually finished, while the skeleton of King's College Chapel seemed frozen in time and space.

On 22 April 1506, Henry and his magnificent entourage rode into Cambridge. They had left London a couple of days earlier, taking the old Roman road north to the shrine at Waltham Abbey, burial place of Harold, the last Anglo-Saxon king, in order to pray before its miracle-working ancient stone cross. On the outskirts of Cambridge, they were met by the official civic party, consisting of mayor, aldermen and the county sheriff, Sir Anthony Mallory, wielding his ceremonial rod of office. As they entered the town gate and approached the centre, it was the turn of the Church to welcome them. The king's party passed rows of friars – Dominicans, Franciscans, Augustinians and Carmelites, recognisable, like flocks of birds, by their plumage of black and grey, white and brown, assembled in greeting and symbolically representing the theological foundations of the university. The king leaned from his richly caparisoned horse to kiss the ornate crosses that each order proudly held aloft. Then he rode past the ranks of senior students, proud graduates of the university, appearing like peacocks after the muted tones of the friars, clad in the bright robes that distinguished each college, liveries of red or blue, green or purple.

The finishing point was the university cross, an object of extraordinary magnificence and antiquity and an essential component of all such occasions. Supported by the cross bearer, under the anxious supervision of the university chaplain (who had organised some necessary repairs in honour of the grand occasion), the heavy cross was made of gem-studded silver, floridly ornamented with niches containing sculptured figures of saints and angels around the Coronation of the Virgin, with the Crucifixion above.

The king alighted, and seated himself on a cushioned bench (no doubt welcome to one who had been on horseback for several hours), in order to receive the university's formal welcome. This combined religious ritual with intellectual stimulation. After the wafting of censers and the sprinkling of holy water, the Chancellor of the university, Bishop Fisher, delivered an oration in Latin which honoured the royal guest and outlined the university's history. Henry then remounted his horse and made a circuit of the town before reaching his lodgings. These were in the most up-to-date and comfortable accommodation that the town could provide, the Queens' College in Milne Street, near the river. The college's name commemorated his own late mother-in-law and Henry VI's wife. Unlike the unfinished chapel of King's College, the Queens' College was complete, built from modern redbrick and neat half-timbering, in contrast to the old walls and rambling gardens of the Carmelite Friary next door.

The baggage train, which had travelled in advance, had already been unpacked. The king went to his rooms, the 'great chamber' on the first floor of the President's lodge, its floor strewn with fresh, scented rushes, to change out of his travelling clothes into the ceremonial robes of a Knight of the Garter. He rested for an hour then set off on horseback again at the head of a cavalcade of Garter Knights. Their progress led them slowly past the unlovely building site towards the small, old-fashioned courtyard of the King's College. Its current chapel, cramped as it was, had been decorated to imitate as closely as possible the ceremonial settings of the proper St George's Chapel: the back of each stall was hung with painted replicas of the knightly blazons and mottoes that were permanently installed at Windsor. Putting up copies was part of a well-established protocol employed on the rare occasions that the saint's own chapel was unavailable, so that the Garter Knights could occupy their set places despite the different venue.

It took three days to celebrate the Feast of St George. Morning service on the day itself was followed by the grand procession. The wardrobe accounts for one ceremony (that of 1489) listed the king's robe 'of sanguine cloth in grain and damask' and the gifts he made to his queen and to his mother (ladies were not elected to the Order but were especially appointed by the king) were similar robes embellished with the white fur called 'pure miniver' (the winter coat of a weasel), and garters with inscriptions sewn in gold thread. He also presented Richard Foxe,* Bishop of Winchester, with

---

*The name can be spelled Fox or Foxe, but the latter will be used here to distinguish him from Provost Edward Fox.

one of these luxury gowns. On the robes of other Garter Knights, the miniver was mixed with a coarser fur, and the garters embroidered with silk. Even the king's horse was clad in white cloth of gold embellished with St George's emblems, while the sword bearer's horse wore the arms of Edward the Confessor.

In 1506, Henry was forty-nine but looked older than his years. Someone flatteringly described him at that time as being 'of body but lean and spare, albeit mighty and strong therewith, of personage and stature somewhat higher than the mean sort of man be, of a wonderful beauty and fair complexion, of countenance merry and smiling, especially in his communication'. But the once reddish-gold hair was a scanty grey-white, his face appeared longer and thinner than ever, with narrow lips sucked in over the few blackish teeth that remained, gaunt high cheekbones, pale eyes set in deep sockets. His health was not good. Although he had secured his position amongst the kings of Europe, had married his son to a Spanish princess, kept his country out of war, and ruled so powerfully that he had needed to summon only one Parliament in the last ten years, the hammer blows of his eldest son's death four years earlier, followed the next year by that of his wife in childbirth, gallantly trying to replenish the line, meant that he now cared more about preparing for comfort in the next world than enduring the painful futilities of this one.

He appeared a devout man by the standards of the time. Observers noted how he listened to a daily sermon during Lent, and then continued his devotions for the rest of the day. Every week, he gave money for the singing of masses. Although it is difficult to distinguish the duty of a king to support religious foundations and charities from the individual's need to ensure that grateful prayers would continue after death, Henry does seem to have been particularly concerned for his soul. Holding together the long-awaited realm had proved as hard a struggle as his campaigns to seize it. He had many deaths on his conscience. But he could offset the guilt and the weight of his sins on the scales that the Archangel Michael balanced at Judgement Day by good deeds and proofs of virtue: the more buildings he erected and embellished, the more he insured himself against Hell or the extended pains of Purgatory.

Henry VII's welcome to Cambridge by unctuous mayor, bailiffs and aldermen, and by the peasantry lining the (temporarily) spotless streets, concealed generations of hostility and misunderstanding. The king always supported the university, but the university seldom backed the town. The expansion of college and student numbers during the fifteenth century made the locals increasingly resentful of the arrogance of masters and Fellows, or the outrageous behaviour of high-spirited scholars. By 1506, there were fourteen colleges (whose Fellows provided most of the teaching in the form of lectures between 6 and 9 a.m.), plus halls and independent hostels for the junior students, accommodating several hundred people, plus staff and servants. All members of the university, including domestics and the suppliers of goods and services, were accountable only to the university courts.

A related grievance was the wholesale expansion of college-owned land and property, which was exempt from local taxation, and therefore put up costs for local people. Indeed the conversion of buildings into student accommodation was so rapid and extensive that shopkeepers and tradesmen claimed they were being driven out of the town, a complaint first voiced when Henry VI was starting to knock down the town centre to make room for his new college. Townspeople also thought that the university had brought about a general decline in law and order. They viewed all visiting strangers as potentially dangerous and subjected them to an earlier curfew than the locals. Notorious disturbances broke out between rival institutions, like the fights between the residents of God's House and St Nicholas's Hostel that lasted for two nights in 1500, and the 1521 riot when groups of students from different hostels invaded Gonville Hall, burned down its gate and stole all its liquor.

Roads were another problem; the university's building boom contributed to their deterioration but the mayor and burgesses always had to pay for cosmetic street repairs before a royal visit. Even though timber and stone were shipped as far as possible by river, then unloaded onto the wharves reached by lanes from Milne Street (many of which Henry VI blocked), they still had to be transported to their final destination by horse- or ox-drawn wagon. The iron-rimmed wheels played such havoc with road surfaces of gravel or sand and made so much noise that, like juggernaut lorries, such carts were restricted from the town centre by fines used to pay for necessary repairs.

The older colleges were constantly expanding, putting up another hall here, an extra range there, while the new ones were barely finished. Just across the road from the king's suite in Queens' College was the redbrick façade of Catharine Hall, founded some twenty-five years earlier. More recent was Jesus College, established by the king's former clerk of the works, John Alcock, in 1497, a clever, ambitious man who survived the transition from York to Lancaster. The latest of all, where labourers still clambered up and down wooden scaffolding, and cranes perilously heaved stones into position, was Christ's College, his mother's special project, and the example to follow if he wanted to earn himself a place in Heaven beside her.

The university's own church, Great St Mary's, was still being rebuilt, a hive of activity embarrassingly close to the east end of King's College Chapel. Henry donated £40 towards the costs of roofing the nave, as well as 100 oak trees from his estates for the necessary timber. This generosity earned him the privilege of an annual mass in that church during his lifetime and after his death (and he made doubly sure of that by arranging annual payments as well). The roof bosses were gratefully carved with Tudor roses, and with a figure of Henry praying at the foot of the cross, surrounded by angels.

Henry had a good week in Cambridge. He visited the university's intellectual hub, the Schools, where theology, canon law, civil law, philosophy and medicine were taught, and whose new library and chapel were proud evidence that learning was flourishing. Here Henry attended a debate whose four main speakers were so impressive that he gave them £20 to share (a handsome sum, considering the daily wage of a skilled craftsman was around 1 shilling). In a further gesture of goodwill, he presented the whole university with £20 for the drink to wash down his gift of fine bucks. Venison was a rare treat because deer-hunting was literally the sport of kings and the preserve of the aristocracy: presenting a carcass to the less privileged was a familiar gesture of patronage. Promoting spiritual goodwill as well, he donated 20 shillings to the image of St George that stood in Holy Trinity Church beside the marketplace, and he gave 6 shillings and 8 pence to the old hermit who dwelled by the chapel of St Anne.

The king kept meticulous records of personal expenditure. He always began his weekly accounts by itemising the charitable donations he made on Sundays (which included many to 'Our Lady of Walsingham'), listed his offerings on saints' days, and allocated alms for the week ahead. His neat account books are the nearest thing to a diary that this most reserved of monarchs left posterity, a curiously revealing record of the daily activities of a king and his responses to people and places, the things he found important and interesting suggested by an extraordinarily varied list of payments for singers and dancers, gambling and tennis, and his many fools.

Henry's accounts for April and May 1506 prove that it was this official visit that forced him to grasp the nettle of Cambridge's unfinished business – completing the chapel of the King's College. After listing the bucks and the gift to the hermit, he recorded a donation of £100 towards the resumption of work on the chapel.

His hosts had undoubtedly been working hard to persuade the king to take financial responsibility for such a daunting project. As well as dining with the Provost of King's, Henry spent much time in the company of Bishop Fisher, who was not only university Chancellor but his host, as President of Queens' College where Henry was staying. The normally austere Fisher spared no expense on ensuring the comfort of the royal party: the college accounts reveal payments for cleaning and sundry other preparations, including the installation of new window glass in the royal chamber. It was no surprise, then, that Fisher claimed the distinction of being the man who focused Henry's mind and purse on what had to be done, and later referred to this April visit as the seminal event which triggered the renewal of work on the chapel, at the king's expense. One of the functions of university chancellors, then as now, was to raise funds by targeting the most appropriate donor for each desired project. Those who contributed to the buildings and finances of the university and the colleges knew that they would be commemorated in the prayers of those foundations for ever, and that anyone who gave benefactions in the form of books or money would also be remembered. During Henry's week at Cambridge, Fisher had the unique opportunity of driving home to his captive guest the needs of the university and of the King's College.

Chapter Four: 'Your Blessed Uncle'

IN THE CHAPEL'S windows, the third most frequent symbol, after the red rose of Lancaster and the green hawthorn bush of Bosworth Field, was a portcullis, the defensive grille that fortified castle gateways, shown in the glass as a grid of vertical and horizontal golden bars. Like the other symbols, it was often placed under a large crown to indicate its royal connections. The symmetry of the form and the glowing lines set against a white background made it fully recognisable from a distance. The portcullis was the heraldic emblem of the Beaufort family and in the context of the chapel it again emphasised Henry's Lancastrian heritage. Henry Tudor was descended through his mother Margaret from John Beaufort, one of the legitimated bastard sons of John of Gaunt, Duke of Lancaster, by his mistress Katherine Swynford. The portcullis was John Beaufort's badge, and was adopted by his son and then by his granddaughter Margaret.

Boosting the family connection was part of Henry Tudor's strategy to make the Yorkist dynasty seem like a temporary aberration from the true Lancastrian succession. Presenting himself as the nephew of Henry VI was one way for Henry Tudor to assert his right to the throne. He had promoted the relationship ever since he became king, referring, for example, to 'the blessed prince Henry VI late King of England, and the present king's very dear uncle'. He used it when it suited him. But he had ignored, for example, a request for help from the Provost and Fellows of King's College in 1499, when they dared to draw to his attention to 'his uncle's great work abandoned, the splendid building left to stand an unsightly fragment'.

The relationship was more complicated than it sounded. As a Beaufort, Henry Tudor was only a second cousin to Henry VI. Both Henrys had a common ancestor in John of Gaunt but were not strictly uncle and nephew at all. But Henry Tudor was a step-nephew through the second marriage of Henry VI's mother to Owen Tudor: their son Edmund had married Margaret Beaufort, and Henry Tudor was born of that marriage.

Another problem in presenting Henry Tudor as the last Lancastrian's true heir was the embarrassing issue of Henry VI's madness. This was glossed over by projecting the latter's image as a devout, other-worldly man, a royal saint and martyr who had prophesied that his own nephew would become king. Henry Tudor and his official historians promoted this story by playing up an actual meeting between the two Henrys that had occurred during Henry VI's temporary reinstatement in the autumn of 1470. Margaret Beaufort had taken her fourteen-year-old son to the palace of Westminster, where Henry VI allegedly predicted that the boy would reconcile the hostile factions.

Henry VII also attempted to stress his uncle's piety by having him declared a saint. Quite soon after Henry VI's murder, his shrine came to rival that of St Thomas à Becket at Canterbury in its reputation for effecting miraculous cures. By 1484, his memory was so popular that Richard III strategically moved his remains from Chertsey to St George's Chapel at Windsor, where Edward IV already lay in a black marble tomb. Here Henry VI's body was placed in a monument in the south choir that became the focal point of a flourishing pilgrim industry, where several hundred miracles were attested during the 1480s and 1490s.

Henry Tudor quickly realised that it was in the family's interest to foster this desirable cult. He began the campaign to sanctify his uncle, and petitioned pope after pope to undertake the necessary enquiries that preceded canonisation. Alexander VI and Julius II in turn agreed to set up commissions to scrutinise the late king's virtuous life and alleged miracles, the necessary preliminaries to any declaration of sainthood. But despite the powers of the Windsor shrine, sundry papal delegates never found the case sufficiently convincing. (Henry VIII finally let the claim drop in 1528.)

Another way for Henry VII to manipulate his uncle's image was through his network of approved chroniclers, poets and historians. Bernard André was a blind scholar whom Henry brought over from France as part of his triumphal return in 1485. Appointed king's poet, André in his *Life of Henry VII* instigated the report that Richard III had murdered the deposed Henry VI, which gave additional moral justification to Henry Tudor's defeat of Richard. The antiquary John Rous embellished the theme in his *History of the Kings of England* (written between 1486 and 1491) whose text created the persona of Henry VI as an unworldly, saint-like figure. Another piece of hagiography was the life allegedly written by John Blacman, Henry VI's personal chaplain, which gave an eye-witness account of his master's saintly behaviour. Published in 1510, it was probably commissioned by Henry Tudor himself.

Given this background, it was only surprising that the king took so long to make the ultimate gesture of kinship by completing that great monument to his uncle's piety, the chapel in Cambridge, in an act of patronage that would help to save his soul, advance learning and, above all, emphasise his family's rightful hold on the crown. Among his carefully itemised accounts of expenditure during the visit to Cambridge in April 1506, he listed the sum of £100 as the initial fee for a contract to be drawn up between Henry Smyth, the royal clerk of the works, and the Provost of King's, John Argentein, 'towards the building of the church of the college'. And Henry pledged himself 'incessantly to persevere and continue till it be fully finished'. It was a start.

A year later, in May 1507, a meeting was organised between the clerk of the works, the king's master mason and the chief mason of King's College to discuss the start of work. Henry returned to Cambridge in July that year, accompanied by his mother and his son and heir Prince Henry, when they stayed at Queens' College for a week, attending functions and debates and inspecting all the building works. King's College had to pay for repairs to the run-down lane between it and Trinity Hall used by the royal party, bought a sturgeon for their dinner and gave the King's Mother a gallon (4½ litres) of hippocras; the university presented the king and his mother with luxurious 'damask water', made from the distilled petals of Damascus roses, to perfume their fingers.

As Chancellor, Bishop Fisher presided over the annual graduation ceremony, which, because Great St Mary's was still inaccessible, had to take place in the largest available building in the town, the church of the Franciscan Friary (where Sidney Sussex now stands). Here, he used the opportunity to make a speech that hailed the king's generosity to Cambridge, both to King's College Chapel and to the university church, and tried to ensure that the bounty would continue. He set the king firmly in the tradition of all those forebears who had helped create the university: Henry III who built the very church they were in that day, Edward III who founded the college of the King's Hall, and of course Henry VI, 'your most holy uncle', founder of King's College, 'that great project, which no one else but you could complete'. After that Henry's death, the university had gone into a temporary decline (the implied cause being the aberrant reigns of the Yorkist kings) but total destitution was narrowly averted when 'your most splendid majesty at last beamed down on us from high like the dawn . . . and raised our dull and languishing spirits'. And Fisher went on to praise Henry Tudor's exceptional qualities, comparing him to great leaders of the past like Moses, Solomon and Charlemagne, and recalling how he had demonstrated the necessary courage to confront the 'numberless plots and treasons, murmurs and rebellions' which he overcame with the aid of divine intervention. An approving God would give him 'a long, happy and prosperous life . . . and after this life, eternal happiness in heaven' because he was going to complete the chapel that Henry VI had begun. Fisher laid on the flattery with an oratorical trowel: this would be 'an immense work, demanding the hands and power of kings, a work which none besides you could bring to fulfilment, a work destined for you alone'.

It was Fisher's clever emphasis on the close family connection that put Henry Tudor under such an obligation to Cambridge. Gradually, however, Henry came to realise that resuming work on this great monument would record *his* kingship as much as, if not more than, that of the pious man whose weak rule had effectively let the rival Yorkists seize the crown. It would reinforce his Lancastrian connections. And it would please his mother. So Henry Tudor swallowed Fisher's bait and agreed to honour his 'uncle of blessed memory', a man whose 'holiness and virtue' he longed to commemorate.

Although he gave a further £300 towards the chapel that July, work did not start for another year. The delay probably arose because the master mason appointed to head the project, John Wastell, was not available any sooner owing to another major commitment, erecting the central tower of Canterbury Cathedral. He was also involved with other Cambridge buildings – extending King's Hall and finishing the new nave of Great St Mary's. Only when these were all complete was he free to give his full attention to the chapel's walls and windows and the ultimate challenge of vaulting the roof with stone. Wastell now had the time and the money to resume work: in 1508 the king gave £1,400 to the project.

Henry had the money but sensed he was running out of time. In the spring of 1507, he was so ill that people feared for his life. In February 1508, he suffered a recurrence of the condition, which was now diagnosed as consumption. He pulled through again, but the rapid decline in his health by the start of the following year made him realise that he was not going to see the chapel finished. This careful, cautious man, who trusted no one, had to secure the future of his project. To save his soul and honour his dynasty he had to ensure the building would be completed, and that would depend on the money continuing to flow after his death.

He made his intentions clear in an indenture with the Provost and scholars dated the last day of March 1509. More than a contract, this document spelled out Henry's wider aims: the king recalled how 'his uncle of blessed memory' had started the chapel, and announced that he himself intended 'to persevere and continue till it be fully finished and accomplished according to the form and intent ordered and devised by my uncle'. As it was more virtuous for a man to undertake acts of charity during his lifetime than willing them by bequests, he was now making available £5,000 to the Provost and scholars, and to their successors, but they must promise to spend this only on the chapel. Recognising the amount of work that remained to be done, and considering his own state of health,

> in the case that the said £5000 shall not suffice for the whole performance and accomplishment of the said building and works . . . and that these not be perfectly finished by our sovereign lord in his life that his Executors after his decease from time to time as necessity requireth shall deliver to the said provost for the time being as much money over and above the said £5000 as shall suffice for the perfect finishing and performing of the same works.

Crucial to that 'perfect finishing' was glazing the wall openings whose proportions and dimensions the blessed uncle had so carefully specified. The windows would link the two Henrys for posterity, with the first Tudor's contribution as important as that of the last Lancastrian. Although completing the Cambridge chapel would fulfil the architectural plan of Henry VI, Henry Tudor had a free hand when it came to determining its decoration and its crowning glory – the stained glass in the twenty-six huge windows that would occupy more space than the walls themselves.

Chapter Five: The Glaziers' Craft

'STAINED GLASS' IS a mundane, inadequate term for the magical medium that Henry Tudor made integral to his buildings. Combining mystical symbolism and dazzling visual effects, it was the most powerful decorative art of the Middle Ages.

The names for the colours of glass were those of precious stones: ruby, sapphire, emerald, amethyst, ultramarine. Glass-making was the most mysterious of all the crafts, a sort of alchemy that converted base materials into glowing gems, with its secrets closely guarded by the families that ran the glass workshops of Europe. The beauty of glass turned the interiors of church or chapel into the Holy City of Jerusalem, as imagined in St John's visions in the book of Revelation: lit up 'like a jasper stone, clear as crystal', its streets 'pure gold, as it were transparent glass', while the foundations of the city wall were 'garnished with all manner of precious stones' – sapphire and emerald, sardonyx and beryl, topaz, amethyst and chrysolite – so bright that the city needed neither sun nor moon to shine because it was lit by the glory of God.

Glaziers brought this fantasy to life, instinctively understanding how coloured glass transmits and refracts light, and casts a kaleidoscopic glow on adjacent walls and floors. Luminescent panels tempered the daylight and created a sense of religious awe. John Piper, a twentieth-century artist with a profound understanding of the medieval medium, likened making stained glass to 'painting with coloured light' because windows illuminate the building and the people within it both literally and spiritually.

The master masons whose brilliant engineering feats created the complex stone structures of cathedral or parish church knew that these were not complete until their internal sacred spaces were articulated and enhanced by translucent windows. Their richly dappled hues played as important a role as the columns, bays and arches in controlling and defining the building. The structural features that marked the phase of architecture called Gothic were the external buttresses and pointed vaults that enabled buildings to soar in height without needing massive walls to support the roof. This meant that window apertures became larger and larger, virtual walls of glass interrupted only by vertical stone ribs that ran up to the roof. The fan-vaulting and huge windows of King's College Chapel were the English culmination of Gothic architecture, the phase called Perpendicular.

Many of the techniques that Henry Tudor's glaziers employed to fill the vast spaces at their disposal were already several hundred years old, laboriously and ingeniously devised to play a role both decorative and functional in Christian buildings from the sixth century onwards. Responding to the changing requirements of the architecture and demands of the patron, subsequent generations of glaziers explored changing facets of style and design, layout and subject matter, and incorporated new inventions, motifs and techniques. Yet the original foundation of the craft was so soundly established that many tried and tested methods were already written down in a manual compiled in the twelfth century by Theophilus, an artistic Benedictine monk, as a textbook for artists and craftsmen of the day. His section on glazing was still viable in the sixteenth century, when Giorgio Vasari drew heavily on it in the prefatory volume to his ground-breaking artistic biographies *The Lives of the most excellent Painters, Sculptors and Architects* (first published in 1550), which described all the tricks of the trade. Although he was a patriotic Florentine artist whose hero was Michelangelo, Vasari recognised the outstanding achievements of contemporary Flemish and French glaziers, whose success he attributed to their stunning use of colour and exceptional skills at painting and firing glass. He claimed that in the hands of northern glaziers, the art of window-making reached a peak of perfection through a combination of luminous transparency, beautiful arrangement and relative simplicity and restraint. Yet his account of the methods used implied that these had hardly changed since the time of Theophilus. He never saw the King's College Chapel windows, but would undoubtedly have ranked them as masterpieces because they exhibited the monumentality and strength that he so admired in the work of his idol Michelangelo.

Although glass occurs in nature, in the form of volcanic obsidian or crystalline quartz, a man-made version for jewellery and vessels had been invented in the Middle East by the third millennium BC. The Romans were the first to discover how to blow it into thin, transparent sheets that filled openings in walls and let in the light but kept out the weather.

The main ingredients of window-glass are sand (silica), a crushed mineral which has been carefully sifted and washed to get rid of any earth or stones, and vegetal ash (alkali) made from dried beech-wood logs or seaweed. Glass-makers combined these powdery components in the proportion of two parts of sand to one of ash, plus a dash of lime (ground limestone) as a stabiliser, in a fire-resistant clay pot and heated them in a wood-fired kiln at a temperature of around 1500°C (2732°F) until they melted into a sticky mass. Theophilus reckoned that it took 'a night and a day' to fuse these basic ingredients together into glass. As the molten mass began to cool, the glass-maker gathered a dollop on the end of a long narrow pipe and blew it into the shape of an elongated balloon; when this was cooling, he split it along its length and flattened it out. An alternative method was to collect a lump on the end of a long rod and spin it into a large disc. Before either type, respectively called muff glass and crown glass, hardened completely, the glass-maker cut it into rectangular panels.

The combination of sand, ash and lime made a glass that was virtually transparent, but with a very pale greenish tinge. This was called 'white glass'. To make sheets of coloured glass, it was necessary to add metallic oxides, a technique already mastered by the sixth or seventh century AD. The glass-maker added oxides, in the form of powdered mineral earths, to the mixture in the clay pot before it went into the kiln – copper for red or green, cobalt for blue, manganese for pink or purple, sodium for yellow. They called the resulting panels 'pot-metal' glass because the fusion took place in the melting pot in the kiln. Different workshops may have specialised in different hues, depending on the quality and availability of local ingredients.

The centre of English glass-making was Chiddingfold and neighbouring villages around the dense ancient forest of the Weald on the Surrey/Sussex borders. There was another important area in Staffordshire. These were thriving local industries whose practitioners' names showed that the founding families had been continental immigrants in the fourteenth century – like John de Alemayne, or the Schurterres, anglicised to Shorter, who provided plain glass for St George's, Windsor. In the sixteenth century, a further influx of glass-making families from Normandy settled in the Weald. Geography determined the location of such workshops: they needed direct access to unlimited stocks of timber to fuel the glass-making furnaces (beech and oak were best) as well as the wood and sand that were the main components. Glass-makers rented areas of woodland for a few years until the supply was exhausted, then moved on. They often combined glass-making with the farming year, shutting down their furnaces in the summer in order to help with the harvest.

But they could not produce the coloured glass that was essential to the glaziers' art. Wealden glass was a distinctive whitish-green, almost semi-opaque, and therefore incapable of achieving the translucency essential to the best window design. For this reason, many medieval patrons specified that their windows must be made of foreign glass. However, Wealden glass-makers continued to produce basic sheet glass, as well as table vessels. It was a dangerous and disregarded profession. 'In Queen Elizabeth's time here eleven Glass-houses which as nuisances, and in regard there were others at Hindhead, were put down by a petition of part of this County', wrote seventeenth-century antiquarian John Aubrey in his survey of the area. However, in France the production of coloured glass was a major industry.

Those who made glass did not make windows. That was the job of the glaziers, a term whose modern connotations dismally fail to convey the status that it once held: respected professionals whose responsibilities covered a whole spectrum of activities, ranging from the basic installation of plain glass in domestic buildings to designing and making elaborate coloured windows for royal palaces and great cathedrals. The term glass-painter was really a better description of what they did, since it was in the sensitive application of painted detail that so much of their expertise lay, but it did not come into use until the eighteenth century. In Tudor times, they called themselves glaziers.

Commissioning glass for a window opening was a luxury confined to the well-off. In the sixteenth century, an acceptable substitute was oiled linen or parchment, as it had been for the previous two or three hundred years: one foreign observer in 1519 reported that English domestic windows might be filled by 'paper or linen cloth, streaked across with lozenges'. Alternatively, window apertures were fitted with grilles of wood or iron to keep out the worst of the weather, though this inevitably meant most of the light as well. In the hall of Corpus Christi College, Cambridge, for example, only the upper portions of the windows contained glass, while the lower just had shutters. No student rooms were glazed, despite Cambridge winter temperatures. The lucky few who could afford glass windows in their homes employed glaziers to install small diamond-shaped panes called 'quarries' (after the French *carrées*, 'squares') held together with strips of lead. Coloured windows were the preserve of the rich – only nobles, churchmen and city officials could afford to commission them.

The modern term 'stained glass' telescopes three different processes, colouring, staining, and painting, each one complex and requiring the application of many hard-won skills. The huge costs meant that patrons had to invest heavily in a glazing project if the windows were to reflect their status and commitment through their glaziers' skills.

The best sixteenth-century pot-metal glass was made in Normandy, where there were estimated to be at least seventy glassworks. Another centre was the Vosges region of Lorraine. English glaziers had to import all the coloured sheets they required from these areas via the port of Rouen or down the Rhine. This added to the cost of windows, expensive not just because of the ingredients and the time-consuming processes of glass-making, but the laborious nature of getting the glass to England. Panels had to be wrapped in straw, packed in wooden crates and transported by slow ox-cart to the nearest river, transferred to cross-Channel ships, and then to London or the other major window-making centres such as Norwich, York and Coventry. Glazing workshops kept limited stocks of different coloured glass, but generally ordered from abroad only when they had received advances against the next project.

In 1449, immersed in the construction of his Cambridge and Eton chapels, Henry VI attempted to encourage the local production of coloured glass in order to install beautiful windows like those of the Sainte Chapelle. He granted a twenty-year monopoly to John Utynam from Flanders, 'who has returned of late to England at the king's command', in order 'to make glass of all colours for the windows of Eton College and the College of St Mary and St Nicholas [King's College] . . . because the said art has never been used in England'. Utynam evidently made extravagant claims to be an inventor, for Henry granted him permission to 'engage in all arts, works, sciences lawful and liberal' and 'to instruct divers lieges of the king in many arts never used in the realm'. He was also allowed to sell any surplus glass without having to pay tax on it, and Henry's measure additionally threatened any other manufacturer with the prohibitive fine of £200 or indefinite imprisonment. But Utynam's schemes came to nothing, nor was there any competition. (However, the document would be cited as the earliest known example of an industrial monopoly patent.)

One way of acquiring coloured glass without having to import it was through a relatively recently discovered technique called staining. When the glazier applied a compound of silver sulphide with brush or spatula to the back of plain glass and fired it in the kiln at a temperature of around 500°C (932°F), the chemicals in the solution combined with those in the glass to create a permanent translucent stain whose colour varied from the palest lemon to the deepest amber, depending on the rate of dilution and number of firings. If applied to blue glass, the silver sulphide produced patches of green, or to red glass, patches of orange. This truly miraculous effect, which epitomised the extraordinary property of glass to transmit both colour and light, was not mastered in the west until the early fourteenth century. The secret lay in an Arabic recipe recorded in a scientific manuscript that Alfonso X of Spain acquired from the Moors. The formula required the correct proportions of silver and antimony sulphide in a solution of minerals distilled from clay or brick dust, whose concentration could be varied according to the effect required. Once the method had been translated and understood, French glaziers were the first to adopt it, followed by the Germans and English.

The whole procedure was extraordinarily complex. Its success depended wholly upon the glazier's understanding and experience of the instability and unpredictability of how the silver compound reacted to the constituents of each sheet of glass. It was not one for an apprentice. The real significance was that one piece of glass could bear different hues without its luminosity being affected by painting on the surface or by dark lead strips joining two separate coloured pieces together. Sixteenth-century Flemish glaziers, including those who made the windows of King's College, excelled in the use of silver stain, an expensive product because of its cost in time as much as in materials.

Another way of getting two colours on one piece of glass was the technique of 'flashing'. Red pot-metal glass (commonly called ruby) was so dense that it let through little light; to offset this, a small molten lump of ruby was dipped into a pot of molten white glass so that the blown sheet was two layers sandwiched together, one red, one transparent, which made it less dense. The glazier then laboriously abraded one of the surfaces, revealing white details on red or vice versa. There are frequent examples in the King's Chapel.

The third colouring process involved painting on the surface of each piece of glass with brush and pigment. This medium was not oil paint, which would have flaked off, but a mixture made permanent through the presence of ground glass or metal in its ingredients. When fired in the kiln at the correct temperature (between 600°C and 700°C, or 1112°F and 1292°F, higher than that required for silver stain), both pigment and panel softened just enough for the painted details to fuse indelibly into the surface. To make the pigment, Theophilus' twelfth-century recipe instructed the glazier to beat copper till thin, then burn it to powder in an iron pan; to this he must add equal quantities of green and blue glass previously ground to powder between two stones, then mix all together and moisten with urine or wine. Italian artist Cennino Cennini, who wrote a practical manual, *The Craftsman's Handbook*, in the late fourteenth century, advised that this pigment should be made of well-ground copper filings, while Vasari, in the mid-sixteenth century, believed it required iron filings, which he described as like rust. Whatever the precise ingredients, they produced a brownish-black vitreous paint, which was the only colour applied to glass during the earlier Middle Ages. The length and temperature of firing were crucial, and it was necessary to heat the kilns up, then maintain them at the desired level during the many hours required to vitrify paint permanently into the glass. (In the absence of thermometers, glaziers had to gauge all temperatures by the quality and colour of the flames.) Then the kiln had to be allowed to cool until the trays that held the painted pieces could be pulled out and laid aside to get cold.

In order to temper the surface of clear glass from too many patches of dazzling white, without impeding the vital passage of light, glaziers sponged on diluted pigment or stippled it with a rag to create a textured wash. Then they stripped much of it off again, removing the paint with the finest tools – the narrow end of a stick, the point of a needle, or a thin brush made from hog's bristle, as recommended by Vasari – all time-consuming but essential embellishments producing a variety of effects that kept the glass alive, its surface rippling as the sun shone or the clouds passed behind it. Painting faces required a range of implements which varied from the narrowest brush tip for the delicate details of eyebrows and beards down to broader strands if more density was needed. Again, the glaziers used the brush handle or some other sharp tip to remove the paint and pick out highlights in features and hair so that they were visible from a distance, not unlike the exaggerations of stage make-up.

The many phases in making a window started with the patron's approval of a small sketch of each panel that the glazier either drew himself or ordered from another designer. This was called the *vidimus* (Latin for 'we have seen'). Both parties kept a copy: it was like a visual estimate or a receipt against work to be done. One remarkable sixteenth-century survival is a set of twenty-four *vidimuses* in pen and wash, almost certainly intended for the windows of the chapel Cardinal Wolsey was building at Hampton Court in the 1520s. There was a Crucifixion in the east window, while those along the north and south walls told the whole life of Christ, from the Annunciation to the Coronation of the Virgin, the same scheme as King's College Chapel. The designs were lightly sketched and incorporated the central stone mullions that divided the upper and lower portions of each window.

Such designs were the basis for a formal contract agreed between client and glazier to set the time-scale (with appropriate penalties for over-running), costs and advances, materials and distribution of labour. Thanks to the careful filing systems of earlier King's College bursars, the contracts concerning the main phase of the windows have survived to provide invaluable information about the expectations and procedures of a large commission. Once the contract was signed, it was up to the glazier and his team to get on with the work, which they did in combination with other projects, large and small.

The glazier had to scale the sketches up into templates for the full size of the window openings. These were called cartoons; for a large scheme, the glazier was likely to commission other professional artists or designers to draw them. By the sixteenth century, they drew on paper, by now a relatively inexpensive medium, but earlier generations had to use the whitewashed surface of a table, rewashed for each cartoon. The draughtsman would put in the 'cut-lines', thicker lines that indicated where the separate pieces of glass that made up each window panel should be cut, with marks or symbols to show the different colours. The glazier sourced and ordered the requisite sheets of glass, coloured and clear.

Then he and his team cut them into separate pieces, getting the right size and shape by laying them over the cartoon and cutting along the thicker outlines. One of the many mysteries of glass is how it seems to have a mind of its own, and despite the most carefully controlled surface pressure and the accurate following of the drawn line, it can often split in a completely unpredictable direction, a risk compounded by a dense or uneven texture. Even modern craftsmen who have the relative luxury of a well-designed rotating carbon-steel blade cannot always control the direction of fracture. How much harder then for the King's College Chapel glaziers and their contemporaries and predecessors to achieve precision in cutting and shaping, using only a poker-like implement made out of iron strengthened by tempering: this meant being beaten into shape while red hot, then plunged into a cold liquid (which, Theophilus advised, must either be the urine of a three-year-old goat fed only on ferns, or if that was really unavailable, the urine of a small red-headed boy). Once tempered, this crude iron point was held in the fire until it glowed, then was applied to the desired outline on the glass. When liquid was added (spit or urine), the sizzling conjunction of hot and cold caused the glass to fracture. In the hands of an experienced craftsman, the break went according to the shape drawn on the cartoon. Medieval glaziers could not afford the time or the materials to get it wrong. The larger the piece of glass, the harder it was to cut accurately, although minor mistakes could be corrected by nibbling away at the unwanted portion with another handy tool with hooked ends, called a grozing-iron.

Once they had cut out all the glass, the glaziers painted or stained on details such as the features of a face, the folds of a garment, the intricacies of a building, as well as tiny marks to show which panel each piece belonged to (the careful King's glaziers always did this). Then the pieces were put in a kiln to fuse the paint permanently into the surface of the glass. Once fired, they were put back in place on top of the cartoon and fitted together with strips of lead into a series of panels that would fill each window opening.

Lead was a metal that was strong and durable yet flexible enough to support a great mosaic of glass against extremes of weather or temperature. The glaziers bought it in shapeless lumps, then worked it into pliable strips grooved on both sides into which they carefully slotted the pieces of glass, and reinforced the joins by soldering them on each side. Called 'calmes' (from the Latin *calmus*, or 'reed'), these strips were originally cast in moulds, but by the sixteenth century glaziers extruded them from a lead mill. Every complete small panel was framed by wider, broader lead strips; the King's College Chapel contract specified extra-strong lead for additional support of those very large windows against the Cambridge east wind. Lead and glass were a perfect combination of the functional and visual. But the balance had to be right: too many small pieces of glass in a window meant more time-consuming and light-blocking leadwork. The final stage was making the panels weatherproof by rubbing them all over with a putty-like mixture of lime, lead and linseed oil that hardened and filled in any remaining gaps.

The essence of good stained glass design lay in its two-dimensionality, the contrast between patches of colour and the dark strips of lead that constrained and demarcated them, like ink outlines framing tinted washes. From these materials, the glaziers created tiers of figures – hierarchies of angels and saints, prophets and apostles hovering around the key scenes from Christ's life, from Annunciation to Ascension, to bring the teaching of clerics alive before the eyes of the congregation. It was an art of set postures, stylised settings and symbols, religious and heraldic. These had not changed very much for several centuries, although the structural advances of Gothic architecture meant that larger windows provided space for an epic narrative cycle. The great windows of King's Chapel display a medium that had truly reached maturity.

What Henry VII found so attractive in the work of modern glaziers was the way they were beginning to change the nature of this ancient craft. While demonstrating their effortless mastery of the familiar old methods, Henry's glaziers were also pioneering revolutionary techniques and approaches. In addition to the monochrome dark pigment, they had access to a range of vitreous paints in different colours, the first generation to employ this new technology. It meant a total shift in artistic aims, because it was now possible to apply separate colours to one piece of glass, like painting in oils on a sheet of canvas. One consequence was that the function of the strips of lead joining pieces of coloured glass together began to change. For it was sometimes easier and quicker to cut rectangular panes of white glass as a ground for painting, rather than labouring with heated rod and grozing-iron to cut awkward curved shapes out of intransient pot-metal reds or blues. This meant that instead of providing strong clear outlines that contributed to the design, many leads merely served to hold the panes of glass together, something to be concealed rather than integrated.

Creating such beauty was not without risk. Most crafts posed some sort of hazard to their practitioners, but the production of stained glass windows involved a whole spectrum – getting poisoned, burned, cut or falling from a great height. Making glass was bad enough: a negligent glass-blower might get his breathing wrong and inadvertently inhale flames and molten glass. (One tip was to remove the end of the blow-pipe from your mouth the second you ran out of breath.)

Lead, the essential framework of every window, was a poisonous metal which glaziers handled all the time, yet hand-washing was unlikely to have played much part in workshop routine. They also ingested it by breathing in the minute particles generated by cutting the strips to the desired length. Another poison in the workshop was antimony sulphide, an essential component of silver stain.

The sharp iron blades that cut lead also cut fingers. Far worse was the prime material, glass, whose needle-like splinters easily embedded themselves into the skin and whose lethal sharp edges could slash through flesh more keenly than any knife. Even if the blood loss was not too severe, open wounds were prone to infection and the chance of fatal blood poisoning.

Another danger was fire. Glaziers' kilns were heated for hours or days at a time to fuse the paint or stain. When the door was opened, as it regularly was to insert or remove the trays of glass, a misplaced spark landing on a stack of fuel might set the whole workshop ablaze, and in the worst cases, the flames could spread to neighbouring timber-framed buildings in the dense streets. John Stow, in his *Survey of London* (1598), mentioned a former glass-making house in Tower Hill destroyed by a fierce fire that was fuelled by the 40,000 billets of wood kept there to heat the kilns. There was also the constant risk of burns and blisters from the red-hot tip of the irons that cut glass and melted solder.

Installing windows required glaziers carrying fragile, heavy panels to climb scaffolding of swaying wooden poles lashed together with rope. Then they had to balance up there in order to ease the glass into an unresisting framework of stone and iron. There is an honourable roll-call of medieval and later architects who fell from scaffolding, from William of Sens in Canterbury Cathedral in the twelfth century down to George Basevi at Ely Cathedral in the nineteenth. Posterity has not recorded the names of glaziers similarly sacrificed in the course of their work, but numbers must be high. The glowing panels set high in soaring tracery are their memorial in more ways than one.

Chapter Six: 'Rainbow Round the Throne'

S TAINED GLASS WINDOWS were as important for communicating political messages as for religious ones. The nature of the medium – its high visibility, large scale and scope for the repetition of key motifs – made it integral to the significance and impact of a royal building. Windows could flaunt Tudor badges as effectively as other media, using bright, recognisable shapes whose colour was as important as their design. Even the windows of his Wardrobe in the suite Henry Tudor refurbished in the Tower of London contained glass roundels painted with the Tudor rose and the Beaufort portcullis. In Westminster Hall, the largest space in London, Henry had the great windows at the west end new-glazed with the arms of England and twelve large panels of roses and portcullises. This glass made a tapestry of translucent Tudor heraldry to complement the gleaming silk and gold threads of the costly hangings on the walls, and reflected the carving over the north door of the lions of England, and a rose surmounted by a crown.

If Henry had appeared to be dragging his feet over involving himself with the Cambridge chapel, it was mainly because he was already heavily committed to other important building projects, especially the two ambitious schemes of his later years, the Savoy Hospital and his memorial chapel in

Westminster Abbey. He had little reason, let alone spare money, to become responsible for another. All these commissions were more than enough to belie his reputation as a frugal, cautious man, even a miser (the hostile interpretation of Francis Bacon, in his early seventeenth-century history of the reign). Henry enjoyed ostentation and extravagant gestures that demonstrated the grand state he believed appropriate to a king and his heirs. Stained glass windows of the highest quality were an important part of the majestic image he sought to project.

Palaces were an essential backdrop for Henry's self-promotion. He spent much time at Sheen, an ancient royal residence by the Thames within convenient rowing distance of London. He began improving it in 1495, but a fire that destroyed all the old parts two years later gave him the opportunity for a fresh start. He renamed the building Richmond, after his father's Yorkshire earldom, which his poets punned into Rich-Mount to express the general luxury of the site. This was Henry's chance to prove himself the equal of other European monarchs by adopting the latest continental styles: Richmond was built of red bricks imported from the Netherlands, while its turreted façade and long, glazed galleries imitated the chateaux of northern France. Visitors honoured by an invitation to the king's apartments approached them by a gallery that was 'paved, glazed and painted . . . with badges of gold, as roses, portcullises, and such other', while the great bay windows, another architectural innovation, contained more Tudor symbols. These all complemented the sculptured figures in the great hall, deliberately selected to illustrate the lineage of the Tudors, starting with the legendary founder, the Trojan wanderer Brutus, grandson of Aeneas. King Arthur was part of the family tree as well, and elsewhere coats of arms juxtaposed these great names with those of Edward the Confessor and William the Conqueror.

Despite the palace's official functions, the king was at his most relaxed here, and the image of the stern, industrious ruler was allayed by the presence of bowling alleys, tennis courts, archery butts and facilities for gambling, dicing and playing chess, all of which he enjoyed. Yet he balanced leisure and pleasure with piety, paying for a friary to be built next door to the palace and physically connected to it by a walkway with gallery above that led Henry directly to the royal pew in the friars' church. Here the king's glazier installed stained glass in the west window, and the rest of the building was sumptuously decorated with paintings and carvings.

At Greenwich Palace too, Henry paid for a neighbouring friary. This scheme was originally devised by Edward IV, but Henry Tudor indelibly associated his own line with the Grey Friars' church by putting himself and his whole family into the east window. The actual glass has not survived, but the brief has been preserved, so specific and flattering that it must have been drawn up for the king's approval. It was for a five-light window that linked the royal family with the saints in Heaven and with their own saintly ancestors. The central images were full-length figures of King Henry and Queen Elizabeth, flanking a 'great red rose'. The king was to be shown 'like a young man…standing in his royal robes of state of purple colour'. Family members featured along the bottom as half-length figures, a standard way of showing the donors of a window. The queen was to be 'like a young lady . . . over her head a cloth of state with valance powdered with portcullises, red roses and white roses', while the portrait of Henry, placed beneath inspirational forerunners the Emperor Constantine, St Helena and St Louis, was to have 'red roses only'. Lady Margaret Beaufort wore 'apparel like to the estate of a Princess or a Duchess and a coronet on her bare head', and her valance was sprinkled with portcullises and red roses. The arms of England and France hung on an adjacent tree.

At St George's Chapel, Windsor, Henry sought to combine patriotism with dynastic promotion. Ignoring the uncompleted choir begun by Edward IV, he commissioned a new Lady Chapel that he intended to be the fitting home for his own tomb, associating it with Henry VI's shrine, already such a magnet for pilgrims. But in 1498, he changed his mind and chose a new location for both these definitive memorials. The Abbot of Westminster, perhaps in a general attempt at fund-raising for his own fiefdom, announced that Henry VI had always wanted to be buried in Westminster Abbey. As this was the time when Henry Tudor was petitioning the Pope to confirm his uncle's sainthood, he warmly backed the abbot's scheme to have the remains moved from Windsor to London. This meant that the work at Windsor slowed down, and indeed might not have been finished at all without the financial support of Sir Reginald Bray, one of Henry's councillors. Although the windows there were not completed till after his death, Henry would have approved of them, a panoramic range of ancestors and heroes, Bible figures and saints, all carried out by the skilled hands of the royal glazier and his team.

His works at Richmond, Greenwich and Windsor all represented additions and improvements to existing buildings. But serious patrons had to start from scratch. One effective way of demonstrating charity was for Henry to provide a new hospital in London. Sheltering the homeless and tending the sick were two of the seven corporal acts of mercy that helped to save the soul from some of Purgatory's torments. (Henry's will specified a third category who needed assistance, 'miserable prisoners', to whom he left money on condition they remembered to pray for him.) At the same time, it was another fine opportunity for promoting the family brand, for the location he chose was the site of the old Savoy Palace, the London home of his Lancastrian ancestor John of Gaunt. This great charitable foundation would prove that Tudor London was the equal of Italy, for Henry copied the whole idea – its rules and regulations, provision of beds for the homeless, cruciform plan, integral chapel and elaborate decoration – from the hospital of Santa Maria Nuova in Florence.

Although he had planned it for a long time, work on the Savoy did not start until 1509, the year of his death. Henry's will reminded his executors of their duty to exhort his beneficiaries in the Savoy 'to give praise to Almighty God for the remission of our sins and the salvation of our soul'. Essential to this process was the 'Doom', or Last Judgement, window in the hospital's chapel that the royal glazier installed. Here the paupers had the opportunity to contemplate their own fate as well as the king's, since it was a condition of obtaining a free night's board and lodging (preceded by a compulsory wash) that they must pray for Henry's soul. As further reminders of his munificence, the royal arms, flanked by roses and portcullises, were carved over the main gateway, the warders' uniforms were embroidered with red and gold roses and they even wore badges in the shape of the Tudor rose.* Each bed had a coverlet embroidered with roses to remind the paupers yet again where to direct their obligatory prayers. After Henry's death, his executors handed over to Westminster Abbey for safe-keeping the sixty-seven bags of money calculated necessary to pay for the Savoy Hospital.

Even more costly was the chapel in Westminster Abbey that came to bear his name. Just as Henry VI had devoted himself to planning his Eton and Cambridge foundations, so Henry Tudor was preoccupied with creating a 'sumptuous and solemn chapel' beyond the east end of the abbey that would be his family's monument for posterity. This was an act of extraordinary confidence, for Westminster Abbey was firmly associated with its founder Edward the Confessor, England's saint-king, to honour whose shrine Henry III had put up a whole new structure in the latest French Gothic style of the thirteenth century. Planning to insert himself and his uncle for posterity in a dazzlingly modern extension beyond the high altar filled with Tudor symbols was Henry VII's way of showing that he was not a usurper but a monarch taking his rightful place among the monuments of England's greatest kings. He buried his infant son Edmund, who died in June 1500, beside the Confessor's shrine.

Henry involved himself in every detail of this building, first getting the ground cleared as ruthlessly as Henry VI had done in Cambridge. Then he devised an elaborate decorative scheme of complementary glass and sculpture that would enhance the architecture and proclaim Tudor supremacy. His will gave the specifications: 'the walls, doors, windows, arches and vaults, and images within and without, be painted, garnished and adorned with our arms, badges, cognisances and other convenient painting in as goodly and rich a manner as such a work requireth, and to a King's work appertaineth'. The results were a tour de force by the king's master craftsmen. Its impact, colour and dazzle earned the building the accolade of *miraculum orbis universalis*, 'the wonder of the whole

* Surviving examples can be seen in the Museum of London today.

world', according to antiquary John Leland, who knew it in its heyday.

Despite the biblical and historical implications of the statues of saints and prophets, kings and martyrs, a hundred inside and another fifty outside the building, much of the ornament was distinctly secular and would have been more appropriate in the great hall of a palace. Below the rows of sculptured figures all the way round the nave were half-figures of angels whose upraised arms joyfully supported crowns, interspersed with motifs of rose, portcullis and the fleur-de-lys that symbolised the kings of France: Henry was proud that among his 'noble progenitors and blood' who already lay in Westminster Abbey, was his paternal grandmother 'of right noble memory, Queen Katherine, wife to Henry V and daughter to King Charles of France'.

The fleurs-de-lys carved in Westminster Abbey were the source for those in the Cambridge windows. In the tracery, there are almost as many fleurs-de-lys (forty-nine) as portcullises (fifty-three), reminding people that Henry was not just a Lancastrian but also the great-grandson of a French king. The ancient badge of the French royal house, the lily, also referred to the purity of the Virgin, and its stylised tripartite shape to the Trinity. But in the Cambridge glass, the repetitions of the deep golden, fleshy plant were further proof of the many distinguished strands of Henry's ancestry.

For his chapel in Westminster Abbey, Henry was particularly concerned with the windows. He insisted that, like the stonework, they must include 'arms, badges and cognisances'.* A seventeenth-century visitor described windows whose every pane contained a red rose or the initial H surmounted by a crown, while nineteenth-century restorers noted other panels with the familiar panoply of Tudor symbols, and the daisy-marguerite that recalled Margaret Beaufort too. In addition to these, Henry commanded that there should be 'images' in the glass, meaning the figures of prophets and saints, to echo the roll-call in the sculpture.

He also knew that contemporary glaziers could create more complex narratives. His third requirement for the glazing was 'histories', whose

---

* A general term for identifiable heraldic motifs.

details Henry had selected or approved himself, for his will referred to the windows' theme having been 'by us readily devised and in picture delivered to the Prior of St Bartholomew's beside Smithfield, master of the works of our said Chapel' as if he had already inspected the designs. The prior, William Bolton, had served as master of the king's works for the last few years, and Henry trusted him.

Henry specified the subject of these history windows as 'the Old Law and the New' – scenes from the life of Christ as told in the New Testament, together with Old Testament predictions of them, thus linking Judaic and Christian belief in a time-honoured tradition. The idea was not new. But Henry intended the familiar theme to be interpreted in the most up-to-date style, combining the modern architecture and decoration of the building in a programme that would show off the innovative nature of the king's glaziers. Instead of whole rows of frontal figures occupying separate, stone-framed panels, Henry wanted the windows to be filled with dramatic Bible scenes set against realistic backgrounds, enacting the drama of Christ's Life, Death and Resurrection in a radically truthful manner. This majestic theme, defined and approved by Henry in his lifetime, provided the exact model for the windows of King's College Chapel: his executors took his instructions for Westminster Abbey as the brief for the Cambridge windows too.

As he implied in his will, Henry knew he would not be alive to see these buildings completed. But he died content in the belief that all would be done as he desired, and trusted his executors to ensure that the chapels would be 'wholly and perfectly finished in every behalf'. The one in Westminster Abbey was ready within about five years of his death. He would not have died in peace had he known how long it would take to finish all the windows of King's College Chapel.

Chapter Seven: Beasts and Badges

IN THE VERY centre of the Cambridge chapel's East Window, immediately above Christ on the Cross, the focal point of the entire glazing scheme, is the figure of a red dragon, a splash of colour which draws the viewer's attention upward into the tracery. This dragon is a four-footed creature with a saurine muzzle and scaly wings whose body otherwise resembles a lion with a rampant tail; above it is the royal standard bearing the arms of England. The vibrant ruby glass makes it stand out as an eye-catching symbol in the largest and most significant window of all, and the one whose tracery contains twice as many Tudor references as all the others. The rest are there too – rose, portcullis, hawthorn and fleur-de-lys – but this is the only example of the red dragon in the glass of the whole chapel. Important enough to fill this key position, its significance was slightly different from the other Tudor symbols. It referred to Henry's Welsh ancestry which, although not part of his claim to the throne, demonstrated yet another aspect of his ancient lineage.

In order to prove his right to rule, Henry VII and his propagandists rewrote recent history and promoted the signs and symbols of the dynasty. The official Tudor view of the Wars of Roses was a bloodthirsty dynastic struggle caused by the unnatural and ungodly deposition of an anointed monarch, Richard II. The usurpation of one line by another was a delicate matter which Tudor historians skirted by implying that Henry's Welsh descent set him apart from the internecine disputes, making him a truly British king capable of reconciling the warring races.

Bernard André began his official history of Henry's reign by tracing the family tree back to the legendary ancient British king Cadwallader, whose descendants would one day rule England again, according to the prophecy made by twelfth-century chronicler Geoffrey of Monmouth. Geoffrey's *History of the Kings of Britain* traced their descent from the Trojan hero Brutus, told of Merlin's vision of a struggle between the white dragon of the invading Saxons and the red dragon of the western British, and predicted the return of a new King Arthur to lead the Britons to victory. Geoffrey described Cadwallader as the last British king, and Henry's grandfather Owen Tudor boasted of his descent from this famous ancestor. Henry's approved biographer, Polydore Vergil, rubbed this in: Owen was 'a gentleman of Wales, adorned with wonderful gifts of body and mind, who derived his pedigree from Cadwallader, the last king of the Britons'.

On Henry's great march from Milford Haven through Wales on the way to Bosworth Field, his battle standard bore the red dragon set against a background of green and white, the distinctive Tudor colours, in order to recruit the popular support essential to fulfil Merlin's prophecy of reconciliation. He presented the actual standard to St Paul's Cathedral (together with another bearing the arms of St George) so that all would remember the symbol of Tudor victory. The dragon became one of the supporters of his coat of arms, and also featured on the revised coinage of the realm.

Some people might have recalled that Edward IV had already played the Cadwallader card to justify his own usurpation (though claiming his descent via the Mortimer line, not the Tudor). But Henry adopted many features of the efficient Yorkist propaganda machine. Edward IV had attempted to revive the cult of Arthur, king of Britain, as indeed had Edward III, a hundred years earlier, when he tried to present *himself* as the new Arthur and founded a short-lived Order of the Round Table, before establishing the Order of the Garter instead.

Henry took all this on board. He reclaimed the ancient prophecy for his own family by naming his first-born Arthur, and arranging for the birth to take place at historic Winchester, home of the Round Table. Chroniclers and poets, headed by Henry's own man André, defined the Tudor victory of 1485 as the start of a new era, yet one which fulfilled and reconciled all the conflicts of the past. Henry was both the new Arthur and the heir of Henry VI. There was even a modest reinstatement of Edward IV's reputation, because Henry needed the support of ex-Yorkists and was married to Edward's daughter: it was not sensible to promote their children's grandfather as a villainous usurper. Henry's authors reserved their real venom for Richard III, the Yorkist scapegoat, now accused of murdering Henry VI as well as the innocent Princes in the Tower. Edward's rehabilitation was even signalled in King's College Chapel, where a few of the tracery glass panels show his variant of the white rose of York, with the sun's rays around it.

Interpretations of recent events were thus expressed in glass and stone by the badges and beasts that decorated the persons, possessions and palaces of those who played their parts in the Tudor drama, a language of signs and symbols that could easily be read by those who understood it. Different motifs had subtly different functions. A 'badge' was a mark of ownership, 'cognizances' or 'devices' referred generally to the arms depicted on different parts of a shield, 'supporters' were the animals on either side of a shield. Depicted in many different materials – carved and gilded in wood or stone, embroidered on rich fabrics, cast out of metal – such designs really came into their own in windows, the main colours immediately recognisable as the family's livery, while their stylised forms told the family's history. The skilled hands of the glazier wrote these crucial messages through the techniques of cutting and staining, painting and leading, celebrating his patron down the length of a gallery or in the heights of a chapel window.

*

Just like New Labour in the 1990s rebranding itself with the aid of a red rose, Henry VII promoted his family by inventing a completely new Tudor version of that well-loved flower. William Shakespeare, writing in the days of the latest and greatest Tudor, Henry's granddaughter Elizabeth, summed it up in *Richard III*, when Henry Tudor delivers the play's closing speech:

> We will unite the white rose and the red.
> Smile, heaven, upon this fair conjunction,
> That long hath frowned upon their enmity.

Shakespeare's words proved the success of Henry's image-makers in fusing the two roses. Edward I had used a rose as one of his badges, while red and white were both Plantagenet livery colours. A red rose was just one of several devices adopted by the Lancastrians, and the white rose, similarly, was one of several Yorkist badges. Just as the rose was long believed to be supreme over all other flowers, so the house of Tudor developed it to elevate itself above previous dynasties.

For Henry, the new rose was an advertisement for his own dynastic policy, the long-awaited coming-together of two warring strands. The proper Tudor rose was composed of two circlets of petals, the outer red and the inner white; an alternative form was a red rose and a white rose springing from the same stem. The combination of the two may have originated in the pageantry that welcomed the new king to York in April 1486. Under a canopy representing heaven, there was an idyllic scene of ingenious artificial trees and flowers, the most prominent 'a royal rich red rose . . . unto the which rose shall appear another rich white rose . . . and thereupon shall come from a cloud a crown covering the roses'. Perhaps this was York's deliberate attempt to insert its own historic emblem into the symbolism of the Tudor dynasty. A rose with red petals surrounding white ones also symbolised Henry's Lancastrian inheritance overriding his wife's Yorkist line, and it completely overwhelmed the flimsy claims of Perkin Warbeck, pretender Duke of York, whose backers called him the White

Rose. So for Henry, the Tudor rose stood for the new dynasty and its power over the past.

The king's followers had to wear their sovereign's distinctive flower, while other retinues were recognised by equivalent emblems. Known as 'badges' (Shakespeare referred to the 'household badge' in *Henry VI*, Part II), they demonstrated the loyalty and allegiance of the bearer to a particular great family. This pared-down motif originated on the battlefield as a simple way of distinguishing friend from foe, for there was no time to decipher the complex armorial bearings on shields. The badge rapidly became a widespread form of family identification that a nobleman stamped as a blatant mark of ownership on the livery of his whole household, on his possessions and on his properties.

Although Henry had a new family badge, it was based on old precedents, and he used other well-established symbols to remind people of his multiply royal ancestry. The most popular were called 'beasts' because they were in the shape of animals. By the fifteenth century, most great men had adopted a distinctive beast badge; a manual for funeral etiquette written in Henry's reign prescribed that each noble should be recognisable by 'a standard and his beast therein'.

The two beasts that supported Henry's shield were the red dragon of Wales and the white greyhound of Richmond. The latter reminded people of his Lancastrian pedigree because it had been adopted by John of Gaunt, Henry IV, Henry V and Henry VI. When the latter made Edmund Tudor the Earl of Richmond, he granted his half-brother the greyhound as a supporter of his new coat of arms. So Henry VII adopted his father's beast and used it as much as the rose and the dragon. When painted, its red and gold collar made a wonderfully rich contrast against the smooth white background of its body. Images of dragon and greyhound were liberally distributed throughout the Westminster Abbey chapel, even in the gilt-bronze surrounds of Henry's tomb: he would have delighted in the rows of hounds and dragons embedded in the railings in snarling confrontation for eternity. In Cambridge, the greyhound appears in profusion in the sculpture on the walls but, curiously, not at all in the glass.

Henry and his mother both promoted the Beaufort emblems. The portcullis in the chapel's tracery was an integral element of the Tudor repertoire and might also have been making the visual pun, Tudor, two-door, because some castle entrances had two portcullises to trap invaders between them. It was also the personal symbol of Margaret Beaufort. Henry's letters patent granting his mother permission to found Christ's College were ornamented by a delicate miniature painting that included portcullises, Tudor roses, greyhound and dragon, and a liberal sprinkling of marguerites. Her glaziers alternated portcullis and rose in the Christ's chapel glass, and in the hall windows at St John's. Her other main symbol was the Beaufort yale, an exotic variant on the heraldic antelope that represented Margaret's father, but had one horn pointing forward and the other back. Two yales supported her arms, like the fine specimens over the gateways of Christ's College and St John's College. At Collyweston Manor, her glazier, a local Peterborough man, misunderstood his instructions and tried to insert a mere antelope in the bay window of the great chamber: she paid a London draughtsman 20 pence for the correct design, and a further 7 shillings to the glazier 'for the changing of the Antelope into a Yale'.

Beasts and badges offered Henry's craftsmen a dictionary of popular images that told the history of himself and his family. In the Cambridge chapel, they ran riot over all over the stonework, and dominated the great windows, where hundreds of Tudor badges in brightly painted glass reminded worshippers for whom they should be praying.

Chapter Eight: Southwark and its Aliens

THESE GLASSY SYMBOLS and the solemn Bible scenes beneath were produced in surroundings that could not have been less ethereal. As if in punishment for their unseemly, un-English talent, Henry's glaziers, like most of the other foreign craftsmen who helped create his public image, were banished to Southwark, the borough with the worst reputation in London, sprawling along the south bank of the Thames. Southwark's unfettered inhabitants seemed to taunt the smug City within its defensive walls on the other side of London Bridge. This was the home of loose women, pleasure-seekers, scavengers and scroungers, those who plied dangerous or unclean trades: dyeing and fulling, butchery and tanning, brewing and baking (Henry VI got his royal bread from the baker beside St Mary Overy). Southwark was meant to contain those whom proper Londoners called strangers, foreigners, aliens. The City's authority did not extend south of the river, and all attempts by pompous aldermen or guilds to control the burgeoning food markets or restrict the work of industrious immigrants were futile and strongly resisted.

Among these immigrants were the Flemings who designed and made the windows of King's College Chapel. The first was Barnard Flower, elevated by Henry VII to the post of royal glazier and given permission by the king to flout the restrictions imposed on his craft by the London guild of glaziers, as long as he continued to reside in Southwark. Then there was his assistant and successor, Henry VIII's royal glazier, Galyon Hone, who had a house and a fine garden in the neighbourhood of St Thomas's Hospital. His colleague James Nicholson also lived here, while Francis Williamson lived in the adjacent parish of St Olave's.

Such men were here because Henry VII admired the superior arts of the continent, and laid out huge sums of money to entice the top craftsmen of the day – glaziers, painters, sculptors, gold- and silversmiths, weavers – to come and work in England. He also understood the benefits to the economy of encouraging as much contact as possible with the southern Netherlands (the area now occupied by Belgium and Luxembourg), a region generally referred to as Flanders, after its largest county: the English gave all its inhabitants the blanket term 'Flemings'. Flanders had flourished under the rule of the powerful dukes of Burgundy in the fifteenth century, and it contained the wealthiest cities in northern Europe, Antwerp, Bruges, Brussels and Ghent. The chief trade was the cloth industry that depended upon imports of English wool. So England and Flanders were mutually interdependent, linked by the constant interchange of goods and traders, merchant ships and passenger vessels carrying economic migrants and religious reformers.

The prosperity of Flanders nurtured some of the most innovative artists of the day, commissioned not only by noble families, but also by rich merchants and dutiful city fathers. With such backing, the trade of art was as prosperous as that of cloth, and glaziers, painters, sculptors and other able craftsmen found that their skills were equally exportable commodities. Those who had travelled south of the Alps became aware, like their patrons, of the revolutionary realism in art that had developed in Italy after the Florentine Renaissance of the 1430s. The movement spread to Rome and then to northern Europe, where artists began to adopt and adapt the novel styles that were based upon the accurate reproduction of the external world rather than expressing the inward-looking spirituality of the earlier Middle Ages.

Realist painting, on glass, panel or parchment, was just one element of the modernity that so impressed visitors to Flanders. It was unfortunate for English craftsmen that most patrons, with the king at their head, believed that the best products were Flemish-made. They coveted luxury fashionable items: robes and hats, jewellery, wall-hangings and panels, weapons and armour, horse-trappings, furniture and carvings, together with many forms of interior decoration, prominent among them painted window glass. Henry Tudor and his court realised that it was often easier to import the craftsmen themselves rather than the finished goods. The king chose an artist from the Low Countries to become his portrait painter, he brought in specialist weavers from Brussels and Bruges to set up a royal tapestry workshop and employed a scholar from Lille to run his new library in Richmond Palace.

Commissioning artworks in the Flemish style helped to contribute to the king's presentation of himself as a confident and cultivated ruler. Worldly wealth positively aided concentration on the next world because the owners of rich goods should always be reminded of the transitory nature of life by the didactic stories told in the shining threads of tapestries or in the jewel-like glass and silver stain of windows. It was unfortunate for English glaziers that Henry Tudor did not think most of them capable of achieving the same high standards as the immigrants who had to live in Southwark.

Southwark was a magnet, a sprawling crossroads funnelling travellers towards the final filter of London Bridge. This double-portcullised check-point was decorated by a grisly forest of tall poles topped with the heads of traitors. In November 1499, the most recent addition to the sinister portrait gallery was the head of Perkin Warbeck, a warning to all pretenders. The City disapproved of the people of Southwark because it had no control over them: the borough was outside its jurisdiction and fell within the wide remit of the diocese of Winchester, whose bishop had his London residence there. His palace and its extensive grounds lay adjacent to the river and to the parish church of St Mary Overy, and gave him easy access to the court and to river travel. Another riverside church was St Olave's, so close to the water that bodies in the churchyard sometimes got washed away, and the Pope offered indulgences to those who paid to mend the wave-born damage to the walls. The Augustinian Hospital of St Thomas gave its name to a whole neighbourhood. Despite such provision, the atmosphere was seductively lawless. In 1527, the Bishop of Winchester wrote to his former protégé, Cardinal Wolsey, concerning the conduct of his clergy of Winchester; he complained only of some minor fornication and adultery amongst the secular clerks in his huge diocese and boasted that it had 'as little openly known sin or enormous crime as any within the realm . . . except at Southwark'.

By Henry VII's day, Southwark was where most Flemish immigrants settled. One contemporary put the pros and cons: 'These great riches of London are not occasioned by [Southwark's] inhabitants being noblemen or gentlemen; being all on the contrary persons of low degree and artificers who have congregated there from all parts of the island, and from Flanders, and from every place.' Like all economic migrants and refugees, they clustered together in order to practise their distinctive skills and trades surrounded and protected by their own people. Like the King's Chapel glaziers, many settled in the parish of St Olave, while others lived within the precinct of St Thomas's Hospital. The arrival of foreigners was not new, but from the middle of the fifteenth century, the trickle was becoming such a flood that speculative landlords acquired fresh properties in the cheapest part of the borough which they converted into crammed tenements to accommodate the newcomers.

The name, generally pejorative, that the English gave them was 'Doche' and it meant German-speaking, 'Deutsche' rather than 'Dutch'. Whether they were North Netherlanders, Flemings or Germans (who confusingly called themselves 'Almayns') it was a satisfactory umbrella term that covered their most obviously alien feature, the incomprehensible guttural language they spoke. Other cultural differences marked them out. Thanks to the flourishing continental trade, the immigrants preserved their distinctive habits and customs by importing and using goods and products that singled them out from their English neighbours. They rejected the smoky open fireplaces of England and pioneered central heating in the form of free-standing stoves decorated with glazed tiles. Their imported pottery imitated that of the aristocracy yet was still cheap to buy because it was mass-produced abroad. Their drink of choice, beer, rapidly supplanted the local ales and became one of Southwark's most vital industries: hops and malt were far more intoxicating than ale-makers' wheat or barley. Andrew Borde's early sixteenth-century *Dietary of Health* noted his disapproval of the strange brew. Beer was 'a natural drink for a Dutchman. And now of late days it is much used in England to the detriment of many Englishmen. It doth make a man fat and doth inflate the belly, as it doth appear by the Dutchmen's faces and bellies.' In 1531, Flemish brewers were legally exempted from the restrictive measures that affected so many other non-native craftsmen. Beer had become the national drink.

It was not just their language and life-style, but above all their unremitting industry that made these colonies of immigrant craftsmen, including the talented Flemish glaziers, seem so alien, the term which became their official title. Being designated an 'alien' meant that your working practice was subject to the imposition of legal restrictions intended to allay the fears and protect the ancient privileges of English artisans and craftsmen who belonged to the powerful guilds of the City of London. 'Alien strangers' came from abroad, 'foreigners' came from the rest of Britain, but they all suffered the same discrimination. This went back a long way. A charter of 1376 attempted to prohibit 'non-citizens' from selling any goods, and another of 1400 declared they must not sell wholesale goods to each other but only to citizens.

The guilds were bodies of merchants and craftsmen who first came together for religious observances and for mutual support, just like the fraternities and schools of other great European cities. These turned into self-regulating institutions who kept their members under tight control and monitored standards rigidly. Their wardens, or 'searchers', had the right to inspect materials, workshop conditions and the finished product, to set rates of pay and regulate career structures. The guilds developed a precise hierarchy, sporting their distinctive liveries in great processions and pageants. London guilds were subject to the ultimate authority of the Lord Mayor and his aldermen, who could award the right of freemanship to master craftsmen, or throw into prison those who worked without official sanction.

When Henry VII came to the throne, the London Company of Glaziers and Painters on Glass regulated the craft of stained glass within the capital, as they had done for the previous two or three hundred years. One of the smaller City guilds, they did not even have their own hall in the fifteenth century but had to hire one from the Brewers' Company for special occasions. Secure in their long-established working practices, and confident of a continuing flow of commissions from the court and City, they did not initially feel threatened by the immigrants from the Low Countries who were gradually moving into Southwark: the 1381 poll tax return for the borough listed only two glaziers amongst more than 100 occupations.

John Stow, in his *Survey of London*, provided snapshots of the company's traditional commissions for City patrons in the fifteenth century, untroubled by thoughts of the future or changes in style. His affectionate and nostalgic view of London, compiled in Elizabeth's reign, attempted to define the puzzling shift from medieval Catholic to modern, post-Reformation times: he had even met people who could recall the days of Richard III. He listed churches and other buildings ward by ward, describing all the fine works that proud past citizens had commissioned for the public benefit as well as for the good of their souls. Stained glass windows played quite a part.

In the Guildhall, the executors of London's most famous Lord Mayor 'glazed some Windows thereof [for the Great Hall] and of the Mayor's Court; on every which window the arms of Richard Whittington are placed . . . Divers Aldermen glazed the Great Hall, and other courts, as appeareth by their Arms in each window.' In the Guildhall's chapel of St Mary Magdalene, another Lord Mayor, grocer John Welles, was commemorated by a window above his tomb and also 'in the East Window, is the likeness of Welles, with hands elevated . . . holding scrolls, wherein is written *Mercy . . .*'.

Not to be outdone, another mayor, Sir Ralph Austrie of the Fishmongers' Company, refurbished St Martin in the Vintry in the 1480s, when he 'new roofed this church with timber, covered it with lead and beautifully glazed it'. In St Helen's, Bishopsgate, Sir John Crosby, grocer, who died in 1475, renewed the whole building and set his arms in the window glass, stonework and roof timbers. Sir John Hinde, draper and mayor, rebuilt St Swithin's in the Walbrook, 'his arms in the Glass windows, even in the tops of them, which is in a field silver, a chiefe Azure, a Lion passant silver, a Chevron azure, three escallops silver'. As well as their expertise in heraldic glass, City glaziers installed likenesses too. In St Anthony's, Budge Row, Henry Collet, mercer and mayor, was 'a great benefactor to this church, the pictures of him, his wife, ten sons and ten daughters remain, in the glass window on the North side'.

Members of the London Glaziers' Company assumed that they would continue to attract the sort of conventional commissions that Stow described. But more discriminating patrons, aware of the poor quality of English glass, now extended their prejudices to the glass-painters as well, because they were too set in their ways. There was an ominous sign of things to come in 1455, when a fight between an English glazier and a Dutch one resulted in the latter's death. When immigrant glaziers from Flanders began flocking into the country in response to the continental tastes of the court, they endured a long campaign of attrition from the jealous guild of the London Company of Glaziers, who rightly suspected they were losing work to the newcomers. In 1474, they delivered a petition to the Lord Mayor and aldermen which nostalgically contrasted the happy time when only Freemen practised their crafts in the City 'without sleight, fraud or deceit' with the present day when 'certain foreign persons and strangers' were unfairly working 'in secret corners' and installing windows all over the City whose shoddy workmanship was exempt from the quality checks that only the company could impose. So they urged the Lord Mayor to let them follow the practice of other guilds by setting up a closed shop and for-bidding incoming glaziers to run workshops within the City. If any alien accepted a commission to install windows within its boundaries (for culturally aspirant aldermen and merchants wanted the latest styles) he must pay the Glaziers' Company a fine. The Lord Mayor agreed to these demands.

By the late fifteenth century, the guild system which had survived for so long was starting to break down in a confusing, unstable England shaken by the long civil war and by the expanding trade links with the continent. Henry VII made his own contribution towards this decay by imposing external controls on the guilds through Acts of Parliament that nationally regulated prices, wages and the terms and conditions of employment. The guilds' hostility to the alien workers of Southwark was a last-ditch attempt to repair a medieval institution that was already fatally undermined. While they discriminated against those from the provinces almost as much as those from abroad, aliens were harder to control because they were happy to ignore the tight structures meant to restrict them, and their marketable skills and well-deserved profits contributed further to the decline of the old ways. The problem was epitomised in the struggle between the London Company of Glaziers and the Flemish glass-painters who won the most prestigious commissions of the day, including the windows of King's College Chapel.

Even before Henry came to the throne, the guilds sought the support of king and Commons to stem the tide of immigrants. In 1468, for example, William Shaw, a protectionist member of the Company of Skinners, egged on a gang of City guild members, made up of skinners, goldsmiths, cordwainers and tailors, to cross the river into Southwark because 'the Flemings there take away the living of English people'. They 'purposed to have cut off their thumbs or hands so that they should never have helped themselves again by the means of crafts'. Fortunately, the mayor put a stop to this just in time. Richard III recognised the popular mood, and his brief Parliament of 1484 passed two Acts, one of which specified stained glass amongst the imports to be restricted. The first measure was mainly intended to address the threat posed by Italian merchants to the local cloth trade, but spilled bile over all the other 'merchant strangers' settling in the City of London and other towns and cities 'in great number and more than they were used to do in days past . . . with their wives, children and households'. These foreigners used unfair practices, such as holding back stock until prices had risen, then refused to spend their profits on English-made goods but sent the money abroad. They also kept themselves to themselves, only trading with other foreigners, with whom they made 'many privy and secret contracts and bargains' to their own benefit but to the general detriment of Englishmen. The Act then turned on immigrant craftsmen generally, who refused to do ordinary tough jobs like labouring but took the soft option of 'making cloths and other handicrafts and easy occupations'. Such selfishness and laziness had grave social consequences: by taking away jobs, aliens caused 'hurt and impoverishment' to the king's own subjects, who 'for lack of employment fall to idleness and become thieves, beggars, vagabonds and people of vicious living'. One solution the Act proposed was to restrict future immigration by threatening to deport anyone entering the country after the following Easter who did not have a work permit from an English employer. Another way to reduce numbers was to forbid foreign craftsmen from taking on foreign apprentices or other staff, under the threat of a swingeing fine of £20 per head. Nor was an alien allowed to employ more than two assistants, which obviously severely limited the amount of work he could take on.

Richard's second protective measure was brusquely entitled 'An Act Against Strangers Artificers' and was aimed directly at the Flemings of Southwark and the other parts of London that were outside City boundaries and so free from the control of the Lord Mayor. These included the 'liberties' of St Martin le Grand, Blackfriars, the Savoy and the parish of St Margaret's at Westminster (where King's College glazier Simon Symondes lived). At the urging of City craftsmen, the Act intended to ban the import of ready-made goods 'from beyond the Sea' because this only profited the foreigners who made them over there, at the same time rendering the English manufacturers of similar products 'greatly impoverished and daily decaying'. These dangerous commodities included pins, pouches, clasps for gowns, shoe buckles, gloves and a whole range of artworks that encompassed painted images, painted cloths and 'painted glass'. The inclusion of the latter meant that the London Company of Glaziers had a hand in lobbying the king and drafting the measure.

The government tried to keep records of immigrants by making them complete an annual *Return of Aliens* which was intended to provide full particulars of where, on what scale and with whom they worked. These laborious lists paint a picture of a vibrant, cosmopolitan London which had accommodated succeeding waves of immigrants, whether merchants, craftsmen or refugees, long-standing and recent, all of whom were endured rather than welcomed. The religious and civic authorities made brave attempts to monitor the influx on moral as well as economic grounds. Later in the sixteenth century, the *Returns* listed not just numbers, nationalities and trades practised by aliens in each parish of the City and its suburbs, but also 'how many are suspected of evil living' or whether they belonged to 'any naughty religion or sect'. These misdeeds were calculated by scrutinising whether they attended their local parish church or the churches that catered for those who had not yet mastered English. Anyone found to have been a criminal or a heretic before they came to England, or who, despite speaking English, did not attend the parish church, was liable to be deported. A modern Home Secretary would have been proud of his Tudor predecessors.

According to the statistics compiled by the *Returns* for the first half of the sixteenth century, the greatest number of aliens were the 'Doche' (meaning German-speakers from Flanders, rather than from the whole Netherlands) followed by Burgundians and French, plus a handful of Italians, Spanish and Portuguese. Some of the commodities they introduced were new to England, but too many were already manufactured in London and elsewhere, and the keen, hard-working and deft newcomers provided undesirable competition for hidebound local craftsmen. The itemised trades and crafts of the immigrants give a vivid sense of the throbbing, clattering, reeking metropolis: blade-smiths, coopers, gold-beaters, printers, spinners, tinkers. Their products ranged from the essential to the luxurious – knives and needles, gloves and hat-bands, fringes and pearls, clocks and locks, tennis balls even. Many of these crafts involved dangerous, odorous or volatile materials and techniques. The use of fire, whether in bakers' ovens, metalworkers' furnaces or glaziers' kilns, was the worst sort of hazard in jam-packed streets – the city of Venice, for example, banished all glass-making to the island of Murano in the thirteenth century – but such conditions were the norm in Southwark.

Being an alien was expensive and restrictive, as the Flemish glaziers knew too well. The various London guilds had the right to impose appropriate penalties on the alien craftsmen who threatened their monopolies, while Edward III, to appease his native-born subjects, had made all aliens liable to double taxation and prohibited them from owning land. Foreigners had long been a useful source of revenue to the Crown, and were officially recognised as such in 1440 when the first Alien Subsidy, or poll tax, was levied on immigrants. This was renewed several times until it became virtually an annual tax. In 1482, when the rate was substantially increased to help pay for Edward IV's war with Scotland, some aliens were exempted but not those from the Low Countries. Henry VII introduced a new poll tax on aliens in 1488, which established five contribution bands but proved very difficult to enforce.

The only way for an alien to avoid having to pay these taxes was by an Act of Naturalisation (which required a twenty-year residence qualification), or by becoming a denizen, an authorised permanent resident, who had been granted a Letter of Denization by the Crown. A denizen received all the privileges of a native – though they could not be made retrospective – but did have to continue completing the *Return of Aliens* in a separate category.

The standard wording of the king's letter granting denization sounded friendly enough. An example drafted in 1509 read: 'the King to all to whom these Letters Patent may come, Greeting. [Name] from henceforth during his life may be a denizen and liege of us and our heirs Kings of England, and that he in all things and by all things may be reputed, treated and governed as our faithful lieges born within our Kingdom of England are reputed and treated, and not otherwise or in other manner.' Then it went on to exempt the denizen from having to pay any 'taxes, tallages, subsidies or moneys' other than those paid by any English-born subject, and entitled him to 'have and possess all manner of liberties, franchises and privileges, and to 'use and enjoy them as wholly, freely, quietly and peacefully as our other faithful lieges'. Applying for such a letter cost money, so many aliens never bothered or simply could not afford the procedure, and those who did not become denizens were no less welcome to Henry VII, because they had to pay far more in taxation.

As the relative stability and prosperity of Henry's reign attracted more immigrants to settle in England, he appreciated their contribution to the economy. Yet the locals continued to resent the incomers. In 1500, a Venetian visitor noted typically English attitudes: 'they have an antipathy to foreigners and imagine that they never come into their island but to make themselves masters of it and to usurp their goods'.

And there was little evidence that second- or third-generation immigrants were assimilating either, because people went on repeating perennial slurs. In the 1560s, there were complaints of overcrowding, and immigrants were accused of living four or five families in one house, causing 'filthiness, infection and pestilence'. The general consensus was that 'the strangers here are commonly uncleanly people'. They were also accused of being unpatriotic, and even those born in England were thought to retain 'an inclination and kind affection to the countries of their parents'. Others deliberately brought their wives over 'to be delivered with child within the City' so that their offspring would unfairly obtain the rights of proper Englishmen.

Foreigners were distrusted on the work front as well, and stirred up dissension by allegedly refusing to comply with the guilds' rules and regulations such as the length of apprenticeships. Disregarding the customs of the country and preferring to trust the standards of their own countrymen were natural responses to immigrants' perceptions of the poor quality of English craftsmanship. It was natural that the Flemish glaziers preferred to settle among their compatriots in Southwark, outside the archaic controls of an increasingly obsolescent system.* And it was Henry VII who

---

* It is ironic that the headquarters of the Glaziers' Company, still an active body today, is in Southwark in the shadow of the bridge their Flemish rivals were not meant to cross.

delivered the greatest insult to the Glaziers' Company, the final proof that they had fallen behind the times, when he awarded the most prestigious post in their profession, that of king's glazier, to an alien, the Flemish immigrant Barnard Flower of Southwark.

Chapter Nine: The King's Glazier

THE POST OF king's glazier dated from the fourteenth century, when Richard II awarded that title to the Master of the London Glaziers' Company. The holder received a daily fee for working on royal projects, wore the king's livery, and had the use of a building called 'the glaziers' lodge' beside the Palace of Westminster, for the scale of royal commissions required more space and manpower than a normal workshop, staffed by a master, an assistant and a couple of apprentices, could possibly provide. Before a terrible fire destroyed much of the palace in 1512, the king's glazier and his team were based in this 'lodge', on the western side of the vast complex that sprawled from the abbey to the River Thames. Here teams of glaziers worked as rapidly as necessary on their sovereign's sudden but always urgent demands for another set of windows for palace or chapel.

When Henry VII came to the throne, he inherited as 'Chief Glazier of the King's Works' one William Neve, appointed by Edward IV in 1476, and renewed in this post for life by Richard III. Neve had advised the king on glazing the east window of King's College Chapel, in the brief period when Richard was trying to reinvigorate the project. Together with the college's master carpenter and the king's sergeant plumber (a man who worked with lead, rather than drains), Neve dined in hall with the Provost and Fellows for two days in August 1484, when they must have discussed their joint responsibilities in the revived building campaign.

Neve was working for Henry at the time of Elizabeth of York's coronation in 1487 (Henry had delayed this for two years after his accession to prove he held the throne in his own right). But it seemed that the king was not wholly impressed by Neve's old-fashioned style, or by that of his colleagues of the London Glaziers' Company. Henry's promotion of the arts to express his own majesty included elevating his artists from fee-paid artisans to salaried master craftsmen, and he awarded the newly enhanced post of king's glazier to a talented immigrant whose skills he had long appreciated.

Barnard Flower came to England from the Netherlandish territories of the Duchy of Burgundy, where Antwerp, Bruges and Ghent were in the forefront of modern art and design. In the 1490s, a temporary economic downturn there, combined with the lure of Henry's stable and prosperous England and its keen patrons, bought the established glazier Flower, like so many fellow craftsmen, to London. By September 1496, he was working for the king, who paid him the fee of £18 20d, probably for glazing the royal palace of Woodstock, which was being thoroughly modernised at this time. Within a few months, Henry was sufficiently impressed by Flower's talents to describe him as 'well expert and cunning [knowledgeable] in the art of glazing'. This was in a royal letter patent dated 6 April 1497, in which Henry stated that he was currently employing the glazier at the palace of Sheen and intended to use his services again: he was therefore granting Barnard Flower an official licence to work in England on condition that he remained in Southwark. More significantly, the king allowed him to employ up to four foreign assistants 'for working and exercising his craft, during our pleasure'. This was a very special exemption indeed, and one which deliberately flouted the Glaziers' Company regulations that limited aliens' assistants to two. It also implied that Flower could not produce the amount of glass that the king intended to commission from him single-handed and that he was only prepared to work with skilled Flemish assistants. His status and abilities, as well as his Southwark address, were enough to shield him from the restrictive policies of the company, for he did not bother to apply for denizenship until May 1514, by which time he probably wanted to regularise the position of his heirs rather than advance his own career.

Henry's letter did not yet call Flower 'the king's glazier' (William Neve may have retained the title until his death some time between 1502 and 1505) but it was obvious that he held the Fleming in the highest favour. This was demonstrated by the number of commissions he gave him.

The royal wedding of 1501 between Arthur, Prince of Wales, and Katherine of Aragon was a fine opportunity for Henry to show that the splendour of his Tudor court was equal to that of her parents, Ferdinand and Isabella of Spain. From the detailed accounts kept by the Offices of the King's Works, it was evident that glass played an essential part in all the grand display, where everything was designed to impress the Spanish princess and her retinue. Flower had to upgrade the windows in the suite of rooms in the Bishop of London's palace where Katherine and her entourage lodged before the ceremony. On this occasion, Flower collaborated with William Neve, for the latter supplied new Normandy glass for the princess's chamber, and reset elsewhere the old glass that had been removed (for nothing was ever wasted). The accounts also reveal that glaziers had a nice sideline in hiring out portable window panels for special occasions, if the client did not have the time or the funds to install permanent ones: Flower and another Fleming, Adrian Andrue, supplied 280 feet (85 metres) of ready-made panels of Normandy glass set in lead frames, which they loaned at the rate of 2½d per foot (0.3 metre) for the lavish but temporary embellishment of the hall in the bishop's palace where the Lord Mayor and aldermen banqueted to celebrate the wedding.

In the spring of 1505, after Neve's death, Flower was appointed king's glazier. He received an annual retainer of £24 'for keeping certain of the king's manors and castles in reparation with glass', a sum that was in addition to the substantial fees he earned for each royal project. He was now a servant of the royal household, reporting to the Office of the King's Works and responsible for recruiting whole teams of glaziers, whose names suggested they were both Flemish and English, to work collaboratively on a range of commissions. Much of this involved the installation of heraldic panels and Tudor badges in the king's various residences, including the palaces of Richmond and Westminster, the old Beaufort manor house at Woking, and the chambers of the king, the queen and the king's mother in the Tower of London, where he also provided some of his ready-made panels for the king's new wardrobe.

The responsibilities of the king's glazier were wide-ranging. He had to be an innovative artist and technician, an interpreter and developer of other people's designs, and a supremely efficient team leader. He ordered and supplied sheets of glass, for which he was paid by the foot (0.3 metre). When working at the Savoy Hospital, for example, he arranged for the superior glass coming from Germany to be taken from the docks at St Katherine's Pool upriver directly to the Savoy site. He also purchased the lead and solder that were integral to window construction. He recruited glaziers to work with him, and co-ordinated different groups, if the project was sufficiently large and urgent. He produced or commissioned preliminary designs, with the approval of Henry's clerks of the works, got them scaled up to the size of the window apertures, then supervised the cutting, painting and staining of all the panels with the required details, from the standard Tudor rose or Beaufort portcullis to reverent images of Christ or Mary, or horrific ones of the demons in Hell. The payment he received for the windows of the Savoy Hospital was 'both for glass and workmanship'. The role of the king's glazier therefore required an exceptional talent that combined organisational and administrative skills matched by the equivalent mastery and understanding of every phase in the making of a window, the most important of which was its effect on the interior of the building. But the success of this ultimate stage could not be gauged until the windows were irreversibly in place. They had to be right first time.

Flower's commissions from the king gained him other patrons who coveted his state-of-the-art windows, for the royal glazier did not have to work exclusively for the monarch. He attracted the attention of the King's Mother, who employed him in her manor house at Croydon, then in the new library of Christ's College in 1507.* Flower might also have supervised the glazing in the chapel at Christ's College, when the older building was expanded into something more suited to Margaret's ambitious plans for her foundation. The King's Mother honoured all her family in its windows, where the present jumble of panels reassembled in the north windows once depicted herself and her son, together with her father and mother and two of her husbands. After her death in 1509, her executors paid 'Symond the glazier' £11 5s 8d for his work, and in 1510 another glazier, Thomas Peghe, reset some of the original windows, and provided new panels as well. Symond's contribution was impressive enough to get him recruited to the team that glazed the new chapel of the King's College.

For Bishop Foxe, Flower glazed the east end of Winchester Cathedral that the bishop had remodelled: since his London palace was in Southwark, Foxe was proud to commission the work of the local immigrant glaziers. Another prestigious patron was Cardinal Wolsey, who became Henry Tudor's chaplain in 1507, then received steady promotions – Almoner to Henry VIII, Bishop of Lincoln, then Archbishop of York in 1514. The ostentation of his buildings provoked indignation because they were 'more like unto a paradise than an earthly habitation'. This included having the best windows. Wolsey commissioned 'Barnard the king's glazier' to fill his London headquarters at York Place with the most expensive glass, made in Normandy, that money could buy, and caused the Provost of King's College to comment about how the archbishop was 'most sumptuously and gorgeously' refurbishing the building. Flower filled the bay window in the hall and the great new staircase with royal arms and badges and in the gallery installed 155 feet (47 metres) of Normandy glass containing thirty-six small badges. While Wolsey dutifully placed the arms of the king and queen in the chapel, its windows also boasted his own status. As soon as the Pope appointed him cardinal, and in November 1515 sent his mark of office, the cardinal's hat (the hat was formally welcomed at Dover and honoured

*The allegorical figures representing the arts and sciences that were removed from the windows in the eighteenth century were likely to have been Flower's.

by a procession all the way to London, where it was greeted by the mayor and aldermen and placed on the high altar at Westminster Abbey), Wolsey paid Flower additional fees to insert eleven cardinal's hats above some of the existing arms. The expenses of Wolsey's clerk of the works on that occasion included 6d for the cost of hiring a boat to go to Southwark in order to speak with the glazier. It was a mark of Flower's status that the clerk had to visit him, rather than the other way round.

What is intriguing now is the discrepancy between the fairly routine work that Flower was recorded as doing, and the many large-scale schemes that have been attributed to him. The building accounts kept by the Office of the King's Works itemised all the payments that he and his men received for extensive repairs they made as well as for quantities of new work. They installed hundreds of panes and panels, virtually none of which has survived. Yet much extant glass of the period is in windows which are anonymous, although their fine quality and advanced designs suggest that they should have been the products of the royal workshop, and were therefore made or supervised by Flower. These include the complete set of windows of St Mary's, Fairford, for which there is no contemporary written evidence at all, figures now in the west window of St George's Chapel at Windsor, some of the glass in Winchester Cathedral, and the pitiful remains of the extensive glazing scheme whose designs Henry VII personally approved for his chapel at Westminster Abbey.

The paradox is that too many royal windows can only be attributed to the king's glazier or his colleagues by the art historian's subjective identifications of Hand A and Hand B, Master This and Glazier That, an uncertain form of identification given the collaborative nature of such projects, let alone the effects of subsequent interventions and repairs. The only place where documents definitively link Barnard Flower to surviving windows is the chapel of King's College, Cambridge.

Chapter Ten: 'Unperfected and Unfinished'

HENRY VII DIED at Richmond, his favourite palace, on 21 April 1509. His will revealed the extensive precautions he had taken against lingering too long in Purgatory. Among his beneficiaries, the friars of Richmond and of Greenwich had to say 500 masses 'for the remission of our sins and the weal of our soul', while other recipients had to pledge 300 masses. He gave his executors discretion to distribute the residue of his estate towards any works of mercy or charity that would be pleasant to God but also 'most expedient for the redemption and remission of our sins and most wholesome and meritorious for our soul'. Leaving money to complete the Cambridge chapel was also a precautionary measure 'for the weal of our soul and for the singular trust we have to the prayers of our said uncle of blessed memory'. He doubtless recalled the solemn warning of Henry VI, whose own Will and Intent concerning the chapel commanded posterity 'to remember the terrible commination and full fearful imprecations of holy scripture against the breakers of the law of God and the letters of good and holy works'. Henry Tudor, confronting death, took this very seriously indeed.

Another item in his will suggested family pride combined with love of luxury, the cloth of gold 'wrought with our badges of red roses and

Henry VI. This was painted in Tudor times, around 1530, to project the image of the pious young man whom Henry VII called his uncle.

Lady Margaret Beaufort. Portraits of Henry VII's mother stressed her devotion and learning. Here she kneels in prayer, contemplating an illuminated manuscript and wearing the ornate head-dress of a widow.

Henry VII. The king in his later years, his face gaunt and his hair grizzled. His clothes are austere yet opulent, with a fur-trimmed robe and a bejewelled cap.

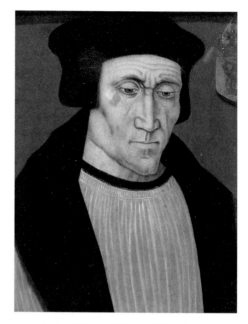

John Fisher, Bishop of Rochester.
The man who persuaded Henry VII to
complete King's College Chapel, but who
was executed by Henry VIII. Engraved after
a portrait by Hans Holbein the Younger.

Richard Foxe, Bishop of Winchester.
The wordly prelate, who as Henry VII's
chief executor was responsible for planning
the windows of King's College Chapel with
the royal glazier Barnard Flower.

Ground Plan of King's College Chapel to show the numbering of the great windows.

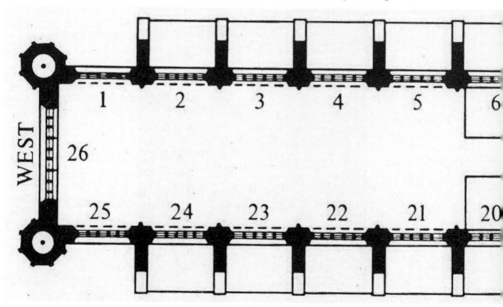

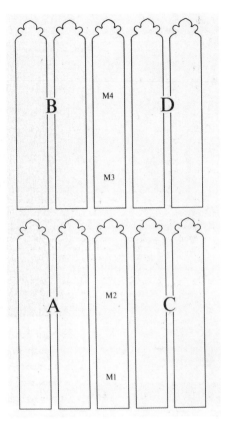

Diagram of a typical window. Scenes B and D show the Old Testament, Scenes A and C the related New Testament subjects. MI – 4 are the four prophetic Messengers.

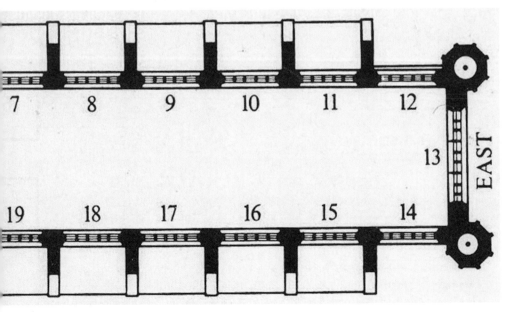

An illustration from the *Biblia Pauperum*. Christ's Entry into Jerusalem (centre) is prefigured by David with the head of Goliath (left) and Elijah (right), with half-figures of prophets above and below. This type of late 15th-century block-book was an important design source for the windows.

Window 2. The Golden Table, and the Marriage of Tobias and Sara.
These scenes prefigure the legendary girlhood of the Virgin, below. This was perhaps the earliest
window, made under Barnard Flower: the fussy half-figures under arches were not repeated.

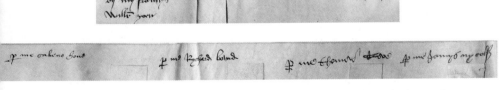

The glaziers' signatures on the 1526 contracts. Galyon Hone, Richard Bond, Thomas Reve,
James Nicholson, Francis Williamson, Simon Symondes.

Window 9. The Last Supper.
Set in a magnificent Renaissance chamber, Christ,
surrounded by his disciples, gives bread to Judas,
who furtively grips the bag containing 30 pieces of silver.

Window 10. The Betrayal of Christ.
Judas kisses Christ to identify him to the sinister
waiting soldiers, while Peter draws his sword to
cut off the ear of the High Priest's servant.

Window II. Christ before Caiaphas, the High Priest.
Christ is surrounded by grimacing soldiers. The Priest's throne bears the anti-papal inscription
'SIC RESPO[N]DES PO[N]TIFICEM?' and his hunting dog is present.

The vidimuses for two scenes
in Window 21,
Peter and John healing the lame man,
and the Death of Ananias. These were
the original working drawings on paper,
which were only discovered in 1964.

Window 21. Peter & John healing
the lame man.
A scene from one of the three Acts
of the Apostles windows. Despite his
dreadfully twisted legs, the man on the
steps of the Renaissance-style temple
will rise and walk again.

portcullises . . . made, bought and provided at Florence', which he left to Westminster Abbey.

Before his death, Henry attempted to safeguard the last sum he gave to the chapel. The document dated 24 March 1509 that conveyed £5,000 to the college specified that 'a strong chest bound with iron having four locks and four keys to shut and open the same shall be provided by the said Provost and set in the treasure house of the said college'. This was to hold the money and might be opened only in the presence of all four key-holders, Provost, bursar, master of works, and the university's Vice-Chancellor.*

After Henry died, the parish priests at Great St Mary's earned 8d for saying prayers in his memory. Great candles costing 3s 2d were lit for the occasion, and 2s was spent on carrying the cross around the town, a ritual that was faithfully repeated throughout the next decade, funded by an annual grant from Westminster Abbey. Bishop Fisher preached the king's funeral sermon on 10 May at St Paul's Cathedral in an address that praised Henry's exemplary death-bed piety and repentance: kissing the crucifix and beating his breast, he had been a model for all. The sermon recalled the king's 'wit quick and ready, his reason pithy and substantial, his memory fresh and holding, his experience notable, his councils fortunate and taken in wise deliberation; his speech gracious and in diverse languages, his person goodly and amiable, his treasure and richness incomparable, his buildings most goodly'. This eulogy so pleased the grieving Lady Margaret Beaufort that she had it published. Yet praising treasure, richness and goodly buildings may not have come too easily to the ascetic Fisher, who expressed his true views on kings and kingship in another sermon that mocked the transitory nature of power and money:

they had all their pleasure . . . hawking, hunting, also goodly horses, goodly coursers, greyhounds and hounds for their disport, their palaces well and richly beseen [decorated], strongholds and towns without number, they had great plenty of gold and

---

* This chest is still in the chapel today, in the exhibition space in the north side chapels.

silver . . . but where be they now, be they not gone and wasted like smoke?

Henry's will described the Cambridge chapel as 'unperfected and unfinished, little or nothing wrought or done since the decease of our said uncle', predictably glossing over the not inconsiderable contributions of Edward IV and Richard III. It proved how important the chapel had become to him in his final years, because he left money 'for the perfect finishing and performing of the said work' and bound his executors to see it through. The executor responsible for the windows was Richard Foxe, Bishop of Winchester, whose task was to liaise again with Barnard Flower, the Southwark glazier whom Foxe had already employed at Winchester.

Foxe was a man the king really trusted. They first met in France in the 1480s where Foxe, a lawyer who had trained at Oxford and Louvain, was studying at the University of Paris. He returned to England to serve under Edward IV, but after the latter's death, he backed Henry's cause, fled to France, then fought beside Henry at Bosworth. Rewarded with the posts of principal secretary and Lord Privy Seal, he rapidly became one of the new king's most powerful ministers, bringing distinction to an administration that was insecure in its early days. A natural diplomat who had travelled widely in Europe, he was also respected as an intellectual and a sophisticated humanist. He served as Master of Pembroke College, Cambridge for twelve years, and founded the first permanent lectureship in Greek at Oxford. In gratitude for loyal service, the king rewarded Foxe with lucrative promotions through the ranks of the bishoprics – Exeter, Bath and Wells, Durham and finally Winchester, the wealthiest of all. Foxe loved the high life, causing the Venetian ambassador to report that he lived like a king.

Henry VIII was crowned on 24 June 1509. As a second son, he had not initially been groomed for kingship but at the age of eleven had to take the place of his brother Arthur, whose sudden death occurred in 1502. Henry VII had adored the older son but was less sure of the younger one. Back in January 1504, the Spanish envoy had reported to Queen Isabella on the new

Prince of Wales, who was likely to become her daughter's next husband: 'the King wishes to improve him . . . if he lives ten years longer, he will leave the Prince furnished with good habits'. But Henry VII did not live long enough to imbue the restraints that his heir so conspicuously lacked.

At his father's death, Henry VIII was not quite eighteen, and so officially still a minor. His grandmother Lady Margaret Beaufort stepped in as temporary regent and served for ten weeks, with the support of Bishop Foxe. This final act of family duty may have helped mitigate the pain of outliving her adored son, and she saw it through with iron determination. Having witnessed the ultimate triumph of the blood line to which she had dedicated her life, in the form of the peaceful accession and coronation of her own grandson, product of the union she had created between York and Lancaster, she died on 29 June, the day after Henry's eighteenth birthday. It was as if she had willed her indomitable spirit to keep going until everything was secure.

Bishop Fisher preached her funeral sermon. He tellingly compared her to a Martha rather than a Mary, and revealed her to be so devout that she wore a hair-shirt. She had named him and Foxe among her executors, the same duty they were performing for the late king. Her will established regular funding for Christ's College, and recalled its original founder 'King Henry VI of blessed memory'. She also made provision for a second foundation in Cambridge, the former run-down hospital of St John, which had previously caught her eye and which she had planned to turn into a proper college, with a Master and fifty Fellows: a codicil to the will instructed her executors to go ahead with this scheme.

Margaret was buried in Westminster Abbey as her will specified, 'within the chapel of Our Lady which is now begun by our most dear son'. Her executors approved the contract for her tomb: her effigy should be framed by a tabernacle 'graven with portcullises and roses', at her feet, 'a beast called a Yale'. (The needy Erasmus earned £1 by composing the Latin inscription that ran around the border.) That is how she lies today, close to her beloved son's much greater monument.

Foxe remained at court as the young king's most senior minister, assisted by his protégé, chaplain and secretary, an ambitious and hard-working young man named Thomas Wolsey, who would emulate his mentor in devoted service to the monarchy as well as in grand living. Henry VIII had promoted him from dean to Bishop of Lincoln in 1514, a post that he held at the same time as being Bishop of Tournai, precentor at St Paul's Cathedral and Dean of St Stephen's, Westminster. Someone with a grudge against Wolsey (who had once thrown him into prison briefly) was Henry Tudor's former historian, Polydore Vergil. His *Anglica Historia*, completed in 1533, implied that Wolsey's meteoric rise had disillusioned formerly loyal counsellors such as Foxe who 'when they saw so much power coming into the hands of one man withdrew gradually from the court . . . before they left, like truly sensible statesmen, they earnestly urged the king not to suffer any servant to be greater than his master'. However, this was being wise after the event, and it was more likely that Foxe was genuinely anxious to retire from court in order to spend more time in his see and on his duties as executor to the late king.

Foxe visited Cambridge several times in the years immediately after Henry Tudor's death to inspect progress on King's College Chapel. Masons were now finishing the walls of the antechapel, the western half of the building. In his Will and Intent, Henry VI had called for simplicity of decoration, and insisted on the absence of any 'superfluity of too great curious works of entail and busy moulding'. For him, the monumental scale and proportions of the building were enough to create beauty through perfect design and execution. But this was not to the taste of the Tudors. Under the supervision of the master mason, John Wastell, the ornamental stone carvers set to work embedding the dynasty's beasts and badges into the fabric of the walls. What the sculptors produced was astounding and eye-catching, an exuberant profusion of the symbols of monarchy, obsessively repeated through the interior of the antechapel.

At the west end, practically the whole wall surface below the window was taken up by giant statues. A dragon and a greyhound confront each other on either side of the royal coat of arms which their front paws support. The dragon rears up and flaps a scaly wing, snarling through fierce-fanged jaws, while the greyhound is serene and sinuous. Its aristocratic muzzle seems to bear a faint smile, and its body is so lean that the ribcage can be seen, rippling beneath smooth skin. Flanked by a huge rose and a portcullis trailing a heavy chain, these figures are almost fully three-dimensional. Suspended above them are enormous gravity-defying crowns that seem to spring right out of the wall. This group of sculptures is repeated ten times around the walls of the antechapel but the carvers revelled in their versatility by refusing to make identical copies. Instead of contemplating the royal arms with their heads in profile, dragon or greyhound may twist around to gaze sternly down at those beneath.

An even larger version of the group is carved outside, on the wall above the west door, whose pointed archway is studded with roses so plump and floridly petalled that they looked like artichokes. The chapel's exterior announced the theme of the interior, for beasts and badges, with the rose predominant, decorated every projecting surface, just like the outside of the Westminster Abbey chapel where the same team had worked. Inside the antechapel, further permutations of rose, portcullis and fleur-de-lys led the eye all the way up the piers that supported the ceiling. On the very vault itself, as if looking down from heaven, the roof bosses at the centre of each stonework fan were carved into roses or portcullises. Painted in bright colours, their details picked out in gold, these dynastic signs would have shocked Henry VI to the core: the contrast of the sculptural riches of the antechapel with the austerity of the choir was the most striking proof of Tudor intervention.

These masterpieces of stone carving were the starting point for the windows, whose upper zones complemented and reinforced them in stained glass which also paraded the symbols of the Tudor kings. The various small openings at the head of each window were filled with permutations of beasts and badges, on a smaller scale than the wall sculptures but just as easy to recognise: sole dragon, green hawthorn bush, red and white roses, golden portcullis and fleur-de-lys, all brought to life by Barnard Flower and his team in vivid pot-metal glass.

Chapter Eleven: The First Phase

B Y 1512, THE antechapel walls and their ornate carvings were complete. These had exhausted Henry Tudor's last bequest, and his executors had to make available a further £5,000 that was intended to cover everything else outstanding, including decorating 'all the windows in the same church with such images, stories, arms, badges and other devisings as it shall be devised by the said executors: and also clearly and wholly finish, perform and end all the works that is not yet done'. This was optimistic in the extreme, because erecting the remarkable fan vault alone came to well over £10,000. Once the roof was up, the window apertures had probably been temporarily filled with panels of 'white' English glass, its impurities creating a muted, greenish light.

Because it was now weather-tight, and because so much money had been spent, the impetus to complete the building seemed to slow down although nothing had yet been done about the crowning glory, the windows. Worried at the lull in proceedings, the Provost and Fellows were forced to remind Henry VIII how his father, 'that prince of most noble renown', had desired to complete the church that his blessed uncle Henry VI had begun. 'The said work is now almost performed and accomplished except for the paving and stalling and glazing of the same, which is not done for lack of money.' And they begged the king to 'command and cause the said executors' to release more funds. This request was accompanied by a formidable list of outstanding items, some of which, notably the 'gilding and painting of the great vault' and the 'two images of kings' outside the west door, were never achieved, while the rood-loft, to be carved with 'imagery and tabernacles', would eventually take a very different form. In the end, Henry VIII did bring some influence to bear, but it was not until the autumn of 1515, three years after the vault was completed and six years after his father's death, that the executors released a further £5,000 to make a start on the final phase. This delay was bad enough. No one could have imagined that it would take nearly thirty years more to finish the glazing.

On 30 November 1515, Thomas Larke, Surveyor of the King's Works in Cambridge, drew up and signed a document confirming that he had 'received of Mr Robert Hacomblen, Provost of the King's college there, one hundred pounds sterling to be delivered unto Barnard Flower the king's glazier in way of prest [an advance] towards the glazing of the great church there in such form and condition as my Lord of Winchester shall devise and command to be done'. Hacomblen (Etonian, Kingsman and author of a commentary on Aristotle's *Ethics*) had been appointed Provost in 1509, soon after Henry VII's death; his duties included the heavy responsibility of seeing through the renewed building campaign.

As for the glazing itself, it was the job of Henry's most senior executor, my Lord of Winchester, Bishop Richard Foxe, to interpret the late king's vision following a scheme the king had already approved. The model was the chapel at Westminster Abbey, whose windows depicted 'the Old Law and the New' in accordance with the designs Henry had seen, which the royal glazier's team had just completed. This established the Cambridge chapel's terms of reference: 'imagery of the story of the old law and of the new law after the form, manner, goodness, curiosity and cleanliness, in every point, of the glass windows of the king's new chapel at Westminster'. The chapels were thus twinned, two architectural masterpieces whose sculpture and glass were inextricably associated with the ruling dynasty.

There was nothing innovative in this decorative scheme. Henry was familiar with all the implications of linking the Old and New Testaments and their many manifestations in art and literature, an attempt to impose a structure upon the whole universe, from God's creation of the world down to the sacrifice of his son. It proved that the past embraced and enshrined the future. Jesus established these parallels himself when, according to St Matthew's Gospel, he predicted his entombment and resurrection by comparing himself to Jonah in the belly of the whale for three days and nights. He also cited Moses and the prophets as a source of explanation for his own life. (Bishop Fisher made Jonah the subject of a famous sermon on the Psalms by comparing the whale to the power of despair that overwhelms the sinner.)

Medieval theologians expanded these links into a whole academic genre known as 'typology', with an incident from the Old Testament providing the prototype, called the 'type', and the associated New Testament scene that fulfilled the prediction as the 'antetype'. Some of the connections that scholars made were tenuous in the extreme, drawing upon esoteric texts to generate a range of obscure and puzzling parallels. But medieval universities measured learning through the conduct of dialectical debates based on the minute analysis of biblical commentaries, a branch of learning called scholasticism. Earlier theologians had found it necessary to generate these sorts of comparisons in order to demonstrate their knowledge of the whole spectrum of scholarship as much as of the Bible itself. A typical university lecture might consist of a quotation or proposition, followed by the citation of all previous authorities on the matter, especially the early fathers of the Church, Jerome, Augustine and Gregory. By the early sixteenth century, radical scholars were starting to challenge these intricate approaches that laid so much stress on allegories and symbols and mystical predications.

The Old Law and the New was a major source for artists from the earliest Middle Ages, in stained glass, wall paintings and mosaics, illustrated manuscripts and ivory carvings. Visual parallels made Bible texts easier to understand, especially when the images were accompanied by words from the relevant verses. Windows were the most effective medium of all, the familiar comparisons shown large and bright, providing prompts for preachers, memory aids for a congregation who could not read, and abstruse topics of contemplation for the learned. The Temptation of Eve related to the Annunciation to the Virgin, the disobedience of one woman being offset by the submission of another; the Return of the Prodigal Son prefigured Christ appearing to the Apostles; the Ascent of Elijah in his fiery chariot predicted Christ's Ascension. There were many such pairings.

There were different ways of arranging them in windows. A glazier might set a particular New Testament scene in the central panel, and flank it with two smaller ones showing appropriate Old Testament prototypes. Or he might install Old Testament scenes in the windows along the north side of the nave, and place their New Testament equivalents immediately opposite them in the south wall. Alternatively, scenes from the life of Christ, accompanied by the relevant prototypes, went along the north wall, while the south wall displayed his Resurrection, his Ascension and the Coronation of the Virgin. An east window almost invariably showed the Crucifixion, immediately behind the altar where the priest conducted Mass, while the Last Judgement went into the west window, to enable the congregation to contemplate the choice between Heaven and Hell as they walked down the nave after the service. Whatever the distribution, priest and worshippers knew all the parallels.

In a college chapel like that of King's, the intended viewers were primarily academics and students, capable of interpreting the subject matter at its most complex and subtle level. This gave Bishop Foxe the opportunity to plan windows whose intellectual content could stand up to sophisticated scrutiny. The real problem, although neither Henry VII nor he fully appreciated it, was one of changing intellectual approaches. In 1515, Foxe was an old man. He had acquired his learning in the late fifteenth century, and he had always put politics before theology. Meanwhile a younger generation of Oxford and Cambridge scholars were beginning to appreciate the pared-down humanistic theology of the Renaissance. This aimed to focus on the words of the Bible itself through the revived emphasis on clear inter-pretations by modern or late classical writers, thus eliminating many of the arcane scholastic interpretations of the Middle Ages. It was this approach which resulted in the Reformation's concern with the Word itself.

Under Foxe's guidance, however, the King's Chapel windows exemplified the old learning in which he and Henry VII had been brought up, the final flowering of a concept that was becoming obsolete. It was ironic that although the development of printing techniques in the late fifteenth century meant that modern window designers had a wide range of ready-made sources in the form of published woodblock illustrations to copy or adapt, these prints preserved and extended the old scholastic parallels that modern scholarship spurned. The King's Chapel windows epitomised this paradox. Their subject matter was the familiar narrative of the Life and Death of Christ, framed within the Life and Death of his Mother, foreshadowed by the relevant Old Testament incident, as had been appropriate for church windows for the past three hundred years. These scenes were so well established that no designer or artist needed, or indeed would have dared, to innovate. Although Barnard Flower and his fellow glaziers were technically capable of revolutionary story-telling in glass inspired by the truthful naturalism of the Renaissance, they had to apply their specialist skills of sensitive painting and precision-based firing to realise formulaic designs that were becoming intellectually out of date. Reconciling these conflicting demands was a work of genius.

The conventional source material for the Old Law and the New came from two essential compilations, the *Biblia Pauperum* (the 'Books of the Poor'), and the *Speculum Humanae Salvationis* (the 'Mirror of Man's Salvation'). Originating as illustrated manuscripts at the beginning of the fourteenth century, they were first published in the Netherlands in the 1460s in editions printed with woodcut illustrations, called block-books. These contained a wide range of pictorial material: the *Biblia* provided two Old Testament precedents for each New Testament scene, the *Speculum* three.

Barnard Flower and his colleagues were familiar with such illustrated editions, as was a well-read cleric like Foxe. As Foxe and Flower both lived in Southwark, it was an easy matter for the glazier to attend Foxe in his episcopal palace there. Foxe knew they had to devise a scheme that was true to the late king's expressed intention, and which would at the same time complement the whole ambience and scale of the chapel. The windows had to provide the right didactic message, but one that was delivered in a manner that enhanced the wide spaces and soaring height, the pale stone, the rippling, lacy vaults and the overblown Tudor symbols in the antechapel. This was the King's College, and it was royal money that was paying for the work: the glass had to let in enough light not to obscure any details of the interior, otherwise the genius of the masons and carvers would not be fully appreciated.

Controlling the light was Flower's responsibility, not Foxe's. The first thing they had to settle was how to distribute the subjects. Using the woodblock compilations as a starting point, they had to decide which Bible scenes to select, and then how to allocate them to the spaces available. The determining factor was the immutable layout and structure of the window apertures, for the stonework frames of the twenty-four great windows of the chapel were already in place, twelve along the north and twelve along the south wall. Each consisted of ten separate openings (or lights), divided by vertical and horizontal stone mullions into two tiers of five lights, together with fifteen small, irregularly shaped openings in the tracery above each window. The East Window had eighteen lights, divided into two tiers of nine, plus thirty-two tracery openings, and the West Window was identical. Yet all this graceful stone carving, the slender mullions and flamelike tracery designed to show off the masons' precision, lead the eye upwards and flood light into the building, provided exactly the wrong sort of frame for the dramatic scenes that were to fill them. The design of the chapel and its windows belonged to the 1440s, when the subjects of stained glass were frequently single figures of angels, saints or kings, Bible characters or benefactors, placed in rows, each occupying one light only and surrounded by its own stone frame; the boundaries between wall and window were often blurred by fantastical architectural details painted onto the glass. Flower's canvas, a great grid intended to display hierarchical rows of frontal figures, was apparently incompatible with storytelling.

An even greater problem was the height of the windows from the ground, perfect for displaying rhythmical tiers of glassy ethereal forms but not for realistic scenes whose characters expressed genuine emotion and responded to one another, and were set against detailed backgrounds of landscapes or townscapes like those in oil paintings. The extended biblical narrative and the sophisticated theological comparisons were complex enough at eye level. Being set 60 feet (18 metres) above the ground would make them even harder to comprehend unless the figures were massive and the colours strong.

Flower's solutions were ingenious. First, he decided that the designs had to ignore some of the vertical mullions that divided each window into five lights, and he gave each scene more space by spreading it across two lights rather than confining it to one. Then he took positive advantage of the two-tiered structure by placing each Old Testament scene immediately above the New Testament one that it prefigured. So each window contained four scenes, two upper and two lower, with the more significant New Testament being nearer the spectator's eye. Another way might have been to spread each scene over all five lights, but this would have required a series of large designs with much detail and many people in them, while the sequence of events intended for the north side, from the birth of Mary to the Crucifixion in the East Window, involved more than twelve incidents. Doubling up, by fitting two scenes into each window, gave space for twenty-four on each side.

This layout left Flower with the two middle lights of each window to fill, and in these he placed the figures of four 'messengers', one below the other, holding scrolls bearing inscriptions of Bible quotations referring to the adjacent scene, the captions that explained the illustrations. To give them some variety (with four in each window, they would total ninety-six), he turned two into winged angels, and made the other two into prophets wearing hats, robes or tunics, and boots. They represented Flower's clever adaptation of two different formats, familiar devices in stained glass and other media: apostles holding up scrolls spelling out their creed, and Old Testament prophets bearing their own words.

The greatest challenge was how to achieve the correct sequence in relation to the layout of the chapel. Although the East Window had to contain the Crucifixion over the altar, the focal point of worship, this event came more than halfway through the copiously illustrated source-books, the *Biblia*, which drew upon the scriptures for its precedents, and the *Speculum*, which incorporated a wider range of material including legendary or apocryphal incidents. In the *Biblia*, the Crucifixion was the twenty-fifth scene out of forty (itself a sacred number, being the number of days Christ spent in the wilderness) and in the *Speculum* it came twenty-fourth out of forty-two. This forced Flower (like other glaziers before him) to expand the post-Crucifixion scenes on the south side in order to achieve the same number as those in the opposite windows.

At the same time, he enhanced the subtle spatial harmonies in the relationship between the north and south walls. In the third window of the north wall, he placed disobedient Eve succumbing to the Serpent's temptation, immediately above Mary humbly accepting the glad tidings of the Annunciation angel; the windows almost opposite it in the south wall showed Mary's death and burial, followed by her Assumption into Heaven and her Coronation by her son. A similar conjunction revolved around the figure of King Solomon, who on the north side received gifts from the Queen of Sheba, above the three kings bringing their presents to the Infant Jesus, while diagonally opposite, Solomon crowned his mother Bathsheba above the scene of Jesus crowning Mary.

Flower had already glazed the Westminster Abbey chapel with the Old Law and the New. That building did not have so many windows to fill but they required a different arrangement because there were three tiers, not two. Flower might have got round this by selecting two Old Testament precursors (as there were in the *Biblia*), one above and one below each New Testament scene. However, this has to remain speculation because the Puritans destroyed all that chapel's glass.

The viewers, however learned, needed some help in understanding what was going on the panels so high above their heads. An experienced glass painter like Flower appreciated both the scope and limitations of his medium: he must place key figures at the lower end of each scene for maximum visibility, and he must exaggerate their expressions and gestures, as if they were actors in a large auditorium. This meant making considerable adaptations from the woodblocks, whose standard rectangular 'landscape' illustrations he had to convert into the attenuated 'portrait' format of the stonework. In order to respect the architectural function of the windows as walls of glass, he had to get the right balance between pale, silvery transparency and stronger tones that risked blocking the light. Characters had to be easily identifiable by the colour of their robes (Christ was clad in purple throughout, the colour described in St John's Gospel), sky and water had to be blue, fields and mountains green. At the same time he had to temper these compulsory tones with enough white glass to keep the vast interior luminous.

It probably took Foxe and Flower several meetings to agree the general outline. Flower formally started work in February 1516, when Thomas Larke, the King's surveyor, handed over to him the £100 advance from Provost Hacomblen. The 1516 glazing contract does not survive, but a subsequent one, that of 1526, referred to the indenture that committed Flower to make the windows 'accordingly and after such manner' as he had bound himself to do. His first task was to produce the sequence of small-scale designs, the *vidimus*, for each window. Although his starting point was the woodblock compilations, he and Foxe were also aware of a wider spectrum of models, like the sensitive and detailed interpretations of Bible scenes by German and Flemish masters. Such works were available in the form of engravings that up-to-date patrons like Foxe collected; these often provided the basis of window designs for Flemish glaziers. Flower may have drawn the initial designs himself or immediately commissioned them from other artists.

Having finally selected and allocated the scenes, Flower went to Cambridge to take precise measurements of all the apertures to be glazed, not least the 400 or so openings in the stone tracery at the tops of all the windows. As they were far too high and awkwardly shaped to be incorporated into the Bible narrative, he decided that their subjects must be the Tudor badges and symbols that he had made so many times before and which would echo those in the sculptures that glorified both Henrys and their illustrious family.

The next step was to commission the full-sized 'cartoons' to serve as the crucial templates for the cutting, painting and firing by his workshop. For these drawings, as for the coloured glass he ordered, he looked abroad, to the top artists of the day. The best designers, like the glaziers, came from the Low Countries and Flanders, and they were capable of applying their visual insights to the decoration of many different materials: large-scale bravura creations like the canvas, plaster and woodwork floats and scenery for processions and pageants, the gold and silken tapestries to dress the walls of public hall or private chamber, coloured glass windows for churches or palaces, or intricate little stained and painted roundels for domestic or civic settings. These designers were primarily painters or engravers, but some painted on glass as well and so understood the peculiarities of this most capricious and demanding medium.

They had many new sources to contribute to the Cambridge windows. Moving beyond the medieval formulae, they and their patrons were aware of the advances in Italian art, and their aim was to assimilate the best of that into their own mature and confident tradition. Many windows already showed the influence of eminent oil painters, such as Rogier van der Weyden, Hugo van der Goes, Martin Schongauer and Lucas van Leyden. Their works, transmitted through engravings, provided the means for reverential borrowings in glass in the precise, accurate mode of the late fifteenth century. This was not plagiarism but homage, and it proved that window-designing was as important as any other art. Around 1500, Albrecht Dürer became the new model, and some of his thrillingly innovative reinterpretations of Bible illustrations were faithfully echoed in the Cambridge windows.

The names of Flower's designers are not known for certain. Some confident attributions have been made on the basis of painstaking stylistic comparisons to the works of contemporary artists who designed windows as well as tapestries and other artworks. Examples of their products reached

England, so the most likely assumption is that the royal glazier, a Fleming himself, approached his distinguished fellow countrymen. Yet, as in the case of Flower himself, it is risky to attribute too much to one man when the outcome depended on teamwork. The master of a workshop had a signature style which established the model for his assistants and apprentices to follow, and often for his rivals and competitors as well. Quirks of style also belonged to a particular era: there was suddenly one definitive way of painting, for example, hair, or eyes, or teeth, which everyone followed for a while then abandoned for the next mode. So it is always dangerous to claim to have identified the work of an individual in a fundamentally collaborative and anonymous medium.

However, the styles of those working in the great Flemish centres at the turn of the century and beyond did provide sources for the King's windows. Recurrent names, signed on their works or listed in contracts and commissions, include Bernard van Orley, and Adrian van den Houte from Mechlin, and the latter's pupil, Dierick Vellert from Antwerp, whom some regarded as being as great an artist as Michelangelo. In the years between 1490 and the 1530s, Van Orley, who became official painter to the regent Marguerite of Austria, designed tapestries for the weavers of Brussels, and earned a brief mention in Giorgio Vasari's *Lives of the Artists*, which also stressed Flemish pre-eminence generally: 'in the art of glass and window painting there have been many masters of great ability in those countries'. Vasari also mentioned van den Houte, who was for a while the official glazier of Mechlin (an almost hereditary position previously held by his father, then by his brother), who designed tapestries and painted on glass as well. Positioning figures on a large tapestry posed similar challenges to laying out a window. Symmetry and narrative were not necessarily irreconcilable. Key figures had to be placed on a large scale in the foreground, and beyond them majestic architectural settings which gave some sense of recession and perspective. Classical literature and Bible scenes were treated just the same way in glass and in textiles.

The most famous Fleming of the day, duly acknowledged by Vasari, was Dierick Vellert, who combined creating designs for others with the most skilful painting on glass. He spent most of his working life in the liberal, cosmopolitan city of Antwerp, where he became a master of the Guild of Painters in 1511. Contemporaries hailed him as the one of the greatest living glass painters, and his burgeoning international reputation attracted widespread commissions. He was one of the celebrated local artists whom Albrecht Dürer met during his triumphal progress through the Netherlands in 1520–1. In his journal, Dürer described Vellert as a painter and a glass-painter, a combination evidently worthy of comment, and they discussed techniques together. In the spring of 1521, Dürer reported: 'Master Dierick sent me the red colour that is found in the new bricks', a russet that he and his German contemporaries subsequently adopted. Dürer responded by giving Vellert a set of his inspirational *Apocalypse* woodcuts as well as his *Six Knots*, ornamental designs based on Dürer's observations of Leonardo da Vinci's patterns. In May 1521, Vellert entertained Dürer lavishly: he 'asked many others to meet me . . . and we had a costly feast and they did me great honour'. Dürer was a star to the Netherlandish artists. Although he assimilated and spread the principles of modern Italian art to the north, in their eyes he remained the greatest master of the late Gothic style. By developing such a rich stock of images in his own engravings, he provided many new sources for the painters and glaziers whom he met. Vellert reworked many of these into his own designs and the glass roundels that he painted. Such creative interaction makes it very hard to untangle the original inspiration behind the Cambridge windows.

As was typical for so many stained glass artists, Vellert's name sank into oblivion over the following centuries, when painted glass went completely out of fashion. The large windows he made for Antwerp Cathedral and at Leiden have not survived, but he did put his name or his monogram to the exquisite roundels that he painted or designed with pen, wash or chalk. They show his ingenious adaptations of work by Italian artists like Mantegna, and his ability to change the rectangular format of his sources into the different constraints of a circle. His designs on paper also prove how much was left to the individual glass-painter to insert the final details: there was no point in a busy professional like Vellert doing gratuitous work for others. By analogy, the makers of the King's windows had the autonomy to be inventive, to put in for themselves the accessories of a costume, the marbled detail of a column, or the many little background vignettes that can hardly be seen without the aid of binoculars today.

There is no way of proving that Vellert was associated with the King's windows. But he was one of most sought-after designers of the day. One set of roundels he drew in 1523 was for a typological Old and New Testament sequence based on some of the block-book comparisons also used in King's College Chapel, which he carried out in the most sensitive and truthful manner despite their miniature scale. Another traditional narrative he tackled was of scenes from the life of the Virgin, the subject that began and ended the Cambridge windows as well. Vellert produced one such series in 1532 which took as its starting point a nineteen-part woodcut cycle that Dürer drew in 1502.

Whoever was responsible for the cartoons and the painting of the Cambridge windows – and there can be no doubt that many hands were involved – the broad influence of Vellert, together with his numerous imitators, was undeniable. In this way, Barnard Flower's commission of the initial set brought the chapel into line with the greatest innovations of Flemish art.

Chapter Twelve: 'Cunning in the Art of Glazing'

BARNARD FLOWER HAD to fit his work on the chapel into a schedule already made hectic by King Henry VIII's demands for more new glass in his palaces and manors than his father had ever installed. The glazing team worked in London, perhaps in the royal workshop at Westminster (if this had been rebuilt after the 1512 fire) or in Flower's premises in Southwark.

Stained glass windows were composed of many separate, lead-bound panels that were assembled on site at the time of installation. Flower divided each long light of the King's Chapel windows into an average of eight panels (though this occasionally varied from six to nine). This meant that every window required approximately eighty panels to fill its ten lights, so the total for the north and south windows alone would be around 1,900 panels, plus a further 400 for the tracery lights above. (This discounted the windows in the small side chapels, some of which were already glazed but were not the responsibility of the royal team.) The project was going to be very expensive in time and in resources.

Flower chose a structure with a strong horizontal emphasis: each window was supported by horizontal iron bars set into the stonework, to which the separate panels of glass were attached by copper wires. These bars were unusually close together, which meant that the glaziers cut quite a lot of the glass into rectangular shapes to match the line of the bars, an idea Flower might have pioneered at Westminster Abbey. These bars were reinforced on the outside by a set of vertical ones.

As royal glazier, Flower was expected to paint significant areas of the glass himself, like faces and hands, especially those of the major figures. Yet it would have been wrong for viewers to recognise any mannerism that was too individual (if they had even been able to do so, considering the height) for this was teamwork. Although he was responsible for the initial designs, bearing in mind he was a craftsman and not a theologian, the cartoons were the work of others and his job was to interpret them in glass, paint and stain.

After Flower's signing of the February 1516 contract, it took him and his men eighteen months to make just the first four windows. This total is known, because the subsequent contract, that of 1526, referred to twenty more that had to be made for the north and south walls, plus the East and West Windows. Flower may also have been responsible for the 396 panels for the tracery openings of all the windows, visually important yet a relatively routine sequence of Tudor symbols and initials, which apprentices could have produced from the same set of cartoons. Below a row of six larger symbols, the tracery of each window also contained a row of eight angels supporting shields bearing the same Tudor emblems; the angular folds of their robes recalled those of late fifteenth-century glass, suggesting a consistently early date, and perhaps the use of old cartoons. As the tracery panels were all relatively small, they would have required less storage space than those of the main windows.

The overall unity of the glass is its most impressive feature, a tribute to the skills of all those involved, not just the known glaziers but their anonymous assistants, apprentices and journeymen, whose contributions all combined to form a transcendent whole. Distinguishing Flower's phase from the later, post-1526, one depends a lot on subjective interpretation, such as deciding whether the minutest features — such as the recurrent undershot jaws, rows of tombstone teeth, or the particular curls of beard or moustache — are the inventions of the glazier who painted them or the cartoonist who sketched them in first.*

Of the scenes or windows that have been linked with Flower, one in particular stands out, preliminary in the sense that it experiments with an arrangement that was not repeated elsewhere. This is the window over the north door (Window 2), the second in the narrative's chronological sequence. It shows two familiar incidents from the life of the Virgin: her dedication to God in the Temple, and her marriage to Joseph. The design cleverly combines aspects of the *Speculum* and the *Biblia* woodblocks: the characters are those of the former, but the layout incorporates a characteristic of the latter, the presence of half-figures of prophets under architectural niches at the top and bottom of each page. These characters hold scrolls which refer to other relevant prototypes. Window 2 also has demi-figures, which alternate with angels in a row along the bottom. The glass also echoes the *Speculum*'s use of three Old Testament prototypes for every New Testament scene: the presentation of a golden table to the Temple (in fact, a legendary rather than a biblical incident) prefigures the dedication of Mary underneath, while the scrolls of the two little prophets refer to *Hester* and *Jepthah,* ramming the message home: the Old Testament Esther was presented to Ahasuerus, while Jephthah sacrificed his daughter to God.

Such half-figures had appeared in the Westminster Abbey glass, but the examples in Cambridge show how they cluttered and compartmentalised the scene, and gave unnecessary prominence to figures who did not play any part in the main action. They also duplicated the scroll-bearing messengers in the central light. This arrangement was not repeated.

Window 2 also differs from the rest in its dominant silvery tones. It contains much white glass, and relatively little coloured, a permutation

---

* Attempting to define Flower's hand by comparisons with the work he is presumed to have done at Winchester, Westminster and Fairford is unreliable because there is no one panel in any of those places that can be securely attributed to him, except by virtue of hypothetical recognition of what he may or may not have done at King's — a dangerously circular argument.

which looks back rather than forward. The exceptional tonal quality and translucency of the glass suggests a particular source of supply that dried up as the glaziers' fashion for imitating oil paintings encouraged glass-makers to experiment with stronger colours. Another distinctive feature is that the main characters are relatively small in size compared to those in other windows, and are placed towards the middle of the light rather than lower down, because that space was taken up by the row of demi-figures. The characters appear a little stiff, assuming poses that lack the momentum or passion of many elsewhere.

Finally, while most of the messengers in the chapel were taken from a limited set of cartoons, duplicated or sometimes reversed for variety of pose, the four here are unique to this window. Perhaps Flower was working from old cartoons, almost worn out from use in a previous commission such as the Westminster Abbey chapel. In other windows, the format of the messengers was developed. Instead of the four equal-sized figures of Window 2, there might be two full-sized and two demi-figures, while many are in motion, twisting and turning as if scrutinising the events in the panels beside them.

Yet despite the 'earlier' features of Window 2, it also had many up-to-date decorative details, notably the carved friezes of lively Renaissance motifs of leafy scrolls and little animals above the compartments of the prophets and angels, altogether a wonderful confusion of old and new.

Another window that showed off an old-fashioned technique was Window 9. One Old Testament scene showed manna raining from Heaven to feed Moses and the Israelites starving in the wilderness, prefiguring the Last Supper below. It was a magnificent example of fifteenth-century-style glass-cutting, for each piece of manna was a circular disc of white glass separately leaded into a deep blue sky. Cutting glass into circles is as difficult as making the round holes to receive them, yet there are seventy of these inserts. Flower and his glaziers showed off their talents in a time-consuming exercise devised to make glass look like precious stones embedded into a king's crown or the hem of a garment. Anyone looking at the white snowflakes of manna in the window knew that it took a lifetime's skill to achieve effects like that. The window's second Old Testament scene, the Fall of the Rebel Angels, has also been attributed to Flower because its design harks back to the late fifteenth century

Window 6 has the actual date '1517' in a small panel at the base of one scene, although its general style is not noticeably early or different. For this reason, it is difficult to argue the case for identifying the four Flower-period windows on the basis of style, content, and nature and colour of the glass, while the many disruptions, repairs and replacements make it hard to define what is original. The Victorian stained glass artist, Nathaniel Westlake, provided an empathetic visual analysis and defined the earliest windows as being in a Dürer-like style, characterised by buildings with horizontal ceilings and large round arches viewed full on, with the sense of space or depth not yet fully realised. The characters' garments had broad folds and floating, ornamental drapery. The colour tones were lighter than in subsequent phases, because there was as yet no use of the coloured enamel painting *on* the surface of the glass that tended to keep the light out, while the leads were still an integral part of the design, outlining and defining the pot-metal features.

As well as establishing the correct biblical parallels and planning the Tudor badges for the tracery, Flower had to concern himself with the future effect of the glass in the building. This had to be an act of faith and of the imagination, but was also based on his own long experience of having installed so many windows elsewhere. One impression he may have been trying to achieve was that of tapestry. It was as if he saw the chapel as a great hall in a king's palace, decorated with beasts and badges, and the walls clad in shimmering coloured glass that appeared to move and glow in sunlight, just as tapestries shifted in draughts and gleamed with the momentary reflection of candlelight or the flames of a fire. The windows' background of flowers and trees, beasts and birds, and grand buildings belonged to the pageantry of tapestry, proving the many connections between designs for windows and designs for tapestries.

Flower also meant the windows to complement the actual tapestries that were hung around the lower half of the walls. This was standard practice. Our modern eyes, attuned to simplicity and restraint and the long history of puritanical reticence in religious buildings, have to reclothe those stark walls not just with the gold and scarlet paint that decorated the carvings, but with shining fabrics too. Henry VI's first chapel (which remained in unexpectedly long use pending the second's delayed completion) had many adornments. Its walls were hung with cloth of gold, its altar draped with elaborate embroideries, hung around with curtains, approached by a Turkish carpet and surmounted by 'a costly canopy of red cloth of bawdkin with greyhounds and hinds of gold'.

One of the royal glazier's many responsibilities was liaising with the college's clerk of the works and its master mason over the actual fitting of the windows because their great height obviously required scaffolding for the installation; but there was no point in assembling this until several windows were ready. In the meantime Flower had no room in his workshop to store the finished pieces, and the college expected to take delivery of the windows it had paid for.

Under the terms of his contract, Flower faced the daunting task of arranging the safe transport of the fragile glass to Cambridge, packed in purpose-built wooden crates protected by straw. We do not know which Flower decided, but his options were road or water. The choice, made in consultation with the college, depended upon the necessary balance between speed and safety, time of year and likely weather conditions. There were various well-trodden routes to Cambridge: the town was a magnet for traders from all over the region because of its market and ancient fairs. And the colleges added to the coming and going, with their many visitors – royals, clerics and students – making regular journeys to and from the town.

Heavy loads often went by road. Fifteenth-century toll records for London Bridge suggest a thriving, long-distance cart trade using well-established routes, with teams of pack-horses drawing goods to destinations such as Coventry or Leicester; it took eight days, for example, for a cart to travel between London and Gloucester. Cambridge was approached from the main road north out of London, which led ultimately to Carlisle, via Waltham Cross and Ware or Royston. The whole medieval road system was punctuated by the shrines that pilgrims flocked to visit. The Tudors, like earlier monarchs, made frequent cross-country progressions and accounts kept by the Royal Wardrobe show that carts and horses were specially commissioned for long journeys. Loads were costed at a daily rate, based on size and weight, which affected the number of horses required, the length of each day's journey and the overall distance.

Boat transport was slower but cheaper, and carriage by sea cost less than carriage by river. If the stained glass panels went by water, they could have been loaded downstream from London Bridge, to avoid having to shoot the rapids between its supporting piles, on to a ship that sailed down the Thames estuary then all the way round the East Anglian coast to the port of King's Lynn, the major depot for the region. Here the crates would be transferred to a shallow-bottomed barge, with oars and a sail, that took the river route to Cambridge through monastically maintained waterways along the Ouse through Ely, then into the Cam, from where they were unloaded at the King's College watergate.

Other itineraries combined water and road, using the River Lea, which flowed from the Thames through the City and all the way to Ware (home of the legendary Great Bed), and then transferring to the Cambridge road. Henry III used this route in 1258 to transport thirty-two tuns of wine all the way from Peterborough to Westminster, first by river to Cambridge, then overland to Ware, then down the Lea and into the Thames. But the Lea was so sluggish by the mid-sixteenth century that the court of London aldermen set up a commission to consider opening it up again, so it was probably not a viable route for the carriage of the King's College glass in the first half of the century.*

Henry VIII's Wardrobe Accounts reveal the day-to-day details of how royal luggage was transported. Delicate panels of glass, paid for by the king,

---

* By 1570, the clearances proved so effective that a horse-drawn barge travelled from Bow, near the Tower, to Ware in just twelve hours.

would have received the same attention. It took a team of nine men and hired tow-horses two days and a night to pull the king's possessions downstream from Hampton Court to Westminster. For land transport, his wagons were of different lengths and types. (The most impressive vehicle required a team of twenty-four sturdy Flanders mares to draw the cannon that were an essential part of the king's armoury.) To cover goods and crates in barges or carts, cow- and horse-skins were soaked in grease to make them waterproof.

In February 1517, when he had completed the first four windows, Barnard Flower submitted further designs to the college for approval and received another £100 to go ahead. But he saw no windows in position because he died in the summer of that year. He never found out whether all the panels so laboriously crafted in the London workshops actually fitted the window apertures perfectly, or whether they needed deft modifications to offset faulty measurements, and he did not learn whether the stone mullion separating the two halves of each scene had an irrevocably divisive effect. Nor did he see how the colours blazed into life as the clouds moved away, how the morning light was so different from the afternoon's, and how the low winter sun made the glass cast spotlights on the opposite walls.

In his will, 'I, Barnard Flower, the King's Glazier of England' divided his goods between 'Edy my loving wife' and his sons Francis and Lucas (who was a glazier too) and requested burial in the Holy Trinity chapel of his local church, St Thomas the Martyr in Southwark. Henry VII had spent a fortune to ensure the safe passage of his soul after death. His glazier had similar concerns but more humble resources: he showed a touching loyalty to his former master by making bequests to the same two foundations that had benefited from the king's will. Henry had left the handsome sums of £200 each to the Friars Observant at Greenwich and at Richmond in return for 500 masses. Flower could only afford 20 shillings for each 'to pray for my soul and for all expiring souls' but this request was more unselfish than the king's. At both these places, he had worked long and hard putting in the king's windows (his will proudly mentioned the Richmond Friary as being 'near to the king's palace'), and at Greenwich he had installed images of the whole Tudor family in the window of the friars' church. He must have retained happy memories of the holy brothers, so admired for their simple life-style and devotion to St Francis.

With Flower's death, the Cambridge project lost its momentum. Henry VIII inherited and outdid his father's love of display, for he too appreciated the status that artistic and architectural projects, including stained glass, would give him among the new generation of European rulers. But finding the money for the chapel windows took low priority – until he and his chief minister, Thomas Wolsey, needed the university's support.

Chapter Thirteen: The Evil May Day

H ENRY VIII'S COMMISSIONS to the royal glazier, and to other
alien craftsmen, were made in a time of growing hostility to
foreigners. Despite Henry Tudor's positive encouragement of
Flemish craftsmen, the traditional fear and loathing of the strangers revived
after his son inherited the throne — not that it had ever gone away. It was
also a time of wider insecurity, as if society was unsettled by the death of
the old king but was not yet certain how his youthful heir was going to turn
out.* Immigrants remained the favourite target. John Skelton voiced the
national mood in *The manner of the world nowadays*:

> So many Easterlings,
> Lombards and Flemings,
> To bear away our winnings,
> Saw I never.

* One odd attempt to appease the national mood was what might be called the 'Hoodies'
Act, a measure of 1511 intended to stop people concealing their identities by covering their
faces and so getting away with 'murder, felony, rape and other great hurts and
inconveniences'. They were now liable to arrest, and faced imprisonment and heavy fines.

Henry VIII's erratic and interventionist foreign policies took their toll on alien craftsmen: despite royal patronage, glaziers suffered as much as anyone else. One way for the king to appease his loyal English subjects was to withdraw some of the rights of denizens. The Subsidy Acts of 1514 and 1515, which were intended to raise the £160,000 that Henry needed to pay for his campaigns against the French and the Scots, reversed some of his father's measures and made denizens liable to taxation at double the rate of natives, just like registered aliens. With the loss of such a useful exemption, the number of applicants for the now doubtful privilege of denizenship naturally declined.

This did not pacify the extremists. Hall's London Chronicle for 1516–17 expressed the national mood: 'the strangers were so proud that they disdained, mocked and oppressed [the English craftsmen] who could not get a living.' In April 1516, someone posted a notice on the door of St Paul's Cathedral complaining that the king favoured the aliens and gave them money: in modern tabloid terms, they were scroungers. City aldermen scrutinised the handwriting on the document but failed to find the culprit.

The xenophobia came to a head in 1517, a year which started so cold that the Thames froze over and people could walk across the ice from Westminster to Lambeth. These extreme conditions were succeeded by a severe and unseasonally early outbreak of the sweating sickness that kept the king and court out of London that spring: they intended to spend May Day at Richmond. This long absence bred a sense of insecurity in the City, the feeling of being abandoned to hordes of foreign merchants and craftsmen. The relationship between English and Flemish glaziers reached rock bottom when members of the beleaguered Company of Glaziers and Glass Painters, irritated by their continuing inability to attract the wealthiest patrons, became increasingly vindictive towards foreign workers. In a petition dated March 1517, the company laid an official complaint against a Dutch glazier, Herry Sutton, unlawfully working in the City 'to the great hurt and prejudice of the whole body of glaziers being freemen'. This was settled out of court, with Herry being allowed to join the company, but was evidence of the general belief that immigrants were taking work from Englishmen.

At the same time, John Lincoln, a City merchant and broker, determined to limit the status and influence at court of the flourishing London community of continental traders and dealers, and complained that 'the merchant strangers brought in all silks, cloth of gold, wine, oil, iron and such other merchandise that no man almost buyeth of an Englishman'. In an age when public speaking was the most potent way of reaching an audience, he sought wider backing for his campaign by begging Dr Henry Standish, a charismatic preacher from the Hospital of the Mendicant Friars, to 'take part with the commonalty against the strangers', using the opportunity offered by the series of popular open-air sermons preached over Easter at St Mary Spital and St Paul's, attended by Lord Mayor, aldermen and huge crowds. When Standish refused to include such provocative material in his Easter Monday sermon, Lincoln appealed to the speaker for Tuesday, Canon Dr Beale: 'You were born in London, and see the oppression of the strangers and the very great misery of your own country. Exhort all the citizens to join in one against the strangers, ravenors and destroyers of your country.'

Beale was sympathetic, and on Easter Tuesday, 14 April, preached a sermon that drew heavily on the 'facts' in a memorandum that Lincoln had drafted. He complained about the rising number of immigrants – 'the strangers compass the city round about . . . they grow into such a multitude that it is to be looked upon' and deplored their undesirable success at business and trade 'which is the cause that Englishmen want and starve'. His peroration called upon his fellow countrymen to protect their land against all aliens: 'as birds would defend their nests, so ought Englishmen to cherish and defend themselves and to hurt and grieve aliens for the common weal.' These inflammatory words alarmed important foreign residents such as Giustinian, the Venetian ambassador, who reported to his Doge the allegations of Dr Beale, including some sexual slurs: foreigners not only deprived the English of 'their industry and of the emoluments derivable, but disgraced their dwellings, taking their wives and their daughters'.

On Tuesday 28 April, a handful of Londoners were arrested for violence to foreigners and thrown into Newgate prison. This so aggrieved others that, according to Giustinian, 'they commenced threatening the strangers that on 1st May they would cut them to pieces and sack their houses'. May Day was a date to fear because, as a public festival, it was an opportunity for large unruly crowds to assemble. The alarmed Venetian insisted on a meeting with Cardinal Wolsey, and even travelled to Richmond to see the king. As a result, on Thursday 30 April, Wolsey summoned the mayor and corporation to his residence at York Place and warned them that 'we are informed that your young and riotous people will rise and distress the strangers'. 'No, surely', said the mayor. 'And I trust so to govern them that the King's peace will not be broken.' He was over-optimistic. His last-minute attempt to impose a curfew that evening was thwarted when Alderman Sir John Munday, heeding Wolsey's warning, attempted to stop two apprentices play-fighting with swords and shields in front of a crowd. Shouting 'Clubs! Prentices!', gangs of youths (their number estimated at 2,000) rampaged through the streets, attacking and looting the houses of foreign craftsmen, particularly the Flemish and French, before plunging into the Italian quarter, where the forewarned merchants managed to resist them. The mob even threatened the Lord Mayor, but finally dispersed when the Lieutenant of the Tower turned his guns on them. Then troops alerted by Wolsey forced open the city gates 'closed by these seditious rebels, who had overpowered the forces of the Lord Mayor and aldermen' and arrested over 400 of the rioters.

By now there were 5,000 men-at-arms in the City, according to Giustinian. On 1 May, they arrested Lincoln and Dr Beale, seen as the real instigators of the riot. On 4 May, the prisoners, 'some men, some lads, some children of thirteen years', were marched through the streets to be tried. Thirteen ringleaders were found guilty of high treason, because they had committed hostile acts on foreigners, thus risking war in a period of peace in Europe, and were sentenced to death. The following week, Lincoln and the remaining rioters, 400 men and eleven women, were also condemned. Lincoln was executed immediately, but tensions remained so high at the threatened execution of so many Englishmen and women, guilty only of their natural suspicion of foreigners, that a deputation of City aldermen and recorders attended the king at Greenwich to beg him to reconsider the verdict. On 22 May, Henry and Wolsey performed a carefully staged act of mercy in the lawcourt summoned to Westminster Hall, where all the condemned were in the dock. The cardinal spoke up for the prisoners and the king magnanimously granted them their liberty. 'And when the Cardinal told them this, it was a fine sight to see each man take the halter from his neck and throw it in the air.'

So the king and his chief minister appeared to yield to the demands of their subjects, which did little to improve attitudes to immigrant craftsmen. If anyone benefited, it was Wolsey, who emerged with enhanced powers. Yet crown and court appreciated rather more than their hostile subjects the high-quality products of aliens, and the discontents bubbled away, fomenting another anti-foreign rising in the city just a few months after the May Day riot.

Acts of violence, people whose faces were contorted with hatred, troops of armed men brandishing pikes, swords and spiked clubs, all appear in the windows, almost as if inspired by these events. Barnard Flower had lived through that period of cruel discrimination that continued to affect his colleagues and successors. He left designs for the windows that included many scenes of brutality. In Window 6, the Massacre of the Innocents, Herod's soldiers butcher children with knives, overseen by a cruel officer on horseback; in Window 10, the Betrayal of Christ, a threatening troop of armoured men assembles to arrest Jesus; in the East Window's Crucifixion scenes, groups of menacing Roman soldiers enforce the terrible proceedings. The bystanders, too, are vicious. Sneering men point at Jesus, mock him by pulling faces and nail him to the cross. The models may be biblical but the mood is contemporary. The glaziers painted with passion and truth, bringing their real world into the Cambridge windows.

Chapter Fourteen: Cloth of Gold

THANKS TO HENRY Tudor's careful housekeeping, his son was able to spend lavishly on the arts. Stained glass was an essential part of his secular magnificence, for its jewel-like Tudor symbols affirmed his power. Another great indulgence was tapestry. Henry owned over 2,000 pieces, at a time when this was the most expensive art form of all; they adorned the walls of his palaces and his many manor houses.

The inventories that listed the contents of the Palace of Whitehall in 1542, and Henry VIII's other goods after his death in 1547, bring to life this court of pageantry and symbolism, where there was no such thing as neutral ornament. His father's newly created Tudor rose was multiplied a hundredfold in a profusion of images overwhelming fabrics and furniture, wood and precious metal. Painted in windows and plastered on the walls, it also decorated most of Henry's personal possessions. There were 'double red and white roses' embroidered on the damask and cloth of gold hangings of the king's ornate bedstead (one of many), with matching counterpane of 'white damask embroidered with a great double red and white rose, in the middle still magnificent' (though 'it is perished in two places with rats'). Carpets and cushions, chair coverings and clothes were also stamped with roses, and they were even embroidered on the tasteful covers of matching sets of close-stools. One set was 'covered with tawny velvet fringed with black silk embroidered with a rose of Venice gold and lined with scarlet'. The message was driven home at the dining table too, where, among quantities of rose-embossed luxury tableware such as basins and ewers, were a gold spoon 'with a rose at the end, half red and half white' and a salt-cellar of gold and jasper 'with a cover of red and white roses'. Even his candlesticks were draped with metallic roses of Venice gold and silver, and decorated tassels.

This leading symbol was accompanied by all the others familiar in glass and stone – the Beaufort portcullis, the fleur-de-lys, the royal coat of arms, sets of entwined initials, from the H&E of his parents down to his own changing tally of wives – but now on an epic scale. Henry commissioned a whole repertoire of 'the King's arms and badges', stitched or spun, like the 'bedstead painted with bice and gilded with burnished gold, with valances of purple gold tissue and crimson velvet, embroidered with the King's arms and badges', the 'counterpane of crimson damask embroidered with the King's arms and four of his grace's badges crowned with garlands bordered round about with an embroidery of yellow cloth of gold and the King's badges fringed likewise about with a short fringe of Venice gold and lined with red sarcenet'. They were embossed on jugs and painted on the frame of one of his myriad looking glasses, 'set in wood, gilded and painted having a naked woman with a child in her hand and in the top thereof the King's arms supported by his grace's beasts'. The naked woman was a nod to the Renaissance but the badges were utterly Tudor.

To promote this ostentation, Henry supported the royal workshops his father had established, and encouraged more continental artists to come to England. As well as experiencing the Renaissance mediated through Flemish and German art, Henry patronised Italian artists directly. He invited to London the Florentine sculptor Pietro Torrigiano, once a fellow student of the young Michelangelo in Lorenzo de Medici's sculpture garden (where Torrigiano allegedly punched the sculptor through jealousy of his talent, causing Michelangelo's famous broken nose and forcing Torrigiano to flee from Florence). For Henry VIII, he created the magnificent tombs of Henry Tudor and his wife, and of Lady Margaret Beaufort, in Westminster Abbey. Torrigiano spent several years in England producing busts and effigies, including those of Henry VII and of Bishop Fisher, as well as an extravagant funeral monument of marble, jasper and bronze for Henry VIII at Windsor. According to Vasari, Torrigiano 'received so many rewards and was so largely remunerated that, had he not been a most violent, reckless and ill-conducted person, he might have lived there a life of ease and brought his days to a peaceful close'. But his restless temperament took him from England to Spain in the early 1520s.

Another Florentine sculptor, Giovanni di Maiano, embellished Hampton Court and other palaces with classical reliefs and ornaments. Yet Flemings and Germans continued to make a major contribution to court art too. Henry Tudor's painter Maynard Vewicke worked for Henry VIII until he was succeeded by Gerard Horenbout from Ghent. Horenbout also designed tapestries and windows, while his son Lucas and his daughter Susannah painted manuscripts and portrait miniatures. (Dürer met the talented family in 1521 before they came to England, and was sufficiently impressed by Susannah to buy one of her illuminations for a florin, though he noted patronisingly that 'it is very wonderful that a woman can do so much'.) Hans Holbein, born in Augsburg, first came to England in 1526, then returned in the 1530s to paint Henry and his court.

A prime opportunity for Henry to show off his wealth, taste and opulent life-style, enhanced by the talents of the royal glazier, was the most lavish summit meeting of all time, the Field of Cloth of Gold, where he met the French king Francis I at Guisnes, near Calais, in June 1520. This encounter was the brainchild of Henry's Lord Chancellor, Cardinal Wolsey, who had only three months to organise the entire exercise. Henry's retinue consisted of almost 4,000 people and over 2,000 horses and the queen's, with 1,100 attendants and nearly 800 horses, was also substantial. Much of their followers' accommodation was necessarily makeshift, in 2,800 tents, but not that of the royal couple or the architect of the meeting, Wolsey. Determined to outdo the French monarch, Henry decided to erect a temporary palace on the green beside the ruined castle of Guisnes. It was Wolsey who had to ensure that everything required for the building was carried out according to the royal will. The rapid construction and over-the-top decoration of 'this burnished summer palace, put up and pulled down in a month' showed off the skills of all the royal craftsmen, their achievement the more dazzling because this was just a transitory structure.

Accounts and letters reveal the epic scale of the project. It involved 500 carpenters, 300 masons, 100 joiners, plus glaziers, painters, carvers, smiths: in all, there were over 2,000 English and Flemish workmen. The building was 328 feet (100 metres) square, set on a foundation of brick, whose upper walls, 30 feet (9 metres) high, were made out of timber and painted canvas. Statues of great warriors such as Hercules and Alexander guarded the main gate. The state apartments within offered generous accommodation for the royal family and for Cardinal Wolsey, whose suite was next to Henry's. Other rooms were on an equally vast scale. The Great Chamber was 124 feet (37.7 metres) long and 42 feet (12.8 metres) wide, larger than the one in the palace of Whitehall. The dining room, 80 by 34 feet (24.3 by 10.3 metres) was bigger than the greatest chamber in Bridewell Palace, and the blue- and gold-painted chapel glittered with the finest 'hangings, jewels, images and altar cloths and copes and vestments that Henry VII gave to Westminster Abbey'. Equally eye-catching were the king's tapestries, which attracted even more admiring comments than everything else.

Completing the works by the time the royal party arrived on 4 June was due to heroic feats of organisation by Sir Nicholas Vaux, one of Wolsey's secretaries, whose correspondence reveals all the anxieties caused by the overrunning and unscheduled extra costs of any major project. But this was on a unique scale, the deadline was immovable and the client, demanding progress yet complaining about going over budget, was Henry VIII.

Like the Great Exhibitions of the nineteenth century, this was an exercise to boast the superiority of English productivity in the decorative arts, even though many of these craftsmen were not native born. They included pavilion makers, armourers, painters, carpenters, gilders and the like, their tasks made additionally complicated by having to do much of the work on site instead of in their familiar London workshops. To demonstrate the English adoption of the latest continental taste, Wolsey even borrowed decorative terracotta plaques in the ultra-fashionable Italian style from the Duke of Suffolk's elegant Southwark residence. As well as the Renaissance motifs, Tudor badges were prominent – and the rose, of course, was everywhere. Vaux reported to Wolsey how John Brown, the King's Painter, and his colleagues 'do make and garnish all the roses – a marvellous great charge, for the roses be large and stately'. And he begged for more money so that 'the king be not disappointed with his roses'. Also prominent were the king's beasts: lion and dragon supported the arms above the entrance to the king's lodgings, dragon and greyhound reared up on the corner turrets.

Crucial to the king's display was the contribution of the royal glazier, Barnard Flower's successor, Galyon Hone. The summer palace was 'glazed with the best glass that could be gotten'. One French official marvelled that half the building seemed to be made of glass, because the otherwise illusionary, theatrical confection had real windows on every side, including 'curiously glazed' oriels whose decoration must have consisted of more Tudor badges. Another eye-catching glazed building was the tapestry-hung chamber where the two queens sat to watch their husbands in the tournament, for a whole week of jousting was scheduled for the festivities, whose other delights included dancing and wrestling.

The accounts list several payments to Galyon Hone, one of £20 for work done in England, and others totalling £68, which included 'setting up the king's glass', while John Tybott received £38 for 4,000 feet (1,220 metres) of glass bought at nearby St Omer. This suggests that the royal glazier had to do much of the work in France: it would have been too complicated, time-consuming and risky to ship glass to London, decorate it there, then send it back across the Channel.

The craftsmen were all at the top of their professions, and knew each other well from previous projects. In addition to the King's Glazier, there was the King's Painter, the Serjeant of the Tents and producer of the entertainments (a former actor), and a lighting expert. Such men were used to creating ephemeral shows, in the form of floats, arches or backdrops for the pageants and processions that contributed so much to a king's public image on occasions such as the official entry to a town or the reception of a royal bride. Court artists knew how to re-create the impact of a Roman triumph, reinterpreting classical buildings in canvas or plasterboard. Such buildings recur in the glass of King's College Chapel, where almost every window displays some form of grandiose architecture: classical façades, pilasters and columns, domed interiors, even triumphal arches, surrounding Old Testament rulers or inventing a Roman Jerusalem. They seem to retain the memory of Henry's glorious visit and all the promise of the reign.

Apart from the terrible weather that fortnight, the only sour note was struck by one reluctant participant in the official retinue, Bishop Fisher, observing the conduct and character of the young king, his patroness Lady Margaret Beaufort's grandson. That autumn, he preached a sermon which began by praising the magnificence of the occasion: the great princes, the rich silks and velvets, the fine tents, the dancing, tournaments and jousting. Yet, he warned, all this outward show of consumerism created envy and meant nothing. If you take away the 'glittering garments, take away the Cloth of Gold . . . what difference is betwixt Emperor and another poor man'. And he went on to attack the worldly ambition of great men and princes 'showing their richness, showing their power', among whom he included 'the king, our master'.

Chapter Fifteen: Galyon Hone, King's Glazier

THE KING'S NEW glazier was another alien. Galyon Hone described himself as 'a native of Holland and a subject of the Emperor'. Born in the Netherlands, he trained as a glazier in Antwerp but had settled in England by 1510, when he worked as one of Barnard Flower's team on projects that included Whitehall Palace, Hampton Court and Eton College.

After Flower's death in 1517, Henry appointed Hone to the vacant position, overlooking, as his father had done, any likely English candidates from the London Company of Glaziers. As Henry VIII put up or modernised many more buildings than his father, with showy glass an essential feature, Hone's status was higher than that of Flower, as was his sense of self-importance. Tantalising glimpses of his private life suggest an obstreperous, energetic character who applied the same drive and self-confidence to his profession, and who achieved a position that would have been impossible without the support of the king.

Like his fellow aliens, Hone lived in Southwark. Evidence of his aspirant life-style and involvement in local affairs came from a bizarre court case when the unhappy parishioners of St Thomas's Hospital (the ward where Barnard Flower had lived too) laid a complaint against the Master and Brethren of what was evidently a run-down and corrupt institution. In a petition addressed to the Member of Parliament for Southwark, Sir Richard Longe, Master of the King's Hawks and Buckhounds, they accused the recently appointed Master of the hospital, Richard Mabbott, of a string of misdemeanours. Hone was involved because one of Mabbott's many crimes was breaking into the royal glazier's garden and stealing sixty young bay trees. This implies an ambitious space in which Hone was emulating the formal arrangements of the gardens of the palaces whose windows he installed: Mabbott obviously wanted one like that too. His other alleged offences included refusing charitable relief to the sick and poor, selling off the church plate ('The world is nought, let us take what we may', he announced), shutting down the free school and failing to preach sermons or employ a priest to sing high Mass. His retort to local residents protesting against his lax regime was: 'If thou like not thy house, get thee out of it!' And there were worse accusations – brawling in the streets, stabbing one Sir Thomas Ladde, and maintaining a mistress called Julyan Foster, whom he set up in a house in Lambeth and put in charge of the good sisters of the hospital: those who complained were put in the stocks or beaten. However, when Ladde called for Mabbott's notorious mistress to be burned, Hone came to Mabbott's assistance and tried to act as peacemaker

In litigious mood, Hone pursued a separate court case against William Rawlyns, grocer, following a disagreement between the two over the repayment conditions of a loan Rawlyns had made to Hone. Both sides submitted a flurry of petitions to the Court of Chancery, Hone claiming that he had fulfilled his side of the agreement, while Rawlyns denied this was so. The outcome was unclear, but Hone's passionate, indignant phrases leap from the scribe's neat italic on the scraps of parchment that survive today. Such qualities also benefited Hone in his role as fearless leader and self-appointed spokesman for the alien glaziers in a period of increasing tension with the reactionary Glaziers Company across the river.

The *Returns of Aliens* recorded the names of Hone's assistants. Although the compiler anglicised their Christian names to the nearest equivalent, their surnames reveal their 'Doche' origin: William Dyurekson, George Cornelysson, John Delhase, William Monserkyn, John Mattyson. Galyon

Hone, however, managed to retain his unusual forename in all documents (though with several different spellings), further evidence of his confident sense of identity.

The turbulent royal glazier and his men contributed to the sumptuous updating and refurbishing of the exceptional number of palaces, country houses and hunting lodges that Henry greedily acquired. Stained glass windows boasting Tudor slogans were the ultimate refinement, complementing the tapestries, rich furniture and sideboards laden with gold and silver that filled the public rooms. As a further luxury, many of these domestic windows were also hung with curtains of costly fabrics – satin or sarsenet, taffeta or damask – although in summer they were taken down and replaced by leafy branches to provide dappled shade.

One of Hone's first projects for the king was repairing all the glass in the palace at Bridewell, next to the Blackfriars. This had been occupied by Cardinal Wolsey, but became for a while the king's main London base after the 1512 fire that put the Palace of Westminster temporarily out of commission. Bridewell remained the place where Henry hosted events of state, such as the reception of the Emperor Charles in 1522, or the elevation of his illegitimate son, in the absence of any legitimate one, to become the Duke of Richmond in 1525, or the less happy arrival of the papal legates in 1528 to discuss the idea of a royal divorce. In all, Henry spent around £20,000 on Bridewell, the money handled by his clerk Thomas Larke, who was also Surveyor of the King's Works in Cambridge.

As a retreat from London when the plague threatened, as it so often did, Henry modernised and extended Hunsdon Manor in Hertfordshire. Here Hone repaired all the old windows and created a whole heraldic symphony in glass during the 1520s and 1530s, displaying 'the king's arms, poises [mottoes], badges and bends set and glazed in the said windows'. At Oatlands and Eltham palaces too, the windows shone with roses, portcullises and hawthorns (for which Hone received 12d per badge) and at the manor house of The More, in Hertfordshire, he installed arms, badges and inscriptions in the huge bay window and clerestory of the king's presence chamber.

Henry's greatest extravagance was Hampton Court Palace, the building first owned by Cardinal Wolsey, who lavished considerable attention on it and decorated parts in the new Renaissance style. But for fear of appearing grander than his master, the cardinal sensibly presented the king with the purpose-built set of royal lodgings there in 1525, and received in return the inferior and now old-fashioned palace at Richmond. They both used Hampton Court over the next few years, while Wolsey carried out further building works. The tipping point came in September 1528, when Henry was about to receive the papal legate, and ordered Wolsey to vacate the premises.

After Henry took over Hampton Court, its further improvements proved so costly to him that Wolsey's successor, Thomas Cromwell, complained: 'What a great charge it is to the king to continue his building ... how proud and false the workmen be; and if the king would spare for one year, how profitable it would be to him.' Galyon Hone was probably one of the workmen referred to, expressing an unseemly but characteristic pride in his craft. Henry had Wolsey's Great Hall knocked down and began a new one. Hone filled all the windows with heraldic panels, which included '30 of the King's and the Queen's arms, price the piece 4s. Also 46 badges of the King's and the Queen's, price the piece 3s.' He also inserted inscriptions, called 'scriptures with the King's word' at 12d each, and 'in the two great windows at the ends of the Hall is two great arms with four beasts in them, at 6s 8d per piece'. The Tudor lineage in glass was almost literally reflected in the rest of the decoration, where other proud craftsmen placed badges, arms and mottoes, carved in wood, and painted with gilt and bice; the king's words were extravagantly inscribed 'in gilt letters with fine gold gilt, price the word 2s'. As a finishing touch, Hone glazed the louvred opening in the centre of the ceiling, which had a huge Tudor rose at its summit and carved beasts, portcullises and roses around. Then he put thirty-six new windows into the king's watching chamber, alternating clear glass with panels containing the royal arms and badges, and he filled with tiers of glass the two floors of the queen's bay-windowed long gallery.

Perhaps it was his work here that fostered Hone's horticultural ambitions and the acquisition of those bay trees. He was employed to put glass into the forty-eight openings of 'the mount in the garden', part of a romantic arbour where Henry and Anne Boleyn played at being rustic lovers. The ultimate folly was glazing the tennis-court windows. The poet Skelton included Hone's contribution in his description of the palace:

> With turrets and towers,
> With halls and with bowers,
> Stretching to the stars,
> With glass windows and bars.

The building accounts for Hampton Court, with their constant mentions of arms, badges and mottoes, only whet the imagination, because the 'improvements' under William and Mary swept away much of the old work, including the riot of royal beasts – lions, dragons and greyhounds – which abounded inside and out, not just set in the windows, but carved on gable ends and turrets, holding weathervanes on the roofs, carved and painted on the walls, and in statue form throughout the gardens.* But Hone left posterity one characteristic mark, scratching his name and a crude sketch of a cardinal's hat into the stonework of the wall opening to the pages' chamber off the gallery that would allegedly be haunted by the ghost of Katherine Howard.

---

* One small fragment of glass of Hone's time is on show in the historical display in the palace and two heraldic panels believed to be from the building are in Earsdon Church, Northumberland.

Chapter Sixteen: Wolsey to the Rescue

HENRY VIII DID not seem to be bothered by the lack of progress in fulfilling his father's last wish, the glazing of the Cambridge chapel. He had no particular involvement with the town, unlike the strong ties that Lady Margaret Beaufort had imposed on Henry Tudor and their need to associate themselves with the chapel's saintly founder. Henry VIII's inheritance was secure. Nor did he want his glazier Galyon Hone diverted from the far more essential work of decorating the royal palaces. So the chapel's glazing stalled after Flower's death.

Bishop Fisher was still Chancellor of the University, appointed to the post for life in 1514 (though he had tried the previous year to offer it to Cardinal Wolsey, who turned it down). Fisher was now the only active surviving executor of the late king's will, for Bishop Foxe was too old and too fragile to worry about the windows any more, and lived in retirement from politics and the court. Unlike most of his fellow clerics, the gentle, devout and conservative Fisher had firmly rejected promotion to a wealthier bishopric, remaining content with his relatively modest see of Rochester. As it was Fisher who originally persuaded Henry Tudor to commit himself to the chapel in 1506, he still felt a genuine anxiety to see it through, for the sake of the university as well as the college. In addition to being Chancellor, he was currently involved with St John's College, where, in his role as executor of the founder, Lady Margaret Beaufort, he was overseeing work that was being carried out by the master mason of King's College Chapel. One of these projects was the building of the chantry chapel that would hold his own tomb. Fisher found the delay on the King's College glass inexcusable, considering that the late Barnard Flower had already made four windows and commissioned many cartoons for the next phase. On his own, he had little weight with the king. But Henry was prepared to listen to the man with whom Fisher had least in common in the world, Cardinal Thomas Wolsey.

Wolsey appreciated the demands, duties and rewards of patronage, for he revelled in surrounding himself with beauty to impress. His first biographer, his confidant George Cavendish, put the words into his mouth:

> With images embossed, most lovely did appear;
> Expertest artificers that were both far and near
> To beautify my houses, I had them at my will
> Thus I wanted nought my pleasures to fulfil.

In the 1520s, Wolsey had his own agenda for Cambridge. He was anxious to make an ally of the university, powerhouse of influential intellects, at a time when the Church was facing calls for reform, and when he needed backing for his own aspirations to become Pope. The impact of continental, humanistic scholarship made college founders and patrons keen to prove their intellectual credentials by supporting the new learning. But some vociferous Cambridge scholars, aware of the greater advances on the continent, attacked the Church's old ways by criticising the lax complacency of monasteries and abbeys, and the pomp and arrogance of churchmen. Those who challenged the status quo too blatantly risked being burnt as heretics.

The internationally renowned humanist scholar Erasmus of Rotterdam had managed to reconcile conventional Christian theology with full awareness of the intellectual advances of the Renaissance during his time in

Cambridge in the previous decade when, despite their apparently profound differences in attitude to the Church, he had become firm intellectual friends with Bishop Fisher. Fisher was the conservative, Erasmus the radical, yet they shared a passion for truth in learning and respected each other's rigorous standards. Erasmus's distinguished presence had also helped encourage stirrings of interest in Church reform, even though the university was initially so keen to prove its orthodoxy that, following Pope Leo X's excommunication of Martin Luther in January 1521, it publicly burned the man's heretical works,

This gesture was timed to coincide with Cardinal Wolsey's first official visit to the town. The proctors' accounts recorded the payment of 2 shillings to the Deputy Vice-Chancellor 'for drink and other expenses about the burning of the books of Martin Luther'. It was clearly a convivial occasion as well as a theological demonstration. Wolsey came to Cambridge to prepare for the reception of Queen Katherine in February. He stayed at Queens' College, where he dined on swan and crane. The mayor and proctors repaired and cleansed the streets in advance of his arrival, suggesting the town was in its usual run-down state. The quality of their gifts signalled the cardinal's high status – wine worth £3 6s 8d, two oxen, six swans, six great pike and a bream. Queen Katherine's visit required more street cleaning and mending. She attended a disputation in the Schools, and received gifts of hippocras and gloves, the latter a standard gift for noble ladies (though Margaret Beaufort had once ungratefully pointed out to an earlier donor the wrong size of her gloves 'which were right good save they were too much for my hand').

In book-burning, Cambridge proved itself ahead of London. It was not until May 1521, that Wolsey, at the Pope's behest, presided over the burning of Luther's books in St Paul's Churchyard before an audience of ambassadors, nobles and prelates. Bishop Fisher followed with a sermon in which he denounced the heretical writings, praised Wolsey and reaffirmed the power of the Pope. He also took the opportunity of drawing attention to the king's almost completed masterpiece, the *Defence of the Seven Sacraments*, Henry's own expression of loyalty to his ally and friend Pope Leo X.

Compiled with Wolsey's encouragement, it demonstrated the king's orthodox stance and gave unquestioning support to the Pope's eternal supremacy over ecclesiastical and secular authority. In October, Leo rewarded the king with the title 'Defender of the Faith'. Henry VIII's intellectual defence of the Pope was not shared by the critical reformers of Cambridge University, some of whom dared to speak out against the Church of Rome, but had to face the choice of being charged with heresy or fleeing the country.

Henry VIII came to Cambridge in 1522, when the town showered him with the usual gifts, on an exceptionally munificent scale – twelve great pike, twelve great eels, eight great tench, eight breams, four swans, two wild and two tame cranes. He stayed at the King's College, where he must have noticed the great blank spaces of the new chapel's windows while attending worship in the old one. Yet it was not his intervention but Wolsey's that finally reactivated the glazing scheme. This, anyway, was the view of the Fellows of the college, who thanked Wolsey for the 'zeal and energy' he had employed in encouraging the king to make funds available for the project to resume. Since Henry Tudor's legacy had run out, Henry VIII was faced with having to pay for the additional work himself, or so said John Caius, in the history of the university he compiled in 1574, when he attributed the completion of the windows and the floor to Henry.

Wolsey's role as intermediary between king and Cambridge began in 1524, when the university requested him to revise its statutes and pledged in return an annual celebration of prayers after his death. He displayed a forceful manner of negotiating and shifted the balance of jurisdiction from town to gown. Coming to the aid of King's College was not entirely altruistic. Wolsey kept a close eye on the latest developments in stone and glass, for he intended to employ the top masons and glaziers on the Oxford college he was founding. Having once been a lowly bursar at that university, he now proposed to create a new college superior in size and decoration to anything in Cambridge or to Bishop Foxe's Corpus Christi College in Oxford. Wolsey gave his foundation the boastful title of the Cardinal's College, which sounded like a direct challenge to King's College. It was not only the King's craftsmen that he intended to poach for his college, but some leading young Cambridge scholars too.

The outcome of Wolsey's involvement was that in 1526, nine years after Barnard Flower's death, the king agreed to make fresh funds available so that the glaziers could proceed.

Chapter Seventeen: 'Surely, Cleanly, Workmanly'

ON 30 APRIL 1526, an indenture drawn up by 'the right worshipful master Robert Hacomblen, doctor of divinity and provost of the King's college in the university of Cambridge, master William Holgylle, master of the Hospital of St John the Baptist called the Savoy beside London and master Thomas Larke, clerk, Archdeacon of Norwich' was signed by Galyon Hone and another three glaziers. The terms of the contract* bound the glaziers 'well, surely, cleanly, workmanly, substantially, curiously and sufficiently' to glaze and set up eighteen windows (sixteen in the north and south walls, plus the East and West Windows), six to be completed and installed after twelve months, and the remaining twelve by 1531. Promising to get six windows up within twelve months must have been an unacceptable commitment, for this condition was hastily modified by a second, otherwise identical, document stating just that all should be up within five years. The contract also specified that they must install the four windows that had already been made under Flower in a clause that acknowledged him as the originator of the whole scheme: the work must be done 'accordingly and after such manner as one Barnard Flower, glazier, late deceased, by indenture stood

---

* It is fortunate and unusual that the contracts survive in the college archives.

bound to do'. And it commanded them to follow in every detail the windows of 'the king's new chapel at Westminster', the definitive model for the new team just as it had been for Flower. No distinction was made: they were simply resuming the project that had started in 1515.

The contract laid down the constructional methods in some detail. The new and the earlier windows must be securely bound with double bands of lead in case of 'great winds and outrageous weatherings'. It also specified the quality and origin of the glass, 'good, clean, sure and perfect Normandy glass'. This was standard wording. Similar terms had been used in the 1513 glazing contract for St John's College, where the roses and portcullises honouring Lady Margaret Beaufort must be of 'as good and hable [easy to handle] Normandy glass of colours and pictures as be in the windows within the college called Christ's College or better in every point'. In the King's contract, however, someone had put a line through the word 'Normandy'. Perhaps the glaziers were reluctant to commit themselves too closely to the exact source in view of future price rises or the availability of supplies over the next five years, or some might have preferred or already possessed stocks of Rhineland glass.

As king's glazier, Galyon Hone was in charge and his name was first on the list. The second was another Fleming, his name anglicised to James Nicholson. Like Hone, he lived in Southwark, in the precinct of St Thomas's Hospital. He already knew Cambridge, having worked on the windows of Great St Mary's church from 1518 to 1519 after the new roof was up. His fees for that ranged from £7 from the university (to *Jacabo nycolsoon*) down to a paltry 2 pence 'for the mending of three holes in the glass of the clerestory'. He was in favour with Cardinal Wolsey, who employed him, after Flower's death, at Hampton Court, and in the Great Hall of the Cardinal's College at Oxford, where Nicholson installed forty-seven sets of armorials and badges referring to Wolsey's state, including his tasselled cardinal's hat, together with 246 inscriptions in the windows. This was a considerable project which Nicholson had to combine with his work on the chapel.*

* Some of these panels survive in the hall windows of Christ Church today.

The third member of the team was Richard Bond, who lived in the parish of St Clement Danes, convenient for the Savoy Hospital where he took over the glazing after Flower's death and installed 'images' as well as the usual quantities of royal arms and badges. The fourth was Thomas Reve, from the parish of St Sepulchre, Newgate. It was significant that although Bond and Reve were apparently English, they both lived outside the City boundaries and were therefore not members of the Glaziers' Company.

Because the scale of the project was so vast and the deadline so tight, two more glaziers were recruited to make the remaining four windows, two on the north side and two on the south. A subsequent contract, of 30 April, bound Hone to provide, for a fee 'as shall be thought reasonable' by Larke and Holgyll, 'good and true patrons [patterns] otherwise called A vidimus' to Francis Williamson and Simon Symondes, which meant they too had to follow Flower's original scheme, whose designs Hone had inherited as royal glazier. They signed their indenture on 3 May, agreeing, like the others, to reinforce their windows with double leads and to finish and install them within five years. Williamson was a Fleming who spelled his name as 'Willemzoen', another of Hone's cronies from Southwark. He lived in the parish of St Olave, then later in the precinct of St Thomas's Hospital. Symondes (who signed himself 'Simenon') may have been English, but, like Bond and Reve, was not a member of the Glaziers' Company because he lived in the parish of St Margaret, Westminster (whose church windows he repaired when they were smashed in the great storms of December 1521). He was already used to royal commissions and to Cambridge, for he had worked on the glazing of Christ's College Chapel in 1509, probably supervised by Barnard Flower.

Their fee was 16 pence per foot (0.3 metre), a rate somewhat above the average. (Local glazier Thomas Peghe received 5 pence per foot (0.3 metre) for installing standard roses and portcullises and 12 pence per foot (0.3 metre) for 'images' in the chapel of Christ's College in 1510.) The fee reflected both the quality of the glass and the skills to be lavished on it. So that the glaziers remained in pocket over the estimated five years, they were to receive a series of advances, starting with down payments of £60, followed by £100 as and when necessary. In return, they agreed to forfeit a deposit of 500 marks if they failed to keep their side of the bargain. (The mark was a notional sum, a term used in contracts: this deposit was the equivalent of approximately £350.)

Symondes and Williamson made a good start on their four windows, because the date '1527' has been inserted twice at the top of Window 1, which was almost certainly their work, as were Windows 3, 24 and 25, three of which employed the same group of messengers, who do not appear elsewhere in the chapel. Barnard Flower had already made Window 2, but otherwise their four were opposite one another at the western end of the antechapel. Using the designs the contract obliged them to purchase from Galyon Hone, they may well have completed their work within the five years specified.

Their Windows 24 and 25, the Death and Coronation of the Virgin, are now almost incomprehensible, owing to the many drastic restorations needed because of the location at the south-west corner of the building, which still attracts the worst of the wind, a swirling vortex where steppe-born gales meet the chapel's immovable bulk. Their relative fragility, compared to the rest, might also result from Williamson and Symondes's use of inferior glass. Their Window 1, on the north side, has also needed many repairs. The first in the whole story, it tells of Mary's parentage and birth, in vivid colours that are only exceeded by those in their Window 3, the Annunciation and Nativity. The precedent above the Annunciation is the Temptation of Eve, who grasps a rosy-gold apple from the sinuous serpent coiled around the Tree of Knowledge. The creature has the upper body of a beautiful woman with long golden hair and bare white breasts, made sinister by red arms and legs – an opportunity for the glaziers to show off wonderful gradations of flashed ruby – and a green scaly tail. Michelangelo's Sistine ceiling serpent has the same female face and serpentine body, with a muscular arm stretching out to offer the forbidden fruit, but Adam greedily reaches for the fruit as well. In the King's window, Eve is alone in her sin.

The designs for these four windows, as for the others commenced in

1526, came from Foxe and Flower's original scheme of 1515. However some of the cartoons made from those *vidimuses* dated from the later phase, for they incorporated elements that reflected more strongly the art and architecture of Italy, providing an ironic portrayal of modern buildings in the Gothic stonework of the chapel. The impact of the Renaissance increased during the lifespan of the project, and it affected windows as much as sculpture and painting. The magnificent Temple in Window 5, the Old Testament dedication of the first-born, has the soaring complexity of a high Renaissance oil painting, while the Temple in the panels below, where Mary presents the infant Christ, is more coherent and logical, as if the designer had improved upon the perspectival problems posed by the example above.

The grandiose impression of many of the buildings painted in the glass suggests that the designers and glaziers of the later phase revelled in showing off a whole range of architecture treated in an almost three-dimensional way. Vistas of receding arcades and towering domes give the impression of looking out through the windows into vast realms beyond. Some are plausible, others fantastic. In Window 11, high up behind the imprisoned Jeremiah (who prefigures Christ before Caiaphas below) is a delightful little round temple that recalls the masterpiece that Bramante built in 1510, San Pietro di Montorio in Rome. In the East Window, Pilate washes his hands against a majestic backdrop of Roman arches and architraves, pilasters and ornate relief carving. There is hardly a window that does not show some form of Renaissance building – familiar from Italian or Flemish painting – either as a frame for the main actors, or else as background scenery, like the many exquisitely detailed fresco-like townscapes in the distance.

Hone and his team were all aware of the latest technological advances in an era of change and development in glass-making, which made a whole new range of colours available, particularly greens, pinks and purples, while tones became stronger and darker as more paint was employed. The inadvertent delays to the project enabled this generation of glaziers to demonstrate more advanced skills and techniques. Their treatment of silver stain was supreme, for they used it to produce a range of stunning effects created from translucent yellows that saturated the glass. Achieving such a variety of tones was a means of identifying the separate characters in a crowd who also had to be spotted from far below: Eve's pale blonde locks, the sinister red hair of Judas at the Last Supper, the golden chain of office worn by Pilate as he washed his hands of Christ, the auburn plaits of Mary Magdalene weeping at the foot of the cross, the flaxen curls of the angel-messengers were all the products of this miraculous compound. By applying stain, the glaziers also cleverly enabled minor figures to stand out from the background. There are myriad groups of gesticulating soldiers, toiling farmers or distant travellers, tiny and absolutely subsidiary to the main events, yet just as visible because they are picked out in warm ambers that lift them away from the plain white background.

The laborious technique of flashing – the abrading of a top layer of red to reveal the white glass beneath – was used with considerable effect to achieve contrasted colours on a single panel, such as the red-rimmed white eyeballs of the grotesque demon attacking Job in Window 12, whose rippling body is also subtly flashed into red strips. The flames of Moses' Burning Bush (Window 3) are also made of flashed glass, while the Harrowing of Hell (Window 15) has a multiplicity of techniques: the jagged white fangs of Hell-mouth are flashed glass, while staining produced green spots on the blue body of the long-nosed demon lurking within the gaping mouth, and the orange of the flames leaping up at Christ's intervention.

In painting, too, the glaziers' versatility had no bounds when it came to their treatment of faces, of the minor as well as the major characters. With the lightest of brush-strokes, they expressed a whole gamut of emotions, both realistically and in a theatrically exaggerated manner. Such contrasts are most extreme in the East Window, from Christ's composure on the Cross and his Mother's grief (tiny, almost undetectable teardrops spill from her eyes) to the toothy grimaces of Christ's tormentors and the Unrepentant Thief.

The greatest charm lies in the details which abound, many seemingly gratuitous in that they make little contribution to the plot or to the often laborious symbolism. The panels teem and heave with life, as if their painters had an absolute *horror vacui* and refused to leave any pane untouched. This was partly practical, because it was necessary to texture the surfaces of the glass in order to prevent dazzle and to modulate the light. But the glaziers were not satisfied with the gentle effects of a stippled wash. In all the scenes in each of the windows, there is a wealth of extra features that can barely be seen with the naked eye, and which cannot have been in the original cartoons. There is no patch of ground free of pebbles, tussocks of glass or little flowers, no horizon without trees, some drawn with almost photographic precision, while lightly sketched townscapes do not depict the Italianate architecture framing the main participants but little Gothic castles with fairy-tale turrets that seem to have been miraculously transported from some illuminated manuscript. The main buildings have fantastical flourishes too: minute centaurs prance along the pediment, bearded dwarves bestride griffins, warriors ride on camels and sirens flaunt their double tails.

Some of these intricacies do help the story along, yet are often shown in far more detail than was strictly necessary, from the perfect rigging and neatly furled sails of St Paul's ship to the almost tangible indentations of the Crucifixion sponge lying in a brassy bowl, from the convincingly drawn camel among Tobias's troop of animals to the supine flock of sheep, like fluffy white clouds, behind Joseph as his brothers cast him into the pit. The city of Nineveh, some 60 feet above the ground at the very top of the upper tier of Window 16, is made forbidding enough by its threatening ranges of high walls, battlements and tiny defensive window apertures to explain Jonah's reluctance to convert the inhabitants. The doctor who circumcises the baby Jesus in Window 4 has spectacles perched on the end of his nose. The wooden tub and ewer in the foreground of the Last Supper add a touch of domestic authenticity while at the same time recalling Christ's washing the disciples' feet. Eve's Tree of Knowledge is heavily hung with tempting ripe fruit. In the Nativity, a tidy bundle of hay lies on a rack beyond the ox and the ass, while in the far background an amazed shepherd, surrounded by his sheep, leans on his crook and gazes at the hovering gold and white angel.

Most delightful of all are the dogs, based on accurate observation which is full of affection too. They occupy the very forefront of a scene, as if mediating between the outside world and the events crammed into the glass. In Window 10, a seated hound, its ears drooping, observes the mocking of the blindfold Christ, while in the next scene, another hunting dog, with pricked ears and whiskery muzzle, its neck boasting a golden collar, sits beneath the throne of its master Caiaphas the high priest, as he challenges Jesus. In Window 22, a little dog cringes and looks plaintively up at the Roman soldier who is about to hurl a stone at St Paul. The real scene-stealer is in Window 19, the return of the Prodigal Son: a blasé dog slumped on the ground scratching itself, completely oblivious to the father's rapturous embrace of its master. Other, more unexpected creatures are the butterfly and the hedgehog in the forefront of Window 7, to embellish the Wilderness where Satan tempts Christ, and the jaunty duck swimming past bulrushes in the stream in which John baptises Christ. The glaziers were enjoying themselves.

Chapter Eighteen: Glaziers at War

THE SEEMINGLY HARMONIOUS combination of Flemish and English glaziers painting dogs and hedgehogs into the King's College Chapel windows masked a very different state of affairs within their trade and within the country at large. When the project resumed in 1526, all foreigners, however skilled, were suspect on political as well as economic grounds.

In 1522, Henry VIII had formed an alliance with the Holy Roman Emperor Charles V, with the aim of invading France. One way for the king to pledge his loyalty to the emperor and their joint cause was by imprisoning all French merchants living and working in London. In order to finance the intended campaign, he summoned the first Parliament since 1515 to approve the subsidies necessary to raise the required sum of £800,000. The proceedings, chaired by Speaker Thomas More, were marked by angry debates in which a new Member of Parliament, Thomas Cromwell, a young lawyer, made his first speech bravely arguing against the war. One of the resulting measures was the Subsidy Act of 1523, an unpopular graduated property tax based upon inspections of people's houses and goods and opposed by Parliament because it represented Cardinal Wolsey's attempt to tighten the crown's financial hold, particularly on aristocrats. Even Oxbridge colleges were not exempt, though they did not have to declare the extent of their wealth as long as they consented to be assessed by Wolsey. He charged King's College £333 6s 8d, the highest rate in Cambridge. The only issue they all agreed was the double levy the Act demanded from aliens.

The price Henry VIII had to pay for getting the controversial tax approved was conceding some of the anti-immigrant demands of the London guilds. The Act 'Concerning the Taking of Apprentices by Strangers' epitomised such populist legislation, for it decreed that any alien craftsman, whether denizen or not, must pay a fine of £10 if he took on a foreign apprentice, and it limited him to two foreign journeymen assistants. For the sake of 'good order and true workmanship', the Act insisted that all such craftsmen must be subject to the inspection and approval of the wardens of the appropriate guild, even those living immediately outside the City. For the sake of fairness, one of these inspectors had to be a foreigner craftsman.

The measure, however, excluded 'stranger' craftsmen working within the universities of Oxford or Cambridge – quite possibly a special provision to cover Wolsey's plans for Cardinal's College – which further fuelled the potent resentments between town and gown by giving additional unreasonable privileges to the universities. Another clause that infuriated the Glaziers' Company granted permission to 'any Lord of the Parliament and every other of the King's subjects to take and retain Stranger Joiners or Glaziers in their service from time to time . . . this Act notwithstanding'. This was clearly a sop to all aspirant patrons of the latest fashions in window and wall decoration, who were, after all, only copying the king. This significant exemption so aggrieved the Glaziers' Company that over the next few years, just when the chapel windows were being made, they lobbied to bring in a new measure that they believed would solve all their problems.

From the mid-1520s, there was an additional factor causing fear of foreigners, like the Flemish glaziers: they might be religious extremists, or heretics. The most devout adherents of the Reformation movement, the followers of Martin Luther, were now fleeing to England as religious refugees escaping persecution in Germany. This was a dangerous strategy, because Lutheranism was just as unpopular in England as it was on the continent. The refugees, however, were not content only to escape, but began to disseminate their own beliefs. In 1526 an immigrant was charged, for the first time, with heresy.

In 1527, Flemings became additionally unpopular when the emperor, in whose territories Galyon Hone and many other immigrants had been born, sacked Rome and imprisoned the Pope. These unimaginable desecrations provided the excuse for more hostile and restrictive measures. The London mob turned on all foreigners and there was another tense May Day, when members of the French embassy were too frightened of attack to venture out.

The warden and Company of Glaziers took advantage of the mood to petition the Court of the Star Chamber in 'a lamentable bill of complaint' dated 10 February 1529. This begged for the urgent enforcement of existing legislation, which, they claimed, was now being completely flouted, in order to protect their craft from the continuing foreign menace. They made the point that while there used to be at least twenty-two glazing workshops in the City, there were now only seven because of unfair competition from the immigrants of Southwark and other areas, who ran at least eighteen workshops employing forty or fifty foreign-born servants and apprentices 'to the great hurt, decay and undoing of the said Citizen Glaziers'.

Wolsey cunningly used the glaziers' specific complaint as an excuse to bring in legislation that affected the whole spectrum of immigrant craftsmen. This was the 'Act ratifying a decree made in the Star Chamber concerning Strange Handicraftsmen inhabiting the Realm of England'. Its wording regurgitated the familiar blend of economic and social problems, even down to the current food shortages, caused by immigrants, and denounced them as the handy scapegoat for all society's ills. It was necessary to restrain 'the excessive number and unreasonable behaviour of the strangers artificers' because they 'continually resort and repair into this realm to the great detriment of our own subjects' who 'for lack of occupation fall into idleness' as a result of which 'they do continually fall to theft, murder and other great offences and consequently in great numbers be put to death'. By deliberately ignoring the existing legislation, the strangers 'daily increase in great richness and in great multitude', salting away their profits over the seas, and even travelling abroad to help England's enemies. The Act insisted that an alien could keep only two alien servants, and that no one who was not a denizen could operate his trade or set up a workshop. Anyone who took on a non-English-born apprentice or assistant had to pay a £10 fine, half to go to the relevant guild and the other half straight to the king's coffers (a smart move first suggested in the Glaziers' petition). However there were two significant exemption clauses. One permitted certain aliens to employ ten journeymen, and the other excluded Oxford and Cambridge from the Act. This demonstrated Wolsey's commitment to the King's Chapel glass, with its optimistic deadline of 1531, as well as his employment of alien craftsmen on the Cardinal's College, Oxford.

The Act also established a new way for the guilds to impose control over rivals working within the City: alien craftsmen had to undergo a prototype of the modern citizenship ceremony (in which candidates swear an oath of allegiance to the queen and sing the National Anthem) by taking an oath 'to be faithful and true to the king ... and obedient to him and his laws' in the appropriate company hall in the presence of the master and wardens. They were forbidden to hold meetings anywhere except in the approved company premises, and they had to obey all the rules and regulations of the Lord Mayor and corporation. All aliens became liable to City taxation, a clause which somehow also covered those working in Southwark though the borough remained outside the City boundaries. Finally, the Act accused foreigners of charging unreasonable prices for shoddy work that undermined the whole craft – a ludicrous and malicious libel considering the demand for quality Flemish-style windows.* Yet this harsh and wide-

---

* *Plus ça change.* The notorious Aliens Act of 1905 was brought in to impose restrictions on immigrants wishing to enter the country, not so much to prohibit potential revolutionaries and anarchists, but as a sop to East London traders and craftsmen who found their fragile economies threatened by energetic newcomers, mainly Jewish.

ranging measure had little impact. The Flemings and other immigrants did not seek denization, nor leave the country, but simply kept their heads down and got on with their work, applying, if necessary, for individual licences that enabled them to continue trading without the sanction of the guilds.

Henry VIII had a new reason for distrusting foreigners. Madly in love with Anne Boleyn and desperate for the male heir that the ageing Katherine of Aragon had failed to provide, he was beginning to contemplate the enormously complex issue of setting Katherine aside by appealing to the Pope for the annulment of their marriage. He believed that the absence of sons was God's punishment for his unlawful union with his late brother's wife, a deed forbidden in the Old Testament Book of Leviticus, and that his marriage to Katherine, only rendered possible by an earlier papal dispensation, was invalid. He needed the support of all his subjects in this controversial matter. But many of the Flemings working in London were subjects of the emperor, Queen Katherine's nephew, who would inevitably oppose Henry's plans for divorce.

Most Londoners remained loyal to the beleaguered queen. So Henry turned on the immigrants in an attempt to curry favour with his own subjects. Following the king's public installation of the hated Anne Boleyn in elegant apartments at Greenwich in 1531, the French ambassador Jean du Bellay noted how 'they wish to accustom the people by degrees to endure her' and reported that Henry had issued a proclamation that 'only ten shop-masters shall remain in London of every nation; and this will remove more than 1500 Flemings'. Yet there was still fear of local protests: 'a search has been made for hackbuts and crossbows, and wherever they have been found they have been taken, and no other weapon remains except the tongue'.

Henry turned the screw harder when he made even those who had bothered to become denizens the target of another Act. This measure was intended to restrict the excessive and increasing numbers of foreigners and their dangerous accumulation of wealth, because, once rich, 'they convey themselves with their said goods to their own country' and this impoverished the king's own true subjects. The Act abolished one of the main privileges of denizenship by making them liable to pay all 'subsidies, customs, tolls, duties and other sums' at the non-denizen rate, which was double that of ordinary subjects.

The king gave special protection to his royal glazier by exempting Galyon Hone from one of the main restrictions. In 1532, he granted Hone permission to employ four more foreign journeymen in his Southwark workshop than the two he was officially allowed, just as Henry VII had freed Barnard Flower from the prescriptive regulations of the Glaziers' Company in 1497. For monarchs, it was a case of 'Do as I say' and not 'Do as I do'.

Chapter Nineteen: The King's Great Matter

CAMBRIDGE, WHERE MANY people fondly recalled Queen Katherine's official visit just a few years earlier, played a key role in determining the legality or illegality of Henry VIII's marriage. His patronage of the King's Chapel windows may have been a factor in the debate. The campaign started in 1529, when Thomas Cranmer, a Fellow of Jesus College, who had already acted for the king on discreet diplomatic missions, advised consulting all the universities of Europe for their opinion on the desired annulment. He was supported in this by Edward Fox, the new Provost of King's College.

Fox was a former Etonian and Kingsman, whose burgeoning career as cleric and diplomat had a useful start with his appointment as secretary and legal adviser to Cardinal Wolsey. This led to service at court as Royal Almoner. Fox might even have added his own voice to Wolsey's in 1526, when the king at last agreed to implement his father's will by paying for the chapel windows.* By 1527, the Dean of St Paul's, in a letter to Henry,

---

* This was what the antiquarian Thomas Hatcher, a King's Fellow in the 1550s, and later university Vice-Chancellor, understood after researching the college's history, for he claimed that it was Fox who had finally persuaded the king.

referred to Fox as 'he in whom you put most trust', and by 1528 even Wolsey called him 'the king's confidant'. In the summer of 1528, following the death of Provost Hacomblen, the Fellows wrote to Henry VIII to request the appointment of a successor, when they also took the opportunity to complain about the excessive costs they were facing 'in building and repairs and in continual suits for their livelihood, wherein they can have no relief without the gracious favour of your highness'. Henry's response was to make his favourite, Fox, their Provost.

Fox was already embroiled in the king's marital problem at that time, for Wolsey sent him, together with Stephen Gardiner, another Cambridge man, as his envoys to Rome to seek the Pope's agreement to remit the decision over the annulment to a local tribunal. On this occasion, Wolsey used his position as papal legate to help raise money specifically towards the costs of completing the chapels at Cambridge and Eton. He instructed Fox to urge Clement VII to grant Henry permission to dissolve certain smaller monasteries (whose annual revenues did not exceed 8,000 ducats), and divert their funds towards the two projects. Clement's agreement was perceived as a triumph for Wolsey's diplomatic skills, his wide influence and powers of persuasion. But it was also a worrying reminder of the power of the pontiff over the church in England.

Meanwhile, Cambridge took its place in the international debate, with passionate arguments presented from the town's various pulpits. The main dispute was between the reformers, headed by Hugh Latimer, a modernising theologian at Clare College, who were prepared to support the annulment, and the traditionalists, centred around St John's College, who were implacably opposed to the idea. Their most eminent spokesman was the university Chancellor, Bishop Fisher, who argued that only the Pope could decide the case. Late in 1529, Provost Fox attempted to intervene on the king's behalf, writing from London to request the Vice-Chancellor, Dr William Buckmaster, to calm both sides down.

Henry then wrote to the university himself seeking its considered response as to whether it was lawful for a man to marry his dead brother's wife; and if not, to confirm that the Pope had no right to have granted

The interior of King's College Chapel looking towards the East End.
The windows are like great transparent tapestries.

The exterior of Henry VII's Chapel, Westminster Abbey, completed by 1512. The lavish Tudor symbol in the stonework were echoed by those in the glass and stone of King's College Chapel.

The carving over the West door of King's College Chapel: Tudor roses, dragon and greyhound.

Tudor signs and symbols in the tracery of Window 5. The royal arms surmount six large examples of red rose, portcullis and fleur-de-lys. Below these, angels hold shields with more symbols, including hawthorn bush, and the initials H&E and H&K.

Window 3.
The Temptation of Eve.
The Serpent is seductively feminine; the glaziers have delighted in showing the details of the Garden of Eden.

Window 4.
King Solomon and the Queen of Sheba.
The kneeling Sheba offers a golden vessel
to the enthroned Solomon, who has been
portrayed in the likeness of Henry VIII.

Miniature of King Solomon and the
Queen of Sheba by Hans Holbein the
Younger, c. 1534. Holbein's comparison
of Henry with Solomon was the source
of the scene in Window 4.

Window 7. A Renaissance
cavalcade in the landscape.
The lovingly detailed
retinue of Namaan, who
washes in the river Jordan
to cure his leprosy, a
prototype for the Baptism
of Christ below.

Window 8. The Triumph of David.
He enters Jerusalem bearing the head of the
Philistine giant Goliath on the tip of his
elevated sword to the welcome of musicians.

Window 9. The Israelites gathering
Manna in the Wilderness.
The white discs exemplify the glaziers'
skills in cutting and leading.

Window 9. The Fall of the Rebel Angels.
The Archangel Michael, in authentic late 15th-century armour, its details picked
out in silver stain, drives the rebel Lucifer into the flames of Hell.

Window 16. Jonah and the Whale.
The drama of Jonah's escape is reinforced
by the strong colours and powerful
interpretation of the whale.

Window 17. Shepherds watch their flocks.
innocently bucolic background to the scene
here Joseph's brothers find he has vanished
m the pit they threw him into: Joseph here
prefigures the resurrected Christ.

Window 23. St Paul's ship.
An authentic Tudor ship waits to carry St Paul on his mission of conversion, as described
in the Acts of the Apostles. Henry VIII would have travelled in such a vessel.

Henry the exemption to commit this act. Was there a hint of bribery, when he emphasised that although he was 'desirous to know and understand your minds and opinions', at the same time he trusted that the university had always found him benevolent and he would be 'glad to extend our authority for your wealth and benefits'? The King's College Chapel windows were due to be completed and installed by 1531, according to the contracts signed five years earlier, but were well behind schedule. Without royal funding, their future was under threat.

Provost Fox became a key figure in the official inquiry held in Cambridge in March 1530. This took the form of a three-day debate which Fox reported back to the king, summarising a great dispute which split the university down the middle. Fox was initially over-optimistic in calculating possible votes for the king, because the syndicate decreed that the Pope did have the right to grant a man permission to marry his dead brother's wife. But then Fox and Gardiner, aided by the persuasive arguments of Cranmer, secured a significant qualifier: such permission was valid only if the previous marriage had not been consummated. This was an effective challenge by the university to the Pope's authority, although it triggered off an insulting interrogation of the queen's virgin status at the time of her marriage to Henry. Most significantly, it proved that it was possible for the king and his men to manipulate the university's decision-making process. The Vice-Chancellor took the blame for the shameful concession, protesting that 'all the world cryeth out of Cambridge for this act, and especially on me', though he found himself in royal favour when he delivered the good news to Henry at Greenwich.

But it was all too slow for Henry and Anne. Wolsey's failure to negotiate a rapid and successful outcome with the Pope led to his impeachment in 1529 and his death, a broken man, in 1530. In the triumphant year of 1527, when he posed as defender of the Pope, who had been imprisoned by the emperor in Rome, the Venetian ambassador compared Wolsey flatteringly to the archangel Lucifer, soaring close to the sun that was Henry VIII.

Two years later, an anonymous verse, 'An Impeachment of Wolsey', turned the tables, again alluding to him as Lucifer but this time prophesying his ultimate fate:

Thou knowest that Lucifer had a fall
And all that follow him shall fall,
Into the pit of Hell.

This moment was depicted in graphic detail in Window 9, the Fall of the Rebel Angels, which may by then have been installed. The image was as familiar in art as in biblical commentary, yet now had a particular resonance for Cambridge and for the king's Great Matter. The scene was placed immediately above that of the Agony in the Garden, in order to contrast the disobedience of a formerly trusted follower with the submission of Christ to his fate. The glass shows God seated on his throne at the very top of the panels, gravely observing St Michael and his fellow angels drive Lucifer and the other rebel angels out of Heaven. They plummet downwards, the length of the narrow lights enhancing the sense of dizzying descent. As they tumble, their fall is hastened by the prodding spears and swords of the vigorous, contorted angels above and they become transformed into scaly demons toppling into the flames of Hell flaring up to overwhelm them: Lucifer becomes Satan.

The whole scene was a triumph of the glaziers' art. The colour tones became richer from top to bottom, contrasting the clarity of Heaven with the all-consuming depths of Hell. The glowing flames and monstrous shapes provided a fine opportunity to display the whole repertoire of technical tricks. Flashed ruby was standard for devils, enabling white eyes to stare out from a red mask, or pointed fangs from a grinning maw. Silver stain tinged scarlet fire with a simmering orange, and painted sinister bands of gold to make grasping talons more fearsome.

Although the design was an old one, borrowed from the images of the devil-angels hurtling towards the ground in Dürer's 1498 *Apocalypse* woodcuts and probably made in Flower's time, Galyon Hone and the colleagues who installed it, like the King's Fellows who saw it, were fully aware of its topical comment on the dangers of overweening ambition, and how pride comes before a fall.

Among Wolsey's posthumous bills, £58 was outstanding to his favoured glazier James Nicholson for work on the cardinal's various properties in the north of England. Even out of royal favour, Wolsey was still planning to live in style and had not scrupled to divert one of the four main glaziers meant to be working on the King's Chapel to promote his own grandeur and display.

Unlike Wolsey, the university, however grudgingly, had given the king the backing he needed, and continued to do so. Provost Fox spoke publicly, in September 1532, in support of the king's renewed alliance with France to counterbalance the emperor's hostility to the divorce. All this might have appeared to guarantee continued funding for the windows. Few yet appreciated a new concern, that most of their familiar biblical subject matter was about to become politically and theologically unacceptable.

Earlier in the century, German Lutherans and Swiss Calvinists had begun to voice their fears of the idolatrous and superstitious arts associated with the beliefs of Catholicism. The year 1522 saw the first attempts to abolish religious imagery in those countries, a factor which caused the exodus to England of many artists who feared the potential loss of work at home. English reformers were initially more relaxed in their interpretation of the new iconoclasm, but by the late 1520s they too were beginning to call for restrictions, and even the banning of certain images such as local saints. Among those proscribed were Thomas à Becket, sanctified as a result of defying his king. The many alien craftsmen from the Low Countries and Germany helped to spread reformist attitudes further.

Despite the fashionable Renaissance details painted in the glass, the overall message of the windows followed the well-established formats of the Catholic Church, which the reformers increasingly challenged. Such attitudes could even render the whole theme of the King's Chapel's windows suspect, for the narrative of the windows was framed by the birth and death of the Virgin, ten scenes showing incidents not taken from the Bible but from legendary and unauthorised texts which the reformers rejected. These included the *Golden Legend* (the first book that William Caxton published), a popular compilation of saints' lives and miracles based on a whole range of apocryphal sources written long after the Four Gospels, which was the main source for the life of the Virgin. Her Assumption and Coronation, as in Window 25, had no textual foundations but were well established in art: Giotto's Arena Chapel frescoes, for example, were devoted to the life of Mary. But for the reformers, the Word of the Bible was the only acceptable source.

Progress on the glazing programme was not helped by the fall of the university Chancellor, Bishop Fisher, a force behind the completion of the chapel over so many years. Fisher had taken Queen Katherine's side in 1527, when Henry first expressed his doubts over the legality of the marriage, and was perceived as so prominent and influential an opponent that Wolsey had tried hard to make him to shift his position. In June 1529, when Fisher was seventy-two, attempting to live peacefully in his see at Rochester, he spoke up bravely on Katherine's behalf in the court summoned to Blackfriars in London to discuss the status of her marriage. Here, Fisher declared that he was prepared to lay down his life to defend the sanctity of marriage, just as John the Baptist had lost his for daring to criticise Herod's adultery, in the form of marriage to his late brother's wife. Fisher's private annotations to the text of the speech with which Henry opposed him contained treasonable comments such as 'arrogance, temerity' and 'I said nothing of that!' He defended Katherine's position to Parliament, and openly criticised Henry's prominent liaison with Anne Boleyn. In 1532, he boldly published the text of the sermon he had preached in 1520 concerning the Field of Cloth of Gold. As well as commenting on the king's extravagance, this made an overt attack on Henry's adultery, for the sermon had made a prophetic reference to Herod, whose finery could not save him from his doom. The printer and publisher of the sermon was William Rastell, nephew of Sir Thomas More, Fisher's companion in opposition to the king's divorce.

Henry finally freed himself from papal control by appointing himself head of the Church of England, authorised by the Act of Supremacy of 1534. The university hardened its own line when it officially rejected the authority of the Pope in the same year. This made Chancellor Fisher's position untenable. His attitude to the divorce was inseparable from his opposition to the breach with Rome. He declined to offer allegiance to the new queen,

Anne Boleyn, by refusing to swear the Oath of Succession that Henry demanded: acknowledging the king's second marriage meant denying the Pope's confirmation of the validity of Katherine's. On 7 March 1534, Ambassador Chapuys reported to the emperor the likely fate of Fisher and More: 'the holy bishop of Rochester has been sent for. He is in great danger . . . the persecution of these men is only because of their having taken the Queen's part.' Henry sent Fisher to the Tower, locked up under the harshest conditions for a whole year while waiting for him to change his mind. But Fisher remained serenely resolute. Henry and his secretary Thomas Cromwell, Lord Privy Seal, rigged the case against him in the show trial they staged in June 1535.

On 17 June, the Court of the King's Bench found Fisher guilty of high treason and sentenced him to be drawn through the city to Tyburn, to be hanged alive, drawn, quartered and decapitated, a gesture of dishonourable and gratuitous brutality by Henry VIII towards his grandmother's favourite. In the event, Henry spared Fisher the very worst indignities; he was beheaded, his body buried at Barking, and his head displayed on London Bridge, to be joined a month later by that of Sir Thomas More, who also resisted the king's will. Fisher's written works defending the Pope's authority were banned, and Thomas Cromwell succeeded him as Chancellor of Cambridge University.

It was rumoured that Cromwell himself gave orders to destroy the revered symbols of Fisher at St John's College. The accounts certainly note that the punning carvings of fish and ears of wheat in the chapel were hacked away, and Fisher's arms were cut from the walls of his chantry chapel.

When he put aside Katherine of Aragon, Henry had lost his main European allies. Facing the combined anger of the Pope and the emperor, he needed to secure the loyalty of the population of aliens, the majority from the Low Countries. He hoped to do this by encouraging more applications for denizenship. In 1534, he extended powers to award the necessary letters patent to his secretary Thomas Cromwell and to the Lord Chancellor. Over the next few months, 127 Netherlanders applied to become denizens, their example quickly followed by a group of French Protestants who had fled from persecution in their own country. At this tense time, even Galyon Hone took the precaution of becoming a denizen, in March 1535, following the example of his colleague James Nicholson, who had done so a month earlier. Perhaps Cromwell had advised them that this step was necessary to prove their allegiance to the king.

Once the university had demonstrated its further capitulation to the king by denying the Pope's authority, following a series of public debates, Henry was prepared to show his gratitude for its loyalty. Paying for the chapel windows had previously been on an ad hoc basis, such as the fine extracted from the Bishop of Norwich in 1534. Ambassador Chapuys reported to his master how 'the king has caused the Bishop of Norwich to be set free, on giving the king 30,000 crowns as a free gift'. According to local tradition, this sum went towards the cost of the windows. Now there was about to be a regular source of funding.

As a part of a wider reform movement, Henry's men were beginning to inspect monasteries and shut down those which appeared to be lazy or corrupt. To speed this up, in January 1535 Henry appointed Thomas Cromwell to the post of Vicar General, with a remit to inspect and review the future of all religious foundations. This meant that Henry could fill his own coffers with the proceeds of shut-down monasteries and other religious houses. Among the countless victims of this policy were the Observant Friars of Greenwich and of Richmond, loved and remembered in the wills of Henry VII and Barnard Flower. Cromwell threw them out and shut their houses down. Henry claimed that he would do good works with the money raised from dissolving the monasteries, and he probably regarded paying for the King's Chapel windows as a suitable cause. He had shown the college special favour by sending his illegitimate son, the Duke of Richmond, to study there in the early 1530s.

This was at a time when the Reformation was beginning to have an increasingly drastic effect on the ornaments and practices of the Church. The king and his ministers issued a series of regulations that licensed the seizing and smashing of relics and images. Cromwell ordered that the windows at St Thomas of Acres in the City of London be removed because they told the provocative story of Thomas à Becket, who defied his king 'so that there shall be no more mention to be made of him, never'. St Thomas's Hospital in Southwark, in whose precinct the glaziers lived, was retitled Thomas Becket's Hospital. It did well enough out of the Dissolution, selling the king some of its lands in return for others owned by former monasteries.

Astonishing restrictions were now imposed on familiar rituals. Pilgrimages were banned, as was talk of miracles and of the intervention of the saints. Religious texts were censored, holy days cancelled, and a whole host of trusted saints became non-persons. And people were forbidden to undertake all the comforting acts of worship they had followed for hundreds of years – processions, chanting, candles, incense, the penitential act of crawling towards the cross at Easter.

The problem with the chapel's windows was they gave out increasingly ambiguous signals. In April 1534, soon after Fisher's imprisonment in the Tower, Provost Fox and the Fellows of King's College invited royal glazier Hone, his colleague James Nicholson and 'another' to dinner. This was to discuss the outstanding work to be resumed because the money was guaranteed, and to deliberate how a well-advanced set of windows intended as a monument to medieval scholasticism and ancient Catholic beliefs could reflect the drastically changing religious climate. The ultimate dilemma was that the most extreme reformers challenged the need for any painted images at all. But this would hardly do, considering that at least half of the windows had been made, and some were already installed, as specified by the 1526 contracts.

The person in charge of reinterpreting their meaning was Provost Edward Fox. Although he had begun his career as secretary to Cardinal Wolsey, the papal legate, his own theological interests were reformist, and he was a pioneer of Lutheran studies. As the man currently responsible for the project and its funding, he had the right and the duty to intervene in the message of the windows by bringing out aspects that would make them more relevant to present circumstances. It was absolutely essential, given the king's new image as head of the Church of England, for the college to be seen promoting the Reformation. It was also the only way to ensure the further flow of money.

Chapter Twenty: The Old Law and the New

READING THE WINDOWS depended upon the connections viewers made between the Old Testament prototypes in the upper register and the New Testament scenes below. (The only exceptions to this system were Window I, and the East Window, which contained a sequence of six scenes telling of Christ's Passion, culminating in the Crucifixion and Deposition, too important in their own right here to need predecessors.) Although Henry Tudor's specification of the Old Law and the New was agreed, designed and begun in Barnard Flower's time, this long-established formula suddenly took on a vital contemporary symbolism: the New Law of Henry VIII, now Head of the Church in England, superseded the Old Law of the Pope's authority. This concept was devised by the teams of political theologians who argued Henry's case for his new role, and his artists illustrated it just as effectively. Whether by creating new visual imagery (as they had done to flesh out Henry VII's invention of the Tudor brand) or by reinterpreting familiar formulae, ranging from published prints to the huge area of the Cambridge windows, his draughtsmen and craftsmen did their job. Court painter Hans Holbein even entitled one of his allegorical paintings celebrating Reformation beliefs *The Old Law and the New*.

The towering Old Testament figures in the upper register of the windows, Moses, David and Solomon, who in their different ways appeared as prefigurations of Christ, assumed sudden relevance as key figures in the case that Henry argued to separate the Church of England from that of Rome. In this, he employed the intellectual authority of Provost Fox, whose 1534 treatise *De Vera Differentia* provided theological justification for undermining the Pope's authority and boosting the king's by citing many Old Testament parallels: Henry was Moses, who led his people into the promised land, Josiah, who reformed his people by banning corrupt priests and destroying idolatrous images, David, who defeated the Philistines and composed the Psalms, Solomon, who built the Temple and was the wisest of judges. By associating himself with Old Testament kings who defended their subjects against enemies who disregarded the laws of God, Henry assumed an imperial authority which outranked that of pope or cardinal.

Prime exemplar of royal power was Solomon, epitome of divine wisdom and supposed author of the book of Ecclesiastes. Henry and Fox now also hailed him as the forerunner of the great Christian emperors Constantine and Charlemagne, while his founding of the Temple in Jerusalem was the precedent for Henry's foundation of the true Church. Solomon appeared prominently in three of the chapel's windows. In Window 12, he was crowned by his mother Bathsheba, as a precursor of Christ receiving the Crown of Thorns in the panels below. This was could also be taken as a subtle acknowledgement of the Tudor inheritance of the crown through the line of Henry VII's mother, Lady Margaret Beaufort: that family's portcullises were, of course, prominent all over the stone carving and in the glass of the traceries. In Window 25, it was his turn to crown her, a prototype for Christ's coronation of his Mother.

The most striking image, and one which was specifically identified with Henry VIII, was in Window 4, the encounter between Solomon and Sheba which prefigured the visit of the Three Kings to the infant Jesus beneath. The scene showed Solomon enthroned, receiving gifts from the Queen of Sheba and her exotic train. Galyon Hone, as royal glazier, painted the most important portions of any window, and he made the connection perfectly clear by inserting Henry's monogram HR, *Henricus Rex*, on the shield held up by a little supporter at the top of the panel. Solomon's handsome bearded face, golden chain and sumptuous clothing were those of Henry's official image as disseminated in portraits and medals.

Hans Holbein was the first to devise this flattering visual parallel in the miniature of Solomon and Sheba that he painted around 1534. This turns Solomon into a recognisable Henry, receiving the Queen of Sheba and her retinue. Sheba kneels at Solomon's/Henry's feet, just as she does in the window, where her demure, pale profile is framed by a fashionable headdress, and she wears a gold-brocaded gown. Sheba's posture in the miniature referred to Henry's supremacy over the Church, symbolised in her submission to him. But it might equally stand, in the eyes of keen reformers like Holbein himself, as a reminder to the king of his responsibilities to the new Church. The lavish gifts borne by Sheba's train might just represent the rewards promised to Henry if he continued to support the reforms. So the image became a significant topic in its own right, going far beyond its role as one of the old typological parallels, which made the submission of Sheba a prototype for that of the Virgin, who is seen in the window below. In the context of a Cambridge college with a Lutheran-sympathising provost, there were many layers of meaning.

Such portraits were a feature of modern glass. Realistic images of patrons and their families, sometimes taking the role of biblical characters, appeared in other contemporary windows. The image of Henry as Solomon hints at his role as a great lover as well as a fount of wisdom, for the Song of Solomon forms an uncharacteristically sensuous section of the Old Testament. Henry's father had been compared to Solomon too. In the pageant that welcomed him to York in 1486, the figure of Solomon, possessor of eternal wisdom, hailed the first Tudor as his equal and presented him with the sceptre of wisdom. And in the next display, Solomon's father David presented the king with the sword of victory, the very same one that had cut off Goliath's head. Henry Tudor emphasised his authority as descending from the ancient British, Arthurian tradition, but his son preferred to associate himself with the power of the Old Testament kings, his true prototypes.

However appealing the parallels with Solomon, it was with David that Henry VIII chose most closely to identify himself during the revisions to his image that followed the breach with Rome. As with Solomon, the presence of David in the windows belonged to the old medieval tradition and had been part of the scheme since its inception. But this now acquired a fresh resonance as a direct compliment to the king in his uncertain new role as head of the Church. For Henry used the image of David to redefine his own position, newly independent of papal control and holding imperial power in his own right. David's power came directly from God, and he had been anointed by Samuel, just as Henry's coronation had made him supreme over England.

David had multiple roles: the shepherd boy who defeated the Philistine giant Goliath and became king of Israel, the musician, dancer and author of the Psalms, the lover of Bathsheba, who bore his famous son Solomon – all these aspects were depicted in many media, and not just in England. David in his beautiful nudity had inspired two great Italian sculptors, Donatello and Michelangelo, and the latter's massive marble statue stood prominently as guardian and defender of the prosperous city of Florence.

Henry owned various sets of tapestries showing 'histories' of David and of Solomon. One was hung in the luxuriously furnished temporary banqueting hall erected at Greenwich in 1527 to impress the French ambassadors whom Henry was trying to woo into an alliance against the emperor. (Whether Hone's glazing skills were required on this occasion is not recorded, but other royal craftsmen were employed to re-create the king's beasts out of papier mâché.) Other tapestry sets hung permanently and prominently at Whitehall, Windsor and Hampton Court, some designed by the Fleming Pieter Coeck who, according to the often critical Vasari 'made excellent cartoons for tapestry and cloth of arras; he had also a good manner', a vital criterion for artistic success in the sixteenth century. Henry had some of these tapestries repaired in 1539, including a *History of David*, while a *History of the Apostles* was relined.

The scene chosen by Flower and Foxe for the chapel window was the moment when David made his victorious entrance bearing aloft the huge head of Goliath on the point of his sword. In one way, this was the conventional prefiguration of Christ's Entry into Jerusalem, the scene immediately below it in the glass. This conjunction was well established in the block-books, which depicted David bearing his sword in one hand and Goliath's head in the other, which he presents triumphantly to a group of rejoicing musicians. The Cambridge design has the head held high in the air, a sensible adaptation for the tall narrow window opening. Although it was in the upper tier, the scene can easily be recognised from the ground because of the giant's massive head, made even more prominent by the yellow stain that makes it stand out from the pale background. But the meaning had a new topicality: David was Henry, Goliath was the Pope, and the real victory was that of England over Rome.

The prominence given to David's sword had its own implications as well, because the sword was the symbolic weapon of the reformers. As such, it appeared on the title page that Holbein designed for the first English translation of the Bible, the Coverdale Bible of 1535. Published under the patronage of Thomas Cromwell and Thomas Cranmer, who had been appointed Archbishop of Canterbury in 1533, the work did not yet have Henry's formal consent. Holbein's woodcut used the familiar conjunctions of the Old Law and the New, but made the king the focal point and the theme reform. Henry, enthroned, flourishes the sword and book in the manner of earlier imperial imagery dating as far back as Julius Caesar, combined with the familiar Christian subject of Christ presenting the book to St Paul and the keys to St Peter. Holbein gave Christ's central position to Henry, whom he depicted offering the translated Bible itself to representatives of the clergy and the aristocracy. But he replaced the flanking figure of St Peter with that of David playing his lyre, although St Paul remains on the king's other side. Thus Holbein brings together David and Paul respectively contributing to the most important sections of the Old and New Law.

David's composition of the Psalms gave him an additional textual authority that became widespread after the Bible was translated into English. Instead of the limited selections that featured in the luxury books of hours which the aristocracy used for private devotion, all the psalms could be read in translation. In the private psalter that Henry's French orator, Jean Mallard, presented to him in 1540, the illustrations turn Henry into David, almost implying that the king himself composed the Psalms. One miniature shows Henry seated reading that same psalter, meditating, the text states, on the law of God; another paints Henry confronting Goliath, while its inscription makes a doubly flattering comparison to Christ. Henry annotated this manuscript copiously, proving deep study and his evident empathy with David the psalmist. It was a bad time for the king, who received the manuscript in the unhappy period after the downfall and execution of his fifth wife, Katherine Howard.

In another Bible frontispiece, Holbein showed Moses receiving the Ten Commandments, just as he does in Window 20 (where the scene is a precursor for the Descent of the Holy Spirit, or Pentecost): Moses rescued his people from the cruel pharaoh after generations of slavery and led them to the promised land, just as Henry freed the English from the Pope. Again, the windows took on a modern relevance that transcended their uncomfortable old-fashioned parallels. Although the hated Martin Luther had first compared the Pope to Pharaoh, it was now entirely acceptable to compare Henry VIII to Moses, as Edward Fox had done. Moses played an important role in the chapel's windows. As the first Old Testament hero hailed as a forerunner of Christ, he is shown five times. God appears in a burning bush commanding him to free the Israelites from Egypt (Window 3), miraculously parts the Red Sea so that they can escape (Window 15), preserves them from starvation in the desert by sending manna from Heaven (Window 9) and gives Moses the Ten Commandments to carry to his people (Window 20). Finally, Moses destroys the false idol, the Golden Calf, that the foolish Israelites worshipped (Window 6). To add to his significance in the chapel, Moses was the only Old Testament character whom the glaziers portrayed in the actual presence of God. When God speaks to him from the bush, Moses is so awestruck at being on holy ground that he tugs his boots off in an urgent movement beautifully captured by the glass painter. In this window, God's violet robe is framed by layers of colour – a red halo, orange nimbus, dark blue clouds and green foliage licked by flames of flashed ruby. Beyond him are exquisite vignettes of a landscape and lake, shepherds, sheep and a drowsy sheepdog. In the lower foreground, a little duck bobs in a stream. Such charming details in the glass all helped to humanise and bring solemn subjects to life. It was easier to accept that Henry was Moses when glaziers made the Old Testament look so modern.

Chapter Twenty-One: The Hand of Fox

EVIDENCE OF HOW Provost Fox steered the windows towards
Reformation conventions lies in some of the messengers' scrolls.
These bear inscriptions taken from Erasmus's updated version of the
New Testament, based on his revision of the original Greek texts and first
published, together with the parallel Latin version, in 1516. He intended this
to supersede the long-outdated 'Vulgate' edition that St Jerome produced
in the fourth century. One quotation from Erasmus's version of Luke's
Gospel appears in Window 9, referring to Christ's Agony in the Garden
(although Erasmus once argued this was a false comparison with the Fall of
Lucifer, which surmounts it in the window).

Other windows illustrate Provost Fox's special area of theological
expertise, the works of Martin Luther, who had used Erasmus's version as
the source for his own translation of the Gospels into German in 1522. So
recently banned and burned, these works were now essential reading for the
modern scholar. Fox even visited Germany in 1535 for discussions with
Lutheran leaders, and the Protestant* theologian Martin Bucer dedicated a
treatise on the Eucharist to him.

* A term first used in 1529.

The sequence of three windows showing the Acts of the Apostles in the south wall of the antechapel (Windows 21, 22 and 23) sits strangely with the layout and design of all the other windows in the building because they disrupt the otherwise logical and coherent typological sequence of Old Testament above and New Testament below. Apart from the East Window, the only other exception to this rule is the early Window 1, the birth of the Virgin. Yet these three south windows contain no Old Testament scenes at all, for their upper tier also depicts the New Testament. This is a striking inconsistency that can only be explained as Fox's alteration to Flower's original scheme of 1515, which Hone otherwise faithfully followed, using the first set of *vidimuses*. But whatever had been intended was now replaced by the latest reformist theology, in response to the urgent need to make the scheme less orthodox and dangerously papist. Already in position were too many potentially unacceptable scenes based on dubious non-scriptural sources, such as the Harrowing of Hell (Window 15), only recorded in the Gospel of Nicodemus, and Christ appearing to his Mother (Window 16), a scene from the Golden Legend that did not even appear in the cycles of Italian frescoes.

Two of the south windows were now entirely devoted to scenes from the life of St Paul, who was a significant figure for reformers. Forty years earlier, in the 1490s, John Colet had given ground-breaking lectures at Oxford on Paul's Epistles, based on his studies in France and Italy, where he absorbed the refreshing scrutiny of Renaissance humanist scholars like Marsilio Ficino and Picolo della Mirandola, who had helped make the old scholastic approach obsolete. The sweeping-away of layers of obfuscation inspired many theologians to provide new readings of familiar texts. Colet wanted to get back to basics and 'follow the mind of St Paul' directly rather than through the interpretations of others. This was how he thrilled the young Erasmus, who first met him in 1499: 'when I hear my Colet, I seem to be listening to Plato himself', he wrote enthusiastically. Martin Luther took this further when he used Paul's Epistles to the Romans as the foundation for his whole criticism of Catholicism. He explained that true faith must only follow the Word, and that genuine belief could not be expressed through external shows like pilgrimages, devotion to images and all the other old rituals. In the 1520s, such views were heresy. Yet by the late 1530s, thanks to the work of scholars like Fox, images of St Paul were no longer provocative but were a demonstration of modern thinking.

Paul's Epistle to the Ephesians defined the sword as God's word, a crucial image for reformers: the sword was the Bible. In the chapel's Apostle windows, Paul is more prominent than Peter, who previously had an equal role in artistic depictions of the Acts. He only appears in the first window, in three out of its four scenes – the fourth scene belongs to Paul – and the other two windows are entirely concerned with Paul. Because Peter was recognised as the first Pope, too much emphasis on him now would be highly inappropriate. In his anti-Lutheran sermon at the book-burning of 1521, Bishop Fisher firmly linked St Peter with the Pope, when he compared Christ and Peter to Moses and Aaron leading the Israelites into the Promised Land: when Christ ascended to Heaven, he nominated Peter to lead his followers on earth. By 1535, Holbein's frontispiece to the Coverdale Bible took pains to diminish Peter's role. One vignette had Christ presenting keys to all the apostles as his delegates rather than to Peter alone, a deliberate contradiction of the orthodox reading of the Gospels, as painted, for example, by Perugino in the Sistine Chapel. The association of Moses with Christ remained valid, but the roles of Aaron and Peter were far more problematic.

There were no obvious sources for Reformation-friendly material in the *Biblia* or the *Speculum,* which ignored the Acts of the Apostles altogether but devoted several pages to the Last Judgement. Yet Fox required Hone to come up with new window designs for the changing climate. The Acts of the Apostles, however, had already furnished the subject matter for another large-scale scheme that the king himself owned, a gift, in happier days, from a Pope.

One building which stood out as a model for Henry VII, and even more for his son, was one of the most famous in the world, the Sistine Chapel in the Pope's Vatican Palace in Rome. Totally rebuilt by Pope Sixtus in the late fifteenth century to follow the proportions of Solomon's Temple in Jerusalem (its length twice its height and three times its width) the chapel was dedicated to the Virgin of the Assumption, and its painted walls told the story of the Old Law and the New. The lives of Christ and of Moses, painted by the hands of Italy's greatest masters, faced each other in the friezes along the north and south walls. Above them marched the images of former popes, while the space below appeared to be draped with rich hangings whose dense folds screened the walls behind. But this was a clever illusion, showing off the artists' skills in a different way, for these were wall paintings pretending to be tapestry. Henry VII would have heard of the marvels of this building (just as he had of the Florence hospital that he copied in the Savoy), and his tiers of carved saints in Westminster Abbey might have been inspired by the rows of Sistine popes. But he died too soon to learn of the ambitious project that Sixtus's nephew, Pope Julius II, had commissioned. In 1508, Julius commanded Michelangelo to paint the chapel's ceiling in a highly distinctive interpretation of the Old Law, voiced by prophets and sibyls interspersed with Christ's ancestors, supporting the vault which was covered with images of the Creation and the Flood.

Henry VIII's emissaries to Rome saw this marvel. The king was also familiar with the name of Michelangelo's rival Raphael, who painted the walls of the Pope's apartments in the Vatican, then assisted Julius's successor, Pope Leo X, to make his artistic contribution to the building, which would equal, if not outdo, those of his predecessors.

Leo's ingenious solution was not to compete with the chapel's painted walls or ceiling, but to commission Raphael to design a set of new tapestries to replace the motley, worn-out selection that were hung on special feast days over the painted simulations on the lower walls. These hangings would commemorate his own distinguished patronage and position. By choosing the Acts of the Apostles as their theme, he sought to reinforce papal power by recalling Peter and Paul, both men martyred and buried in Rome, as the joint founders of the Church he led. By showing the deeds of healing described in the Acts, he referred to his own perceived role as a healer of the Church's ills, and also got in a pun on his family name, for *medicus* would recall the Medici too. At the same time, the tapestries must relate to the biblical scenes painted on the walls above them, making yet more Old and New correspondences: the tapestry of the Conversion of Paul hung below the painting of the Nativity, the Calling of Peter below the Finding of Moses.

This was not a novel idea, for the Acts of the Apostles had featured in the arts of the Church since the fifth-century frescoes of *San Paulo fuori le mure* in Rome. They appeared in French Gothic stained glass and illuminated manuscripts, and Giotto included two scenes of Peter healing in his radical fourteenth-century fresco cycles at Assisi. Raphael was a subtle and sensitive interpreter, and was one of those versatile designers who, like his Netherlandish contemporaries, could turn his hands to other media as well. In 1515, the same year that Barnard Flower started on the King's glass, Raphael produced a set of ten tapestry designs for the Sistine Chapel that depicted significant events in the lives of Peter and Paul as described in the Acts of the Apostles. These were sent to Brussels to be woven by the master weavers in the workshop of Pieter van Aelst. Seven tapestries were completed by Christmas 1519, and the remaining three followed by 1521. The weavers retained and copied the cartoons in order to produce several more tapestry sets. One of these, woven with silk, gold and silver, came into the hands of Henry VIII, avid collector of fine hangings. It was subsequently claimed to be a well-chosen gift from Leo X in gratitude for Henry's robust defence of the papacy in his *Seven Sacraments* of 1521, a luxurious material complement to his title of Defender of the Faith.

Leo's choice of imagery to reinforce papal power was subverted by English reformers through the new windows that Fox commissioned from Hone. In these, some of Raphael's actual designs, as well as the general theme of the Sistine tapestries, were now reworked to give the opposite message: it was the king, not the Pope, who was supreme. It was also a way of keeping up with the Vatican. No Michelangelo could ever paint on the intricately carved ceiling, but the glassy walls could imitate Raphael's woven decorations.

Not all Raphael's designs were appropriate. While it was theologically essential to bring in a revised interpretation emphasising the role of Paul, some of the Sistine tapestries laid more emphasis on Peter. Fox and Hone had to provide twelve separate scenes to fill the three windows. Four of these followed Raphael closely: Peter and John healing the Lame Man, the Death of Ananias, the Conversion of St Paul, and the Sacrifice at Lystra. One of Raphael's frescoes in the Vatican, the iconic *School of Athens*, provided the model for a fifth scene, that of St Paul at Damascus. That left another seven which they and the cartoonists had to devise through the ingenious adaptation of established motifs. Paul's Farewell to the Faithful, for example, has in the background the ship in which he is about to embark: a very similar one featured in the painting of Henry VIII's departure for the Field of Cloth of Gold, a work that hung at Hampton Court.

As if to prove the later and separate nature of the Apostles windows, two of the original small designs for Window 21, Peter and John healing the Lame Man, and the Death of Ananias, plus another for Window 19 (Christ's Appearance to the Apostles), survived together. They were only identified as the designs for the Cambridge windows in 1964 when they were found tucked into an album in an American college library. They prove that the *vidimuses* for all three scenes had already been adapted to the shape of the windows; the sketches for each pair of tall narrow lights indicate the dividing central mullion and the curves of tracery at the top. These were working drawings, marked up with a grid of squares for the iron support bars at the back (the *ferramenta*) so that important details of the design would not overlap with these structural features.

Being able to compare these drawings with the finished product in the windows gives an extraordinary insight into the cartoonists' techniques of adaptation and their sensitivity to the space available. In the finished version of Peter and John healing the lame man, the latter's twisted leg has been modified from that in the drawing to make it appear more prominent in the glass, while the gate in the background, left plain in the drawing, has been embellished with painted swags and garlands. These sorts of detail were left to the discretion, judgement and available time of the glass-painters, who had the opportunity to leave their own distinctive stamp – even though such touches of individuality were far too small to be distinguishable in the soaring height and blazing colours high in the chapel's walls.

Another feature that separates the Apostles windows from the rest is that four of the prophet-messengers were firmly identified with the evangelist St Luke, because they were accompanied by his symbol of the winged calf. Referring to him so prominently was further proof of the college's Lutheran tendencies in the late 1530s. St Luke was widely believed to be the author of the Acts of the Apostles, which read like the direct sequel to his gospel. It was he who accompanied Paul on his conversion missions to Greece and Rome, and who carried on the good work after Paul was martyred. In 1530, Martin Luther hailed Luke's teaching that faith in Jesus was the only justification. So it was right that the explanatory messengers were linked with Luke, the actual author of the narrative in those windows whose texts they held.

Other elements in these late windows could be taken as discreet Lutheran propaganda, yet not sufficiently blatant to offend those who resisted the more rapid course of reform, like the king himself. Window 11, Christ brought before Caiaphas, contained a sort of pun. Inscribed on the High Priest's throne were the words *SIC RESPONDES PONTIFICEM* ('Is that how you answer the High Priest?'). As the word *Pontifex* could also mean Pope, and as there had once been a Pope named Caiaphas, the anti-papal message was there for those who wanted to see it. The idea was familiar enough in Lutheran iconography, such as the Nuremberg woodcuts of the early 1530s where the specific image of a Pope replaced that of Caiaphas: such source material was easily accessible to Flemish cartoonists. Another image that attacked the established Church was in Window 7, the Temptation of Christ, where Satan appeared in the habit of a friar, an inadequate disguise for his horns and cloven feet. The presence of the Repentant Thief in the East Window also supported a reformist reading, for the concept of penitence was an important element of Lutheranism. A similarly repentant figure was the Prodigal Son (Window 19), whose return to his father's house was a familiar motif in medieval art but here uniquely represented a prototype for the Incredulity of Thomas, below, whose doubts were forgiven by Christ.

While Hone had to commission new designs for Fox's revisions, some of the other windows that he and his team installed in the 1530s showed recognisable quotations from artists in favour with the popes. If anyone had noticed this, the painters' reputations would have outweighed disapproval of the patron. The cartoonists thus borrowed various details and motifs from Raphael's Vatican frescoes, such as a figure from his *Expulsion of Heliodorus*, the ultimate source (though possibly mediated through tapestry) for the graceful woman trying to protect her baby, with her head turned away in three-quarter profile in Window 6, the Massacre of the Innocents. Just as Raphael's Sistine tapestries complemented Michelangelo's ceiling frescoes, so Hone's crucified thieves in the East Window had the contorted muscular bodies of the Sistine nudes. Michelangelo's *Entombment* (which he painted in Rome around 1502) seems to have inspired the three Marys at the Tomb in Window 17. Another allusion was to Leonardo da Vinci's *Last Supper* in Milan. The version in Window 9 acknowledges the original in the pure Renaissance architecture of the carefully coffered ceiling, although it uses a boldly receding perspective for the table, which was the only way to fit such a strong horizontal element into the narrow vertical opening. This was probably borrowed via Pieter Coeck's tapestry version of the scene rather than being copied directly: Coeck had seen the work when he visited Italy, an essential training process for so many early sixteenth-century Flemish artists.

The impact of Dürer and Memling was still present, as in the Scourging of Christ (Window 12), lifted from the former's Passion cycle. But some of Hone's cartoons reflect a new generation of northern Renaissance artists, such as Lucas van der Leyden, in the scene of Christ Crowned with Thorns, again in Window 12.

The career of Provost Fox flourished. In 1535 Henry promoted him from Archdeacon of Leicester to Bishop of Hereford. In 1536, he headed the team of bishops determining the tenets of the new faith, their conclusions defined as the Ten Articles. In 1537, he chaired the commission that Henry appointed to flesh out the Articles, and was responsible for compiling their conclusions under the title of the *Bishops' Book*. Fox's preface invited the king, in his 'most excellent wisdom and exact judgement', to make any necessary corrections: Henry submitted 246 alterations.

At the same time, Fox was trying to oversee the completion of the chapel, now made additionally urgent because the old chapel collapsed in 1537 (just after Evensong, so fortunately no one was hurt). Though long superseded in significance by its towering neighbour to the south, the old chapel had remained in use until the other was ready. But its maintenance had clearly been neglected. As if in preparation for the move, Fox made an inventory of its contents in 1535, updating the previous version of 1506 that included many of the original acquisitions from the 1450s. There were copes of white cloth of gold, chasubles of black cloth of gold, orphreys sewn with stars and flowers, and, for the image of the Virgin Mary, a black velvet cloak, and a bonnet of cloth of gold for her Son. Such things were not easily compatible with Lutheranism.

In addition to many of its windows, the new chapel still lacked the screen and choir stalls that were essential for services. These were commissioned during the brief reign of Anne Boleyn, from 1533 to 1536. There was no proper floor, because the paving was not completed until the late 1540s. The sumptuous high altar, carved, engraved and gilded in London, probably by the king's Florentine painter, Antonio Toto (who had made the altar for the Westminster Abbey chapel), was not brought to Cambridge until 1544, but perhaps the old-fashioned one from the former chapel served temporarily. So although the new chapel came into use in 1537, it still occasionally turned back into a building site, with scaffolding and tarpaulin, wood-shavings, dust and a hard-earth floor, and too many clear-glazed apertures still awaiting their vitreous tapestries.

Chapter Twenty-Two: Dissolution

EDWARD FOX DIED in May 1538, before he was able to grapple with the king's emendations to the *Bishops' Book* or see the latest windows in position. Archbishop Cranmer inherited the editorial problems, while Fox's successor, Provost George Day, had to cope with the chapel. Day was not a Kingsman, but very much the king's man as former chaplain to Henry VIII. He was now also appointed the university's Vice-Chancellor and was seen as a safe pair of hands in difficult times. Yet having the king's approval did not necessarily mean guaranteed financial support for the college. Shortly after Fox's death, in June 1538, Henry approved a payment of £232 15s 9d for unspecified 'works' within 'the new church of the King's College' which could have been for windows, stalls or flooring. But evidence of the college's general impoverishment in these years is implied in a letter that Provost Day and the Fellows wrote to the king in the summer of 1539. Clearly hoping to benefit from the general redistribution resulting from the Dissolution of the Monasteries, they begged for alleviation from their current poverty by the reallocation of funds that the college had previously granted to two religious houses that were now shut down. They pointed out that although their numbers were as high as the Founder had intended, outgoings now exceeded income by at least £100, with the result that Provost, Fellows and scholars could only afford to draw two-thirds of their due salaries. The king granted this request in September 1539.

Meanwhile, the glaziers laboured on, doubtless grumbling at the further changes needed in a project that was already far behind schedule. But the delays and alterations made more work for them by their having to put a new slant on the dubious subject matter that was already in position. The three Apostles windows may have replaced other Old and New Testament scenes that were already completed although not yet installed. According to the now hopelessly old-fashioned block-books, the typological cycle concluded with several scenes from the life of Christ's Mother: the Virgin with Sts Dominic and Francis (unacceptable once the friaries had been shut down), the Virgin as Protectress (too Roman), and the Virgin Visiting the Places that Jesus Knew (apocryphal). Such scenes had probably been part of Flower's original scheme but were no longer theologically acceptable because the events they depicted were not described in the Gospels. With no scriptural foundation, they could not truly represent the Word so revered by the reformers.

Some of the Cambridge glazing team welcomed these changes. James Nicholson had become an increasingly committed supporter of the Lutheranism that was academically rife in Cambridge, and also in Oxford, where he had worked for Wolsey on Cardinal's College. Painting newly meaningful images like David and Goliath for the Cambridge windows must have given him great satisfaction. A surviving *vidimus* from his earlier commission for Cardinal Wolsey, the chapel at Hampton Court, reveals how a commissioning glazier coped with sensitive theological issues. Nicholson submitted two designs for the Crucifixion East Window, one of which included two angels gathering Christ's blood, while the other omitted them. This was a time when devout reformers were starting to challenge the doctrine of the Eucharist, though Wolsey could hardly be counted among their numbers. Perhaps Nicholson and his designer were trying to introduce what they found preferable, while covering their backs.

As further proof of the scale of Wolsey's commissions, another *vidimus* of the 1520s from the same workshop survives (in the National Gallery of Scotland, Edinburgh) for the east window of his chapel at York Place. In some ways, this was a conventional window. Below the Crucifixion was a row of kneeling figures who included the cardinal himself, flanked by Peter and Paul, facing a king, a queen and a princess, attended by Sts George, Henry and Katherine. It had obviously been planned well before the divorce. The presence of St William of York and St Thomas à Becket in attendance at the Crucifixion and Resurrection makes it a firmly English commission, but again the annotations and written suggestions for alternative scenes (showing how flexible subject matter could be even at the design stage) are in a Flemish hand that suggests Nicholson's involvement. In the glass of the Cambridge chapel too, there is evidence of the aliens' language: in Window 6, the Golden Calf, the text of the first commandment, 'Thou shalt worship no other god but me', is not in Latin but in German.

Further evidence of Nicholson's work for Wolsey can be detected in panels now in the windows of Balliol College, Oxford. These were made from the same design and by the same hand as those for Wolsey's Hampton Court chapel and were perhaps intended for the never-completed chapel of his college. Some of the figures bear a striking resemblance to those in Cambridge, notably the head of Pontius Pilate, with its cruel face, beaky nose and flowing moustache, beard and hair.

While he was working for Wolsey, James Nicholson met Thomas Cromwell, the cardinal's most trusted legal adviser, who was in charge of funding and overseeing the building of Cardinal's College. Despite being employed by this prince of the Church, the two men found they shared reformist sympathies, for Cromwell's views were very much in line with what was being disseminated in Cambridge. After Wolsey's fall, Cromwell helped disband the Cardinal's College (it was later refounded by the king as Christ Church College) and Nicholson continued to work on the Cambridge project, where there was still a daunting amount to do. At the same time, his strong beliefs encouraged him to expand his activities to include printing and publishing reformist literature.

In 1534, the same year he and Hone dined at King's College with Provost Fox to consider the necessary revisions to the glass, Nicholson wrote a sycophantic letter to Cromwell which flattered the latter for being not only a good master, but also 'the only patron unto the Truth' and begged for his support in a new enterprise: Nicholson intended to print an English edition of the Bible, so far only published abroad in the controversial translation of Cambridge man Miles Coverdale, former Augustinian friar, 'so that the pure word of God may at once go forth under the king's privilege'. If Cromwell would only back this scheme, urged Nicholson, he would be more worthy of remembrance than St Augustine himself. This was still controversial. Wolsey and Thomas More had passionately opposed the idea of translating the Bible into English, because it gave the literate direct access to the Word and did away with the necessary mediation of clerics. The always orthodox Henry VIII only gave half-hearted support on the same grounds, that unrestricted access was a dangerous thing. Nor should the Bible be read aloud, but only perused silently by the literate.

The first Coverdale Bible was published in 1535, although not by Nicholson, and Cromwell promoted it to the king. But Nicholson lost Cromwell's favour in 1538, when he issued a pirated version of Coverdale's translation of the New Testament that contained so many mistakes that another publisher, Richard Grafton, had to correct it. Grafton wrote disparagingly to Cromwell that although Nicholson had printed the New Testament in Latin and in English, citing Coverdale's version, the latter 'never saw the book till after it was printed. The thing is so foolishly done that he is grieved that the printer has so defamed his learning by adding his name thereto, and also that the common people are deprived of the true sense of God's word.' This brought an end to Nicholson's brief publishing career, but he did have the glazing to fall back on.

Thomas Cromwell, Lord Privy Seal, succeeded Fisher as Chancellor of Cambridge University. In 1535, the king additionally appointed him Visitor to the university, with a brief to bring the whole institution under tighter control. New royal injunctions of 1535 concerned the university and its reform. Cromwell intervened directly in the curriculum, regarding both the subjects taught and the manner of teaching them. The browbeaten university had to submit to its Chancellor's demand that all members sign a pledge of loyalty to the king and renounce the authority of the Pope. Cromwell appointed Thomas Leigh of King's College as his deputy to oversee these reforms and ensure that all the colleges submitted inventories of their goods to him. A further problem was the new wave of antagonism between gown and a town unsettled by the price rises caused by inflation, and the long-standing problem of control over Stourbridge Fair. Cromwell warned the mayor and bailiffs not to interfere with the rights of the university, but things got so bad that the king summoned all parties to Hampton Court in 1537.

In 1538, the measure dissolving the larger monasteries destroyed the four orders who had lined up to welcome Henry VII to Cambridge in 1506, shutting down the Augustinian, Dominican, Franciscan and Carmelite friaries. Vice-Chancellor Day wrote to the king to congratulate him for suppressing such pernicious institutions, and begged that their buildings might be converted into colleges. The Act had many adverse effects on Cambridge. Abolishing monks and friars may have freed their premises for university accommodation but also cut the heart out of the town, resulting in further decline and dismay. Those who had contributed so much to teaching and learning were sacked, and their charitable, educational and artistic contributions ceased.

Henry VII must have turned in his grave when his son and Cromwell shut down the shrine at Walsingham in 1538. Barnard Flower had put in new windows after Henry Tudor's death and Wolsey made a pilgrimage there in 1517 to give thanks for recovery from illness. But Erasmus mocked the place, sneering at its seductive jewels, gold and silver and the Virgin's milk in a crystal flask. In July 1538, 'the images of Our Lady of Walsingham and Ipswich were brought up to London with all the jewels that hung about them, at the King's commandment, and divers other images . . . and they were burnt at Chelsea by My Lord Privy Seal'. Henry Tudor had even mentioned one of these treasures in his will, a silver and gilt statue 'that we have caused to be made, to be offered and set before Our Lady at

Walsingham', now just part of the loot that Cromwell melted down. Those who soar too close to the sun risk burning their wings. Window 9, the Fall of the Rebel Angels that prefigured Wolsey's end ten years earlier, now referred to Cromwell instead. Having lost the king's favour by arranging his disastrous marriage to Anne of Cleves in December 1539, he was toppled by the orthodox faction led by the Duke of Norfolk and was executed for treason in July 1540.

Cromwell's successor as University Chancellor was Stephen Gardiner, the king's former secretary, Master of Trinity Hall and recently elevated to the bishopric of Winchester. Though he had been instrumental in arguing the case for the divorce, and had written *De vera obedientia* (1535) to defend the king's supremacy, Gardiner was now seen as a relatively conservative figure who caused a local scandal in 1545 when he publicly attacked a ribald student play, *Pammachius*, because it mocked the rituals of the Church. In the same year, the university had a narrow escape when the Act for the Dissolution of Colleges enabled the Crown to seize more institutions. But a preliminary commission of inquiry reporting to the king confirmed the general state of poverty, and the colleges were allowed, for the moment, to retain their status, buildings and estates.

Despite so much change and upheaval, the king continued to pay for the chapel windows. Money was now no object because of the streams of gold flowing into the royal coffers from the former religious houses. This meant, paradoxically, that Galyon Hone was kept busier than ever on other duties, glazing the dissolved properties that the king was avidly converting for his own use. Hone repaired all the windows in the former Dominican friary at Guildford, and the old cathedral priory at Rochester, where he installed 'two arms of the king's and the queen's set up within the lodgings, thirteen badges of the king's and the queen's and twelve scriptures with the sword'. This composite symbol which acknowledged Henry's divine authority to rule also went into the windows of the Dominican nunnery at Dartford, after it was converted into royal accommodation. Here in December 1541, work on the building, where Hone earned 21s 4d 'for glazing and repairing the windows of the King's house', was overseen by Sir Richard Longe, the king's long-serving Gentleman of the Privy Chamber and arbiter of the case of Richard Mabbott of Southwark who stole Hone's bay trees.

There were signs of pressure in the Cambridge windows now, notably those on the south side of the antechapel, suggesting lack of time or lack of supervision. The most blatant mistake was inserting the wrong inscriptions on the scrolls held by the four messengers in Window 18, the Road to Emmaus, and the Supper at Emmaus, which were all quotations from the Acts of Apostles and intended to refer to incidents in Window 21. But the error was not spotted until Window 18 was inexorably in position, and so the same texts had to be repeated in Window 21. Nor were the other Apostles' inscriptions correct: indeed two refer to events that were not illustrated at all, the High Priests in Council, and the Arrest of Paul, implying some very late revisions to enhance the status of Paul even further by omitting scenes that presented him in a less positive light.

Any hopes of glazing the West Window with the Last Judgement, as specified in the 1526 contract, vanished when that topic became too controversial. The old block-books had illustrated several separate incidents. Just as the East Window's six scenes centred on the Crucifixion, so those in the West Window might have been expected to expound the Last Judgement through depictions of Doomsday, the Damned going to Hell, the Blessed with Christ, and the Rewards of the Righteous. But Henry's Reformation had banned the saints who were meant to intercede for Christians' souls to keep them from the torments of Hellfire. As for Purgatory, from which the souls awaiting Judgement were expected to emerge with renewed hopes, this was a doctrine the reformers had utterly undermined. They argued that Christ's sacrifice on the Cross forgave everyone's sins, so that those who truly believed in him automatically achieved salvation and had nothing to purge after death. If Purgatory imposed further punishments, then this meant Christ's suffering had been in vain. And the idea that the rich could buy themselves remission time while the poor could not was offensive: it was typical that Julius II, like so many popes before him, sold indulgences to diminish time spent in

Purgatory. Nor was it any longer possible to ensure salvation through performing good works, unless such deeds were done through the genuine love of Christ and not just to earn exemption from sin. This would have shocked Bishop Fisher, who took a hard-line stance on Purgatory, and advised his flock to alleviate the extended torments of their deceased loved ones by purchasing indulgences to shorten their time there. And it would have been incomprehensible to Henry Tudor, for whom the completion of the chapel and its windows was essential in reducing the pains he so dreaded.

So the West Window, temporarily filled with white glass, was left to the last. As if the Provost and Fellows realised that this was likely to be permanent, in 1541 they installed the external iron support bars already fitted to all the other windows 'to protect the glass from the effects of the wind'. This work was undertaken by Roger Young, a local glazier, at a cost of £6 7s. It was curious that the college accounts for this still referred to the building as 'the new chapel', almost as if the older one, defunct since 1537, still had a more vivid identity. It also suggests a real sense of finality: a local man put in the bars because all the great London glaziers had left.

Chapter Twenty-Three: Wives and Windows

THE DECORATION OF the chapel revealed not only the changing religious climate but also the king's turbulent marital history. The coded language of the windows in Cambridge, and in Henry's many other residences too, was designed for those informed people who could relate them to contemporary events. These ranged from Henry's new status as head of the Church of England down to his personal relationships with his ministers and his wives. It was all too frequently the royal glazier's job to substitute for a panel that had suddenly become embarrassing, one that was up-to-date and politically correct.

Henry's marital history was recorded in glass and stone, carving and textiles. The original logo of H&K was replaced by H&A. There was hardly time for H&J, which was then succeeded by a lonely HR, Henricus Rex. However, any H&Ks which survived became relevant again to honour another two wives named Katherine. It was not just their initials that needed replacing, but also the family and personal symbols of their own beasts and badges. Recording the changing queens was one of the tasks that kept Hone and other royal craftsmen busy over the years.

Katherine of Aragon's symbol was the pomegranate, emblem of the Spanish royal house. A pomegranate and a rose appear above the respective figures of Queen Katherine and Henry VIII in the window of the early 1520s now in St Margaret's, Westminster, as well as being associated in metalwork and sculpture of the period. Although the two symbols were conjoined into an entirely new badge to symbolise the permanence of the union between the two dynasties, this does not feature in the tracery glass of the King's Chapel, which was concerned with Henry Tudor's pedigree. However, there are pomegranates among the stone carvings.*

Galyon Hone's extensive commissions to celebrate the union of Henry and Anne Boleyn in 1533 included substituting Anne's arms and badges for Katherine's at Greenwich Palace, and installing new glass painted with the revised royal arms in the north and south windows of the Great Hall in Westminster Palace. This was part of a whole extravagant ensemble of new statues, painting and gilding in honour of Anne's long-awaited coronation banquet there. At Hampton Court, Wolsey, soon before his fall, had already tried to disarm the king's resentment and Anne's hostility by flattering them in glass. Despite their mutual loathing, he installed Anne's armorials in various windows. Hone now put another three in the east window of the chapel, and replaced the figure of St Katherine with one of St Anne: the reference to St Anne, the mother of Mary, was a flattering way of linking the queen with the Virgin. In the pageantry celebrating Anne's triumphal progress through London after her coronation, when she was pregnant with the anticipated male heir, she was welcomed by the figures of St Anne and the Virgin, significantly comparing the child's lineage to that of Christ. It was Anne's arms, replacing those of Katherine, that featured in the glass of the great hall that Henry rebuilt at Hampton Court, including badges 'set in the old garlands of the [former] queen', a way of saving glass and money. At the same time, Hone took the opportunity of replacing Wolsey's motto of *Dominus Mihi Adjutor* (repeated twenty-eight times) with more appropriate new inscriptions.

Hone also commemorated Queen Anne at Ampthill Castle, Bedfordshire,

* The panel of heraldic glass in one of the side chapels combining Henry's and Katherine's arms probably came from the college's Old Court and was a later insertion.

which Henry bought in 1524 and remodelled into a luxurious hunting retreat and convenient halt on royal progresses; here he temporarily banished the newly divorced Katherine of Aragon. Then Henry resumed occupation and lavishly redecorated it for his new bride. In the autumn of 1534, Hone installed the queen's badges in the windows of the king's dining chamber, the queen's dressing chamber, and in both their official bedchambers, as well as putting in many other new windows, including the 'great bay window' in the king's dining room. In 1536, he installed more badges in the queen's dining room, together with new glass for her bed-chamber and privy chamber. At Knole, one of their favourite retreats, even the firedogs were embellished with a cosy H&A.

In King's College Chapel, the arms, initials and badges of Anne Boleyn – her falcon, bull's head and the griffin (a lion with an eagle's head and wings) that was one of her heraldic supporters – all appear in the carvings of the dark oak screen that divides the antechapel from the choir. Commissioned to celebrate the marriage, this tribute to Anne in modern Renaissance style took the form of a unit of rood-screen, organ loft and choir stalls. The stalls may not have been started until after 1536, because they do not bear her initials, but elsewhere these are copiously entwined into curlicues, cherubs and swags of flowers. For the screen, these were even more Italianate than some of the ornamental details in the glass because it was made by top Italian or French wood-carvers. Its triumphal arches survived as a tribute to Henry's imperial claim to outrank the Pope, but many of its details became sadly redundant after Henry had Anne executed on 19 May 1536.

Eleven days later, he married Jane Seymour. By the autumn, the stained glass figure of St Anne (the one that replaced that of St Katherine) in the chapel at Hampton Court was removed. It had lasted less than a year. The building accounts listed 'item, for the translating and the removing of images of Saint Anne and another of Saint Thomas in the high altar window of the chapel, price the piece 6s 8d – total 13s 4d' while Jane's arms were hastily added to the carved spandrels in the great hall. Then Hone returned to Greenwich Palace to replace Anne's arms with those of Jane in the windows there. It was quite a simple matter to convert Anne's falcon badge into Jane's phoenix, and another economical modification was to turn Anne's leopard supporters into the panthers that held up Jane's shield. The unicorn symbolised Jane too, for it would only surrender to a true virgin who represented the Mother of Christ herself, evidence of the virtue and holiness of the short-lived queen and mother of Henry's only legitimate male heir.

Queen Jane gave birth to a son, Edward, on 12 October 1537. He was christened three days later in all the pomp and glittering magnificence of the chapel at Hampton Court, whose sparkling glass was Galyon Hone's special contribution to the event. Amongst grateful recipients of the happy news was the University of Cambridge, which received an official letter from the queen announcing that 'we be delivered and brought in childbed of a prince . . . for the love and affection which you bear unto us, the knowledge thereof should be joyous and glad tidings unto you'. But Jane was dead within two weeks. There was hardly time during the brief marriage to commemorate her in the glass or stone of the chapel (although her heraldic arms are now inserted in the windows of one of the small side chapels.) However, the East Window recorded her achievement in giving Henry a male heir, who was proclaimed Prince of Wales a few days before his mother's death.

Dominating the whole chapel, its tracery glass glorified the dynasty on a scale even greater than in the heads of the other windows. In addition to the recurrent symbols of rose, portcullis and fleur-de-lys, there was the red dragon, the initials of Henry VII and Elizabeth of York, and now a new device, the traditional ostrich feathers and motto, 'Ich Dien', of a Prince of Wales, in panels placed symmetrically on each side of the window. The reference to the prince gave further emphasis to Henry's image as King David, who was succeeded by his glorious son Solomon, just as Prince Edward would inherit Henry's magnificent legacy.

Hone installed glass that was meant to impress Henry's fourth bride, Anne of Cleves, the match negotiated by Thomas Cromwell to establish an alliance between England and a Protestant German state. Eligible sister of the Duke of Cleves, Anne was due to land at Deal in December 1539, and would spend one night in Canterbury en route for the wedding in London. For this brief stay, Henry converted a building which dated back to the very beginnings of English Christianity, the now dissolved abbey of St Augustine. His builders strove overtime and in the dark to get it ready for her: the accounts reveal the purchase of candles to work by, and charcoal for fuel to dry out the newly decorated rooms, whose walls and beams were ochred yellow and red. Here Hone installed the arms and badges of the king and the queen-to-be, the swan of Cleves, to complement identical motifs painted on the walls. Such careful preparations did not compensate for Henry's shock when he met his unattractive bride, who did not resemble Holbein's charming portrait of her at all. The marriage was dissolved six months later, and brought down the man who arranged it, Thomas Cromwell. After the king's death, Anne lived in the dissolved Dominican nunnery at Dartford, where she was doubtless able to appreciate Hone's panels of 'scriptures with the king's word'. Anne's arms can now be seen in one of the side chapel windows at Cambridge, but this was a much later installation.

In July 1540, Henry obtained an annulment from Anne and married Katherine Howard, niece of the Duke of Norfolk. The 'K' in the East Window at Cambridge referred to her rather than to Katherine of Aragon (though based on the earlier cartoon) and confirms the window's late place in the sequence, as also implied by the Prince of Wales feathers, quite apart from its mature and mannered style. Hone installed the Howard arms in various rooms at Ampthill Castle and in the former priory of Rochester. But after Henry had Katherine executed in her turn in February 1542 for her alleged adultery with courtier Thomas Culpeper and others, a local glazier was hurriedly called in to remove her arms from all the windows. The popular identification of Katherine Howard as the Queen of Sheba in Window 4 of King's College Chapel is hard to sustain, given her fate.

The initial K in the East Window remained relevant for the sixth royal bride, Katherine Parr, whom Henry married in July 1543, but this is the only tenuous reference to her in the chapel. There is no evidence that this queen visited Cambridge but, as a learned woman, she was fully aware of the current symbols of Reformation imagery that the windows explored. In her *Lamentation of a Sinner* (1547), she made the familiar comparison so thoroughly expounded in the windows:

> Moses, a most godly, wise governor and king hath delivered us out of the bondage of Pharaoh. I mean by this Moses King Henry VIII, my most sovereign favourable lord and husband . . . and I mean by the Pharaoh the bishop of Rome who hath been and is a greater persecutor of all true Christians than ever was Pharaoh of the children of Israel.

Chapter Twenty-Four: Continuing Hostilities

A S IF HE DID not have enough to do glazing the chapel and all the dissolved monasteries that the king had seized, Galyon Hone was kept busy in London defending his craft against the resentful Company of Glaziers. His team of Flemings and Englishmen represented a fair balance but still irritated the company because Hone had not invited any of its members to participate in the prestigious though much-delayed Cambridge project.

One unpopular alien was a prosperous Flemish glazier called Peter Nicholson, probably a relative or perhaps even the son of James, for they both lived within the precinct of St Thomas's Hospital, Southwark. In November 1536, two members of the Glaziers' Company had brought an action against Peter Nicholson before the Court of the Barons of the Exchequer demanding that he must be fined for employing seven rather than the two alien assistants permitted by the Act of 1523. But the glazier used delaying tactics, feigning ignorance and asking for more time to respond, in the hopes that the action might founder. The company, undeterred, made a formal complaint to the king, in the form of a cringing petition addressed to Thomas (now Baron) Cromwell: 'be so good, Lord, unto your humble suppliants that we may have the

King's laws to proceed against one Peter Nicholson the Glazier'.

They stressed his offence as a 'stranger' of employing five illegal 'stranger assistants to do only your lordship's work alone' – proving that Cromwell himself was a patron of the Flemish style – and protested that Nicholson was obtaining far too many commissions through setting his men to work not just in London but also in Flanders. For 'he bringeth glass ready-wrought over to England', meaning that he was importing stained glass panels made abroad to fulfil the local demand. Bringing in finished windows was strictly forbidden because it took away yet more commissions from London glaziers, 'whereby our English men cannot be set in work', and also deprived Customs and Excise of all the tax he should have paid on imported sheets of glass. The petition concluded with the familiar moan that 'these strangers will utterly undo us' and curried Cromwell's favour: 'We shall pray for your long continuance in health and high preservation.' They demanded that Nicholson pay them a substantial fine for breaking the law and in compensation for all the hypothetical fees they had lost.

The outcome of this case is unknown; but a glazier in such high demand and with such important patrons as Nicholson should have been able to ignore the immediate complaints. The recurrent calls for the imposition of all the established restrictions simply proved that the alien glaziers were happily infringing previous legislation. And it was foolish of the company to try to act against the man who was installing windows for Thomas Cromwell himself. But this was just before Cromwell's sudden fall, as dramatic as Wolsey's had been. One of the many things held against him was the fact that he had pandered to foreigners by making so many of them denizens. Yet the underlying distrust of foreigners was demonstrated when neither aliens nor denizens were allowed to participate in Henry's call for musters to defend the coast during the 1539 crisis following the alliance between the emperor and the king of France.

The continuing conflict with France caused a renewed outcry that there were too many immigrants, which resulted in more restrictive measures. In 1541, yet another Act of Parliament, 'the Act Concerning Strangers', attempted to deal with the 'infinite number of strangers and aliens of foreign countries and nations which do daily increase and multiply in excessive numbers, to the great detriment, hindrance, loss and impoverishment of his Grace's natural true lieges and subjects of the realm, to the great decay of the same'. This Act stressed how the incomers had 'infringed, frustrated and defrauded' all previous laws, and how they had improperly obtained denizenship by 'divers letters patents obtained by the crafty suits, inventions and practices'. So the measure insisted once more that they must obey the law, and not employ more than four alien servants, on pain of the swingeing fine of £10. It even included a clause referring specifically to stranger-artificers living in Oxford or Cambridge, who, for once, were forbidden to employ more than two alien apprentices or journeymen. But there were two significant loop-holes. One gave the king the right 'to grant to any such alien any special liberties or privileges . . . to be plainly, wholely and particularly expressed, specified and declared by special words'. Secondly, any lord of Parliament was allowed to employ six alien servants. Yet despite all this, the imperial ambassador Chapuys commented in 1541 how foreign craftsmen were virtually replacing English ones and, instead of leaving the country, as people hoped, they were embedding themselves more securely by becoming denizens. According to the Subsidy rolls of the time, foreigners, mainly from the Low Countries, were now in the majority in some of the City wards, quite apart from their dominance in the areas outside, like Southwark.

The Glaziers' Company next tried to come to terms with the demand for their rivals' work by establishing pre-emptive controls. According to an agreement negotiated between two wardens of the company, Robert Nelson and Robert Marlyng (a former Master), and the Southwark glaziers, headed by James Nicholson, the Glaziers' Company licensed the Flemings to work 'lawfully and quietly' within the City, on condition that they paid an annual fee to the company of 2 shillings, plus a 'fine' of 10 or 13 shillings per project. The company in return pledged the sum of 20 marks (the equivalent of £13 6s 8d) not to molest them. But the indenture, sealed and signed by both sides, became worth nothing when James Nicholson, who had taken charge of the Flemings' half of the bond, died, and his widow remarried and handed it over to her next husband. Unfortunately, he happened to be the current Master of the Glaziers' Company, William Hornby. Without the protection of the special agreement to work in the City, and despite the Flemings' claim to have been regularly paying their dues, the duplicitous Hornby and a fellow warden had four of the foreign glaziers now working without authorisation in the City arrested and thrown into gaol.

They went too far. One of these men was Galyon Hone, never a man to take things lying down. Imprisoning the king's glazier was *lèse-majesté*. Henry VIII, like his father, had always steered an uneasy course between propitiating English craftsmen while preferring the work of foreigners. Now forced to commit himself, he overruled the company and ordered the release of their hostages. Hone, confident in the backing of his royal employer, immediately brought an action in the Star Chamber against the Master and the Glaziers' Company for unlawful imprisonment. He may have had right on his side but the verdict was inconclusive: although foreigners should not have been working in the City, no individual London guild had the right to make any agreement to control non-guild work without the sanction of the Lord Mayor. Therefore the indenture was void, and there was no technical cause for complaint.

In December 1541, the company submitted another petition that suggested their desperation. This time they appealed to the Lord Mayor's Court. First, they asked permission for 'six honest Englishmen' to be made Freemen entitled to glaze in the City, which was obviously one way of keeping work in English hands. Secondly, they made a general plea for only the right sort of strangers – those who were 'good workmen and of honest conversation' – to be licensed to work in the City. This expressed the wider national fear of all the foreigners who were rendering decent English craftsmen 'utterly undone and not able to keep any house by reason of the great resort of strangers into this noble city, whereof the most part of them know not their occupation', the Court ruled that any persecution of foreign glaziers must be suspended pending a future decision.

From then on, Hone, feeling increasingly secure, waged a personal campaign against the Glaziers' Company. He urged his fellow Flemings and other outsiders not to pay any of the 'fines' – in effect bribes – demanded for working in the City, where all the merchants continued to commission windows from the Flemings. He refused to commit himself to attend meetings with the company, saying offhandedly that 'he could not tell whether he would come or not'; and he successfully persuaded his colleagues, including the unpopular Peter Nicholson,* not to do so either. Instead they 'held privy meetings among themselves', which was technically illegal. As a result of this lack of co-operation, the company alleged, young men became reluctant to sign on as apprentices, while those who had laboriously worked their way up to the rank of Freemen complained that 'the Strangers have as much liberty as they'.

As war with France loomed, the mood against immigrants hardened and an Act was passed in 1544 that compelled all 'strangers' in England to become subjects of the Crown or face expulsion. The Glaziers' Company resumed their particular feud in the summer of 1546, when they complained about their rivals to the king in the form of a petition delivered to the Star Chamber. This named Galyon Hone and another three Flemings, alien denizens Francis Williamson (who had made four of the Cambridge windows), John Gasbright and Gerard Lenthurst, and accused them, despite the previous prohibitions and brief imprisonment, of continuing 'to practise the feat and craft of glazing within your said City contrary to the said customs, usage and liberties'. The petition tactfully but reproachfully reminded the king that, because of his 'weighty affairs and causes' he had not had the 'leisure to examine and finish the said matter'. They denounced Galyon's previous action against them as 'feigned and untrue', accused him of a treasonable refusal to contribute towards the costs of the king's wars (the company of course had done so), and protested that the foreigners were still practising their banned craft within the City yet 'utterly refused' the company's offer to make them Freemen. And they demanded the right to impose fines again, since the previous case had never been fully resolved.

---

* Although his name does not appear in the 1526 contract, Hilary Wayment believes that he made some of the later King's windows.

They named a further six strangers working illegally in the City, together with twelve non-Freemen English glaziers also working there unsanctioned. Finally, they called for the banning of an innovative, time-saving, lead-working device that the Flemings had invented —which really did prove how reactionary the Glaziers' Company was.

Their petition ended with a veiled threat to the king: it was not just the company but the whole City that was affected by such open flouting of laws meant to defend its 'liberties and customs'. 'If it be not shortly redressed, the Citizens of your said City shall not be able to do your Majesty and your heirs such service as they have done in time past.' And they demanded that the offending glaziers be subpoenaed to appear before the Court of Star Chamber itself. This was a test case for the king, not just about window-makers but about the loyalty of his subjects. The City had spoken. He needed the backing of the Lord Mayor and the companies, masters and liverymen. All the ancient tensions between court and city surfaced again, but the king could not afford to antagonise the old institutions.

The response of Galyon Hone and his colleagues was that they were perfectly prepared to obey the law and pay their reasonable dues. But the Glaziers replied that they did not believe them, and demanded judgment with costs. Their subsequent submission to the court, dated 18 October 1546, provided further evidence against the Flemings and again accused Galyon Hone, Peter Nicholson and a Godfrey Trice, who also lived within St Thomas's precinct, of treason, because they had refused to contribute to 'the king's wars'. This time, on 27 October 1546, the verdict went in favour of the company, which was granted permission to license and charge foreigners for working in the City again. As a further blow against progress, the state-of-the-art lead-working gadget was decreed 'doubtful and not suitable to be used within the realm'. The Lord Mayor even impounded one example, which he passed to the Lord Admiral, hoping, perhaps, that the navy might be able to turn the cunning Fleming invention against England's enemies.

It is unlikely that these legal diversions caused further delay to the Cambridge windows because the East Window had now been installed and no decision had been taken to proceed with the West Window. Although the Last Judgement was no longer acceptable, the great size of the window made any alternative problematic. It might have been feasible to insert something uncontroversial, like more Tudor badges or other armorials, but the enormous scale and cost were deterrents.

By 1546, Hone and his colleagues would have welcomed any such commission. Although they had responded to Fox's reformist alterations in the 1530s, all glaziers had noted an ominous decline in the demand for biblical windows, and the closure or contraction of religious buildings. In Southwark, the priory of St Mary Overy was shut down, and the friars' church became the local parish church, also sucking in the small neighbouring church of St Margaret's. That was closed and its treasures transferred: 'the sacrament of the altar was solemnly brought in rich copes with torches burning from St Margaret's to St Mary Overy' and the bells were moved as well. At the start of the decade, when he was still working on the chapel glass, Galyon Hone was a prosperous man who employed five servants in his Southwark household. But in the new climate, the work was drying up and his finances declined. The annual *Returns of Aliens* traced the downward graph: the value of his goods dropped from £40 (a very comfortable sum) in 1541 to 20 shillings in 1545.

Chapter Twenty-Five: The King is Dead

I N 1545, KING'S COLLEGE was the wealthiest in Cambridge. There were thirty-eight Fellows, twenty-four scholars and sixteen choristers, together with deans, bursars, lecturers and priests and a range of servants who included butler, cooks, cellarer, scullion, barber, groom, stable lads and laundress. (College statutes specified that the latter, being a woman and therefore dangerously seductive to impressionable young clerics, must not live within the college, and must be old enough to be unattractive; even so, she was not permitted to exchange the laundry directly with her clients, but only through an intermediary servant.) Other facilities included a barber's shop, vineyards and a hut for the swanherds. More importantly, there was someone responsible for the maintenance of the chapel, the Keeper of the Church, who received £20 'for all necessaries of the same'.

When Henry VIII died, on 28 January 1547, the chapel windows were still unfinished. It was thirty-two years since the glaziers started work, but industry was not enough: they needed backing and money as well, and these had been erratic. So it was still impossible to appreciate the full impact of their talents on the interior because the West Window was filled with white glass. This great blank zone let in too much light, creating a glare which diminished the subtle harmonies of amber and blue, ruby and

green, gold and silver that the glaziers had so carefully crafted in all the
other windows.

Henry VIII's son Edward was nine when he became king. Precociously
learned and more devout than his father, he, with his advisers, Protector
Seymour and Thomas Cranmer, Archbishop of Canterbury, pushed
forward the iconoclasm of the Reformation with an extremity bordering on
fanaticism. They relished the smashing of statues and the pulling down of
roods and altars, and unleashed a wave of destruction far greater than that
of the previous reign. Henry VIII had been well aware of the dangers of
tampering with the arts and rituals he still respected, and had tried to rein
the reformers back in 1540. In that year, when a hot dry summer and
resulting drought brought dysentery, plague and starvation, Henry commanded his bishops to tell the people to pray and to resume the penitential
processions throughout the parishes that he had earlier banned. His
Injunctions said nothing about windows, nor were they mentioned in the
first restrictive measure passed by his son.

But as attitudes became more extreme, Article 28 of Edward's
Injunctions of 1447 called for the removal, extinction and destruction of all
'monuments of feigned miracles, pilgrimages, idolatry and superstition, so
that there remain no memory of the same in walls, glass-windows or
elsewhere within their churches or houses'. This was the first time the
reformers specified glass amongst the items to be destroyed. Local glaziers
were now paid for 'defacing of the sentences and imagery in the glass
windows' and replacing them with clear glass. In Cambridge, it was
unthinkable that anyone should dare to speak up for any change to the
West Window, prematurely filled with the correct sort of plain glass.

Such limitations in subject matter had a further disastrous effect on the
glaziers' fortunes, whether they were aliens or Londoners. Galyon Hone was
probably grateful for the modest commission to install six panels with the
arms of the new king and the college in the Provost's Lodge in Cambridge
in November 1547, for which he received the fee of 16s 10d, and he did
similar armorial work at the Tower and in Whitehall Palace. He died in 1551,

and his son Gerard, who married the niece of one of the master carvers of the King's Chapel, inherited his father's workshop. Like so many others now, Gerard Hone could only make a living by installing clear replacements for smashed stained glass, or by producing innocuous heraldic panels. Edward VI recognised the demand for such work when he appointed Peter Nicholson as his new royal glazier on 21 February 1550. Once again, and despite the apparent victory of the Glaziers' Company over the aliens in 1546, the king awarded the position to a Fleming and not an Englishman.

The sheer impracticality of Edward's Injunctions calling for the removal of offensive images in glass, resulting in smashed panels, twisted leads and the hazards of wind and rain distracting the congregation, moderated attitudes. The Royal Injunctions of 1553 banned more artworks but included a tempering coda 'preserving nevertheless or repairing the walls and glass windows'. Edward's stringent policies even led to the temporary removal of the altar from King's College Chapel, at a cost of 16 pence, but it was reinstated and earned a brief reprieve under Mary Tudor, who succeeded her fanatical brother after his death in 1553. However, in Elizabeth's reign the altar was destroyed for the fee of eight pence, to be replaced by a table, while some of the ornate, gold-embroidered chapel vestments were recycled into costumes for the stage.

After Elizabeth became queen in 1558, she made it an offence to smash windows without proper consent, though this was partly on the pragmatic grounds that it cost so much to replace them. Although it was too late to save the contents and decoration of many churches, the functional role of windows often outweighed their dangerous subject matter. Writing his *Description of England* in 1577, William Harrison noted how

all images, shrines, tabernacles, rood lofts and monuments of idolatry are taken down and defaced; only the stories in stained glass windows excepted by reason of extreme change that should grow by the alteration of the same into white panes throughout the realm are not together abolished in most places at once, but by little and little suffered to decay that white glass may be set up in their rooms.

The spreading puritanism of the reign meant, in fact, that 'white' or transparent glass became popular on aesthetic grounds because it represented the purity and symbolic beauty of clear light. However, symbols of the monarchy were safe. Peter Nicholson retained his post, now becoming the queen's master glazier, and installed arms and badges for her at Collyweston, home of her great-grandmother Margaret Beaufort. He died in 1569.

In King's College Chapel, the West Window remained an awkward blank sheet, but the college maintained the others carefully. Its account books list a painstaking series of repairs and restorations that carried on into the next century and beyond. In 1570, £20 was spent on 'two panes' from the chapel. There cannot have been any local glaziers capable of such sensitive work, for the panels had to be taken to London and back again. In 1590, Window 1, at the north-west corner, required major restoration. All the glass was removed, the stonework repaired, and new ironwork put in. But this was not sufficient, for further treatment was required on this and on the two opposite windows in the early years of the seventeenth century. This was the set attributed to Francis Williamson and Simon Symondes, the weakness of the windows implying either that they were less able craftsmen or that they had used inferior glass.

Stained glass had a brief renaissance in the first half of the seventeenth century, when Charles I and Archbishop Laud encouraged the revival of the arts and rituals of Catholicism, and biblical windows were again installed in the chapels of some Oxford and Cambridge colleges. But the Commonwealth brought this to an end. One of Oliver Cromwell's henchmen was the 'Parliamentary Visitor' William Dowsing, licensed to seek out and destroy 'superstitious images'. His interpretation of this term included most of the medieval stained glass of East Anglia.

In December 1643, Dowsing spent several days surveying Cambridge, a place particularly suspect because several of the colleges had backed the king and happily participated in the 'Laudian' revival, as it came to be known, by turning their chapels back into pre-Reformation state, with altars and cloth of gold, incense and music. One Cambridge scholar sarcastically described how Dowsing 'by virtue of a pretended commission goes about the country like a Bedlam, breaking glass windows'. Another lamented: 'Lord, what a work was here. What clattering of glasses!' However, like a good civil servant, Dowsing kept careful records of his visitations in his diary of destruction.

On 26 December, he came to King's College Chapel, the fifth building to be inspected in a long day that had already involved him in an unpleasant argument with the Fellows of Pembroke College about what he might or might not do to their chapel. A man of humble origin, he strove to hold his ground against the convoluted arguments of professional academics. Then he had spent three hours in the chapel at Queens' College, removing its offensive chancel steps. So by the time he reached King's Chapel, he was thoroughly exhausted and the winter afternoon light was starting to go. This may be the only explanation for the survival of the windows, given the contemporary destruction of those with virtually identical subjects in Henry VII's Chapel at Westminster Abbey.

Dowsing's journal entry was perfunctory: 'King's College, Dec. 26. Steps to be taken, and one thousand superstitious pictures, the ladder of Christ, and thieves to go upon, many crosses and Jesus writ on them.' The mention of 'steps' meant removing the chancel steps leading up to the altar rather than remembering to bring a ladder to smash the windows set so high in the walls. 'One thousand pictures' was his natural response to the overwhelming quantity of windows, which included not only those in the antechapel and choir, but also all the glass in the side chapels, which was much easier to reach. His main impressions were of the East Window and the two prominent ladders on either side of the cross in the Deposition scene on the upper right. (These would have been quite long enough to reach the windows: he must have had steps and ladders on his mind all the time.) His eyesight was keen enough to spot that the crosses in the Crucifixion and Deposition scenes were inscribed with Christ's name. His comment also proved that the Crucifixion scene was there and was visible, contradicting later suggestions that many panels had been removed or whitewashed earlier in the year (precautions taken by some other churches during the nationwide visitations of 1643). The chapel's organ had been taken out prior to his visit, because singing was not permitted in services. The college accounts do have an intriguing entry earlier in the year for '51 foot [15.5 metres] of glass new leaded in the east window of the chapel' at £2 11s, and in the following year, the fairly large sum of £12 3s was spent on 'work on the windows in the chapel'. It was just possible that some of the glass had been taken out, and then returned, but the earlier intervention was probably some necessary lead renewal as part of the routine maintenance.

The college also paid Dowsing a fee of 6s 8d. This was not a bribe, however miserly, to leave the glass alone, but was the standard rate he charged for surveying. Despite his comments, nothing happened to the glass. There were undoubtedly hundreds of 'superstitious' pictures, but the sheer height and scale of the windows were daunting. And as Commonwealth soldiers were currently quartered in the chapel, he must have taken into account the undesirability of causing any disruption at that time, which would not have been appreciated by Colonel Oliver Cromwell, 'Lord of the Fens', Member of Parliament for Cambridge and in charge of East Anglian troops based in the county. A contemporary reported:

> nor was it any whit strange to find whole bands of soldiers exercising in the royal chapel of King Henry VI . . . the commanders themselves . . . chose that place to train in, whether in policy to conceal their mystery [trade], or out of fear to betray their ignorance, or on purpose to show their soldiers how little God's house was to be regarded, let the World conjecture.

But they must have respected God's house after all, because the college's thorough accounts do not list any significant damage resulting from the occupation. Perhaps the Provost and Fellows promised Dowsing that they would do something about the windows at a more convenient time, then simply kept their heads down and waited for the problem to go away. This was how some other colleges saved their treasures.

The story that the Puritans destroyed the original Tudor glass in the

West Window was the mistaken assumption of the eighteenth-century Cambridge antiquarian Francis Blomefield. Another local expert, William Cole, believed however that the window had been deliberately left plain so as to let enough light in to show off the rest of the building. He reported the unfounded tradition that all the other windows had been taken down and hidden in the organ loft to protect them from Cromwell's men.* But he sensibly concluded this was untrue although 'it was a wonder, being so very beautiful and regular a set of scripture history, that they were spared by these enemies to all beauty and regularity'.

King's College Chapel was lucky. At Hampton Court, the Crucifixion East Window that James Nicholson glazed for Cardinal Wolsey's chapel became an inevitable target:

the popish pictures and superstitious images were also demolished and order given for the new glazing of them with plain glass . . . among the rest there was pulled down the picture of Christ nailed to the cross, which was placed right over the high altar, and the pictures of Mary Magdalene and others weeping at the foot of the cross.

* This was the basis of the Reverend Sabine Baring-Gould's short story 'The Chorister' (1874), in which a plucky King's choir-boy hides the windows from the Roundheads but is shot by them and expires on the chapel's altar.

Chapter Twenty-Six: Enlightenment

OVER THE YEARS, the college employed generations of glaziers to repair and conserve the windows. Without the external hazards of extreme weather, vandalism and even bird-strikes, well-made stained glass windows are capable of surviving for centuries, as long as the lead framework is regularly strengthened or renewed. Without this firm yet flexible support, the glass begins to crack and split. During the eighteenth and early nineteenth centuries, only the most rudimentary lead-reinforcing work was done because glaziers simply lacked the necessary techniques to deal with sixteenth-century glass. They had minimal experience of reproducing the mosaic effect of pot-metal glass and its defining lead lines, because enamel painting had become the norm, and windows were made from rectangles of clear, thin glass decorated with a palette of colours applied with the brush.

Attitudes began to change around the middle of the eighteenth century. Reacting against the classically formed taste of the Age of Enlightenment, the embryonic Gothic Revival movement inspired a renewal of interest in the chapel and its windows. An early eighteenth-century visitor, Frenchman Guy Miège, was among the first to record the erratic history of the building, and he admired 'the painted glass in the windows, which may stand in competition with most structures of the like kind throughout Europe'.

The real pioneer in making the windows better known, quite apart from encouraging the wider appreciation of medieval stained glass, was former King's College student Horace Walpole. Already fascinated by the unfashionable art and history of the later Middle Ages, he wrote *A Memoir of Henry VI* when he was still a Cambridge undergraduate. He dealt with the windows in his ground-breaking survey of the history of English art, *Anecdotes of Painting in England* (1761), which proved that he had a real understanding of the glaziers' craft. His old friend from Eton and King's, the Reverend William Cole, fellow antiquarian and expert on local history (who wrote a four-volume history of King's College) informed Walpole of the existence of the 1526 indentures that named Galyon Hone and the others. In his chapter on the arts in the age of Henry VIII, Walpole recorded all their names and hailed them as 'considerable painters in any reign': one of their *vidimuses* would be an asset to any collection of drawings. He realised that the high standard of the windows at least partly resulted from 'obtaining the best designs for their work', correctly identified Raphael's cartoons as one of the sources and sensibly speculated that these had come via Flemish tapestry makers. Raphael's *Ananias and Sapphira* provided the model for one of the finest windows of all (Window 21 in the south wall, one of the Apostles group.)

Walpole understood how glass-painters worked because he had employed them to restore his own considerable collection of early stained glass, now displayed to maximum effect in the windows of his architectural fantasy, the villa at Strawberry Hill. Amongst the 450 panels he bought from agents, dealers and salerooms were many roundels painted by the men who might have designed the King's windows, and perhaps a few from the chapel itself – not, mercifully, from the great windows, but from the side chapels, whose decorative quarries had suffered considerable disruption and relocation. In the guidebook he compiled to Strawberry Hill, Walpole mentioned 'a rose impaling a pomegranate, the device of Henry VIII and Katherine of Aragon' in the window of the Green Closet, together with 'a crown in a thorn-bush between the letters H and E', the symbol of Henry

VII. There was another of these in the Round Drawing Room and the window of his bedchamber included a panel with Anne Boleyn's arms. In his Star Chamber stood a copy of Torrigiano's bust of Henry Tudor, and in the Holbein Chamber was exhibited what Walpole proudly believed to be Thomas Wolsey's cardinal's hat. Canaletto's painting of the interior of King's Chapel hung in the Waiting Room to the Great Parlour, and the pièce de résistance was the fan-vaulted ceiling of the Long Gallery, re-creating in papier mâché that of Henry VII's Chapel in Westminster Abbey.

By 1769, there was considerable interest in the King's windows, and so many visitors demanded information that the chapel's clerk, Henry Malden, compiled the first guidebook to the building. Malden was undoubtedly hoping to liberate himself and his colleagues from having to give endless, exhausting explanations of the carvings and the glass. His endearing preface also cited personal reasons for writing – the hope of alleviating the financial distress caused by the needs of 'a numerous family, of a wife disordered in her mind, of a husband endeavouring to relieve her under that calamity'. His guide was competent and usefully issued in a handy pocket-size 'intended chiefly for those who shall make use of the book while they are surveying the Chapel'. Chapter Five offered 'a full explanation of all the curious paintings on the windows' and helpfully set out the explicit links they made between the Old and New Testaments in a neat format that listed the upper and lower, and left and right, subjects of each window for ease of comparison. He identified the form of the windows as Gothic, following Walpole's stylistic rather than condemnatory use of the term, and confidently boasted that 'there is scarcely found anything of the kind equal to them in Europe'. The glass itself was 'all wonderfully painted beyond the limits of description . . . with colours inconceivably beautiful'. He denied the rumour that it had all been removed and hidden to protect it from puritanical destruction; his only error lay in repeating Cole's suggestion that the West Window was deliberately filled with clear glass to make the chapel lighter.

The next attempt to record the chapel's glass was in the early nineteenth century, in the form of detailed engravings of the East Window and one of the south windows, together with an explanatory booklet written in the hopes of boosting sales of the drawings. The artist and author was Joshua Baldrey, a local engraver and print-seller who had a shop in Trinity Street. In 1809, he published engravings of his drawings of the East Window (5 guineas plain, 6 guineas hand-coloured), but custom was so slow that nine years later he issued *A Dissertation on the Windows of King's College Chapel* (1818), in the hopes of disposing of his remaining stock of prints by giving it 'a greater publicity' (an extremely early use of the term in its modern sense). It was also meant to be the way of subsidising his engravings of the south window. His text sought to explain the exact subjects of the drawings, with the wider aim of making the neglected beauty of all the windows better known. He drew heavily on Malden's guidebook, and gave the impression of a chapel packed with tourists who required 'a much longer time to properly examine [the windows] than is generally allowed'. Other problems included extreme brightness, too much iron- and lead-work, and the many incompetent and inaccurate repairs and replacements. It was only with the aid of Baldrey's engravings that visitors could truly appreciate that the glass contained 'the great essentials of History Painting' (the highest form of art, according to the Royal Academy's criteria), demonstrating the glaziers' use of brilliant colour, anatomical knowledge, foreshortening and perspective.

Baldrey had made himself an expert on the windows. He gave a convincing explanation of the technical contrasts between sixteenth- and early nineteenth-century window-making, pot-metal versus paint, and therefore 'totally different from one another', and he speculated that the glaziers named in the 1526 contracts were not necessarily the people who had designed the windows. This was the opportunity for a swipe at Horace Walpole (unnamed, but easily recognisable as the 'late Noble Author' who had attempted to vindicate Richard III) for his citation of Raphael as a fundamental source, an excuse to launch Baldrey's novel theory that, despite borrowings from 'the Italian, Venetian and Flemish schools', the real designer of the windows was Hans Holbein, a man truly 'equal to such an undertaking' and one who understood the craft too, having once been a glass-painter himself. Baldrey also claimed to identify Holbein's distinctive style of portraiture: because it was his friend Erasmus who had recommended him to his patron Sir Thomas More, Holbein portrayed four of the messengers as Erasmus.

Baldrey described his feat in drawing the East Window as difficult, dangerous and time-consuming. He worked with the aid of a telescope, perched 'a great height from the ground' in the Organ Gallery on top of the screen. He had no assistance at all, and had to estimate the exact measurements of all the apertures and panels through a lens that could only encompass a circle of the glass 'less than twenty inches [40 centimetres] in diameter' at any one moment. As for the south window (he chose Window 21, Walpole's favourite and the first of the Apostles sequence), he found that even harder to draw because it involved having to erect, at his own expense, a scaffold on top of the Organ Gallery.

His pamphlet ended with a plea for sympathy that rivalled Malden's poignant preface. Baldrey described himself as 'a man with a large increasing family; experiencing much sickness; and from the unpropitious state of the times, struggling with great difficulties'. A raffle to dispose of some of his East Window engravings had failed to attract enough subscribers but was just temporarily postponed. If he could only get enough backing, Baldrey announced his mission to devote the rest of his life (he was then sixty-four) to drawing the windows in the chapel. His dream remained unfulfilled, because he died in poverty ten years later. However, the Holbein theory became rather popular when it was given wider distribution in an updated version of the official guidebook compiled by Chapel Clerk James Cook in 1829. This misleadingly expanded Baldrey's original idea by suggesting that many of the messengers were portraits of important people of the day.

In the 1830s and 1840s, Gothic Revivalists enthusiastically tried to imitate the art and architecture of the Middle Ages. Copying the exact styles and subjects of stained glass was an essential part of this process, and many modern glaziers made themselves familiar with old techniques and mannerisms. King's College became more confident about employing a glazier who had mastered authentic medieval glazing skills to clean and conserve the windows, which were now in serious need of attention. Work began in May 1841 when 'Mr Hedgeland' was engaged to take down and repair the first panels in what was intended to be an ongoing programme. But within a few years, his approach became the cause of controversy.

John Pike Hedgeland had begun his career as an architect, then specialised in the restoration of windows. The illustrated account of his acclaimed treatment of the fifteenth-century windows of the church at St Neot's, Cornwall, probably brought him to the attention of the college as the best man for the job. Between 1841 and 1849, he cleaned and repaired the north and south windows of the choir, at the rate of two to three scenes a year. But growing doubts were expressed about the impact of his methods when the newly cleaned windows were reinstalled. This was partly a natural response to the changes in any well-loved work whose ancient patina has been removed by conservators in search of the pristine condition: hostile reactions to the cleaning of the Sistine Chapel ceiling were typical of such criticism.

By the summer of 1843, the college was sufficiently anxious to seek the opinion of Augustus Welby North Pugin, leading exponent of the Gothic Revival. As an architect and a perfectionist designer, Pugin believed that adopting medieval style was the only correct moral response to the disturbing, industrialised world of Victorian Britain. He designed the stained glass windows for his churches but found that most contemporary glaziers were incapable of achieving his demanding standards of authenticity. His understanding of medieval glass was unrivalled, so he was the most appropriate person for the college to consult.

'Mr Pugin's Opinion on the Restoration of the Windows of King's College Chapel', dated 16 September 1843, was not too unkind. He totally appreciated the general point that cleaning old glass inevitably made it seem harsh and bright. Yet the fact that the restored windows 'did not originally appear as they do now' was because the layers of corrosive dirt that had been removed had actually made the blues and rubies appear richer. He concluded that Hedgeland's restorations 'were as well done as could be expected', though he doubted that the high costs were worth it in view of the 'roughness' of new glass in contrast to 'that which is mellow and toned down by antiquity'. Satisfied for the moment, the college continued to employ Hedgeland on the great windows in the choir, and awarded him the ultimate accolade of a commission to make an entire new window to stand alongside the earlier glass masterpieces, next to the East Window itself. The need for another window resulted from recent modifications to the King's Parade façade of the college. Henry VI had intended the chapel to adjoin an accommodation range that formed the eastern side of a quadrangle. For this reason, there was no lower window opening at the south-east end of the chapel because this would be blocked by the adjacent building – which was never started. In 1828, the site at last received an eastern boundary in the form of Wilkins's low screen wall. The alterations provided the opportunity to insert a window below the existing one at the corner (Window 14). Hone's men had glazed the upper opening with one Old and one New Testament scene, Ruth and Naomi in mourning, as a type for Mary grieving at the foot of the Cross. In 1841, Hedgeland moved these panels and their two Messengers down to the lower tier, so his new window filled the upper space they had vacated.

Needing appropriate subject matter for this most sensitive location, the college selected yet another aspect of the life of Moses, when he elevates the Brazen Serpent on to a cross-shaped pole, a standard prototype for the Crucifixion and one which had appeared as such in the block-book illustrations. Hedgeland did not attempt to create a new version but took for his model Rubens's famous 1611 painting of the subject, which had been recently acquired by the National Gallery. Considering its position next to the East Window, Hedgeland's painted glass is unobtrusive enough not to distract attention from the others. But he committed a cardinal error: he ignored the layout of all the other windows by spreading his design over all five lights, instead of having two separate scenes with Messengers in the middle.

Hedgeland earned over £5,000, paid out of the college's Chapel Fund, but there was such a chorus of disapproval over his restorations that in the autumn of 1849 the college decided to dispense with his services. An article in the *Manchester Guardian* on 21 November 1849 attacked his 'work of destruction' and emphasised the loss of colour, bad drawing and unnecessary repairs at an exorbitant fee of £300 per window. This impelled Hedgeland to write to the editor refuting charges 'calculated to do me an irreparable injury', and he claimed that Pugin himself had praised the restorations. At the same time he began to bombard Vice-Provost George Williams with a succession of letters angrily defending his reputation.

By the following spring, the beleaguered Williams drafted a memo for the college which summed up the problems – the windows' 'dull and monotonous appearance', the thin wash which weakened the rich colour of the repaired glass, and the insertion of too many copied faces. He then approached Pugin, offering him the opportunity to be 'again heard on the subject, for the authority of your name is decidedly great' and enquired delicately whether he might like to 'alter or modify' his opinion. Pugin replied that it was some time since he had visited the 'magnificent chapel' but his recollection was that the windows 'provided a most <u>unfavourable</u> impression on my mind' and he expressed 'considerable regret that the restoration was ever commenced'.

The Vice-Provost took the precaution of getting a second opinion. On the same day that he wrote to Pugin, he also contacted Charles Winston, another eminent authority on medieval glass, whose recent book *An Enquiry into the Difference of Style Observable in Ancient Glass Painting* (1847) had praised the *cinquecento* style of glass-painting epitomised in the King's windows as the greatest of all. This book was a daring challenge to Pugin, who believed that only the glass of the early fourteenth century approached perfection. Williams explained that he was reluctant to have any more windows cleaned for the moment, and asked Winston if he thought they had been seriously injured. Winston made a special visit to Cambridge and sent his comments in a letter of eight densely written pages. On balance, he approved of the general effect, praising 'the good done by bringing to light the exquisite handling of the ancient artists' and he had been unaware 'until the other day of the fine art that is displayed in the windows' because it combined 'dignity of conception and purity of drawing'. His main criticism was reserved for Hedgeland's replacing so many old pieces of glass with modern copies, especially the faces. He concluded by anticipating the happy results from 'making public, as it were, the hitherto hidden treasures of the King's College windows'.

This did not vindicate Hedgeland, whose work Winston summed up as 'not as satisfactory as it might have been' and a warning: 'I tell you honestly, I am afraid of Hedgeland!' He advised the college to continue the restoration under a different glazier, and recommended Hedgeland's assistant, William Jay Bolton, not from any 'feeling of favouritism but simply from a sense of duty'. Bolton, who had been assisting Hedgeland for the last year, was already a respected glass-painter in his own right. Fascinated by the King's windows since a childhood visit, 'he then and there founded his taste upon the study of their colour and method', according to his daughter. The son of an American, he had moved to the States in 1836 where he set up a stained glass workshop producing windows in the early sixteenth-century manner so admired by Winston. He returned to England in 1848 and established his own workshop in Cambridge. His memories of assisting Hedgeland included being perilously winched up in a basket to the very top of the windows he had to clean.

Hedgeland took the news of his dismissal very badly, and was mortified that the college had consulted Pugin and Winston without informing him or giving him the chance to defend himself before 'a competent and impartial judge' who would expose 'the proceedings of my enemies'. The affair unhinged his mind and became an obsession that drove him to pester the college for a further three years. A new Provost, Richard Okes, got embroiled in the spring of 1853, when Hedgeland complained directly to him that the Vice-Provost had not yet fulfilled the promise made 'two years ago' (his underlining) to respond to 'the misrepresentations made by certain individuals', and reminded the college that he was still seeking compensation for 'this great injustice' which had rendered him 'subject to many disadvantages'. He was recompensed in a way when his glass-painter son, George Hedgeland, was championed by the influential Winston, who hailed his West Window for Norwich Cathedral as 'the best window of modern times'. It was due to Winston's book that the many different styles of medieval windows came to be appreciated from the 1850s, making it possible to set the King's glass in its wider context. Bolton wrote two short articles on the history of the windows, but the first serious study was that of artist and art historian George Scharf, who published his 'Artistic Notes on the Windows of King's College Chapel' in the antiquarian periodical *Archaeological Journal* for 1855 and 1856. Here he discussed in detail their sources and iconography, and emphasised their Germanic rather than Italian parallels.

Unnerved by its experiences with Hedgeland, and having lost the services of Bolton, who gave up making stained glass to train for the Church, the college was reluctant to court further controversy by continuing with the restoration programme, let alone commissioning another window. But the huge West Window still contained clear glass that unbalanced the subtle harmonies that the original glaziers and architects envisaged. In 1868, a generous donor came forward who wanted to glaze the great space, and had the money to do so. He was Francis Stacey, a Welsh alumnus of Eton and King's, a prosperous barrister with a rich wife, no children and a fortune inherited from his uncle. The aim of the proposed window, as he stated immodestly in a letter to Congregation, the college's council, was 'to equal if not exceed in splendour and magnificence the glorious originals'. The firm he chose, Clayton & Bell, was admirable. They had been making stained glass since 1855, and their broadly medieval style was innovative rather than pastiche-like, combining their experience of restoring old glass with the appreciation of fashionable Pre-Raphaelite line and colour. And they used the new high-quality 'antique' glass, made as a result of experiments sponsored by Charles Winston to rediscover the properties and effects of genuine medieval glass. But instead of the Last Judgement specified in the 1526 contract, they proposed an epic *Te Deum*, hierarchies of angels, saints, apostles and religious praising God, including some 'Historical personages' such as the recently deceased Prince Consort.

Stacey and Clayton & Bell were obdurate about the change of subject, and the college set up the 'West Window Committee' which took two years to reject the scheme and tried to call in another designer altogether, John Hardman Powell, nephew and successor of the man who made windows for the demanding Pugin. The committee also had to grapple with the fact that some members of the college did not want any coloured glass in the window at all. Clayton & Bell, alarmed at the idea of losing such a prestigious commission, finally agreed to design a Last Judgement, and submitted their *vidimus* in the summer of 1872. This required some considerable modifications (for a start, the college objected to the presence of nudes amongst the Damned) but work on the window at last started in 1875. There was a flurry of anxious correspondence when Clayton & Bell asked permission to take it to Paris to star in the Exposition of 1878, but this plan came to nothing when they found that the allocated exhibition space was not big enough.

Their interpretation of the Last Judgement did not attempt to divide it into separate scenes to match the six in the East Window, but treated it as one enormous canvas with different but connected zones. In the upper tier, the focal point is the central figure of Christ Enthroned, exactly facing Christ on the Cross at the east end of the chapel. He is framed by the arch of a majestic colonnaded building that echoes the grand scale of the Renaissance architecture in the other windows, and is flanked by ranks of angels joyfully blowing the last trump. Below them are seated rows of saints and apostles, whose strong, well-drawn features resemble those in the earlier glass: Clayton & Bell had clearly studied it thoroughly. In the lower tier, immediately under Christ, St Michael holds his scales of justice. To the left, angels welcome the Blessed into Heaven, among whom, rising from his grave, is Henry VI in the conventional place for a patron and donor, at the very bottom end of a light. He is a serene young man holding a model of his chapel. On the other side are the Damned, who always offered more scope for glass-painters, in Victorian as in medieval windows. Clayton & Bell have done well here. The flames of Hellfire lick around grimacing, contorted figures whom avenging angels lash with fiery swords, the vision made more dynamic by the use of a vermilion glass which glows on the dullest day and positively blazes into life as the afternoon sun passes behind the west wall.

This is the brightest part of the window, whose overall colours are warmer but rather darker than the rest of the chapel's glass. Altogether absent are the silvery-white tones of the earlier glass, and there is a lot of leadwork to distinguish the hundred or so characters, who are fussily drawn on a smaller scale than those in the original sequence. It is almost a shock to look from the nineteenth- to the sixteenth-century windows, and to realise how the earlier glaziers achieved an impression of effortless simplicity and strength. The tracery of the West Window is more successful, setting vivid royal arms and badges, among them a prominent Tudor rose, against the same strong blue as in the East Window. Henry VII and Henry VIII are commemorated here, accompanied by the arms of the latest patron, Francis Stacey.

In an explanatory pamphlet, Clayton & Bell emphasised how the work was 'in fulfilment of the original intention', the scheme of Flower and Foxe. On 22 April 1879, the Eve of St George's Day, the college celebrated the installation of the window with an inaugural service, which included a performance of Louis Spohr's oratorio *The Last Judgement*. Then 120 guests feasted in the college Hall on a six-course meal that featured *soupe à la reine*, salmon, sweetbreads, braised capon or saddle of mutton, victoria pudding, and ices. Among the glees sung were 'Sir Patrick Spens', 'Auld Lang Syne' and 'King Witlaf's Drinking Horn'. Henry VIII would surely have approved.

Finale

ONE OF THE guests at the 1879 feast that honoured the West Window was a precociously erudite sixteen-year-old schoolboy who had been invited because he was one of the elite group of King's Scholars at Eton. The whole event made such an impression on him that he kept the dinner menu and the seating plan, on which he proudly underlined his own name, Montague Rhodes James.

Today, we mainly associate M. R. James with his chilling tales of the supernatural. Their menace is quiet. There is little gore here, the violence takes place offstage, and the evil deeds committed are not the work of flesh and blood villains. Yet the reader experiences a palpable fear because of the irruption into the organised, rational life of a well-meaning don or cleric of an unearthly, vengeful *thing*, just glimpsed from the corner of an eye, scuttling away into the darkness, but always there, lurking in the background and waiting with studied patience for the final, fatal opportunity to strike. James's long fascination with the King's Chapel windows is rather less appreciated, yet is another manifestation of his all-encompassing imagination and sense of the power the past has over us.

His interest in stained glass began in the 1870s at Eton, when the inaudible sermons in the chapel that Henry VI built 'inevitably led to long contemplations of the furniture and adornments, especially the windows'. Most of these were Victorian, and the few surviving medieval fragments had been brought together in a 'kaleidoscopic' arrangement in the West Window. But the colours were good, especially the blue. He later noted that Galyon Hone had worked at Eton as well as at King's, and he attributed to Hone's hand the set of medallions illustrating the Liberal Arts in the windows of one of the halls.

James learned to love medieval glass and sculpture on a school visit to France in 1880, and, as an undergraduate at King's, developed this interest by a tour of the northern French cathedrals. He travelled with a companion on a double tricycle with solid wheels, so unwieldy and noisy that 'all horses shied at our approach'. For the next thirty years, he spent part of each summer vacation cycling around France to study its art and architecture.

James's academic career in Cambridge was exemplary. His early passion for medieval manuscripts and Christian iconography earned him a Fellowship at King's, which he later combined with appointments as assistant director, then director of the Fitzwilliam Museum. Chapel attendance was compulsory for all undergraduates, and James's involvement with the building intensified when he was made dean in 1889, with responsibilities for the chapel, its services and its choristers. Detailed scrutiny of the windows on such occasions inspired James's first supernatural story, 'A Night in King's College Chapel'. But this was not yet meant to cause prickles down the spine or a nervous glance over the shoulder, even though it started with the narrator dozing off in the chapel one evening and accidentally getting locked in. When he saw the arms of one of the huge figures in the glass begin to move, his first reaction was one of horror, which quickly turned to amusement when the character Reuben (one of the brothers who threw Joseph into the pit) pulled out a pipe, lit up and began to complain, off duty at last.

The idea for the piece came to James when he was still an undergraduate, for an earlier fragment of the tale survives that he later expanded. The story was a delightful flight of fancy that envisaged the people in the windows coming to life at night. They do not conduct themselves with appropriate biblical dignity any more, but chat or argue, just like ordinary men and women. Yet the humour and the light touch only arose from his intimate knowledge of the glass, not just its theological implications but its current condition, and how the original glaziers had arranged the panels. James put in many wonderfully inventive touches: the first person to speak initially sounded metallic, but grew more natural as he went on, the manna made a rattling noise as it landed on top of the choir stalls, and the animals all behaved badly – Jonah's whale splashed Tobias's mother, Daniel's lions got out of control, and Tobias's dog wouldn't stop yapping. Personal feuds included the Children of Israel throwing manna pellets at Reuben, forcing him to complain to Moses; and Eve and the Serpent challenged Mrs Job over her insulting comments about Adam's nudity. Even the red-eyed demon stopped tormenting Job and took his side against his nagging wife, while Job escaped to have a quiet cigar in the Garden of Eden with Adam and Elimelech, the latter the deceased husband of Naomi, who had urged him to get up and take a well-earned break.

The story also demonstrated James's awareness of the state of the glass and its need for conservation. He made all the Messengers assemble, like a gathering of servants, in the West Window, where they socialised so enthusiastically every night that they got their scrolls mixed up and even caused some of the writing to rub off. The final straw was when the four St Luke-alikes delivered their arcane medical treatments to poor Enoch, who only dared to cough away the dust when the organ was playing loudly. As his figure was the most incomprehensible in the jumbled panes of Window 25, the narrator expressed fears that if the doctors went any further, Enoch would be too far gone for the college ever to mend him.

This story was written as a light-hearted counterpoint to a more sober article about the windows in the *Cambridge Review* for May 1892, in which James noted reproachfully that 'intelligent members of the college have been known to pass through their nine terms of residence and to carry away no recollection of the glass in the chapel'. He also took the opportunity to slate J. P. Hedgeland's 1845 window, with its 'hideous copy' of Rubens's *Brazen Serpent*.

These two very different pieces of writing reflected a concern for the glass that led James to organise a long and costly project to restore and relead the windows that Hedgeland had not been let loose on. This was undertaken between 1893 and 1906, at the rate of approximately one window per year: one in the choir, all those in the antechapel, and the East Window, none of which had been touched since 1765. The stained glass firm commissioned by James was that of C. E. Kempe, one of the largest and most successful of the day. Kempe had first intended a career in the Church, but then turned to art. He trained with Clayton & Bell, and also worked with William Morris & Company, including their decoration of All Saints' Church, Jesus Lane, Cambridge. Emboldened by this experience, he set up his own stained glass studio in 1869. Kempe formulated a distinctive house style inspired by late fifteenth- and early sixteenth-century Flemish glass, so had a sympathetic understanding of the era of the King's windows. Equally useful was the firm's extensive experience of medieval restoration work.

M. R. James flung himself into the project. In November 1892, he invited Kempe to prepare a report on the state of the glass, and had this printed for circulation to the Governing Body, who had to give the go-ahead before any funds could be committed. Kempe noted decay in the supporting ironwork, loose leads and many cracks in the glass, especially in the East Window. He first advised that it would be possible to restore the windows *in situ*, but having discovered that the supporting iron bars could be easily removed because the rebates in the stone were mainly filled with 'lime and hair', not hard cement, he decided that the glass could all be taken out.

James worked closely with Horace Jackson, the glazier Kempe allocated to supervise the work, and he described their progress in his affectionate memoir of life at Eton and King's. There was a scaffold with many floors 'from which every part of the window could be got at with complete ease ... great was the excitement of going all over it, settling what mistakes must be rectified, what glaring modern patches should be taken out and replaced by neutral tinted glass, and what ancient patches were worth removing and preserving'. This was a unique chance for eye-level, close-up investigation, and it led to many discoveries, not least that 'the original painters of some of the inscribed scrolls had been so lazy or stupid as to duplicate them or put them in the wrong window'. James took a critical view of Hedgeland's 'pretty severe' repair work of the 1840s, and was only grateful that this had been confined to five windows on the north and seven on the south side of the choir.

But he and Jackson could make little sense or any logical reconstruction of Windows 24 and 25 at the south-west end, the Death and Coronation of the Virgin. Whether this most unacceptably Catholic of topics had been deliberately damaged during the Reformation or under the Puritans, or whether it was because the original glaziers had used inferior glass, these windows remain incoherent despite James's best efforts, but were at least put in sound condition.

There was just one awkward moment, when Kempe and the college had a disagreement about money. In May 1896, the Bursar queried Kempe's estimate of a £200 advance against the summer's forthcoming work, and this made Kempe threaten to withhold his men's labour until 'this unfortunate question' was settled. This, he pointed out, was a risky procedure because they were missing the good weather. However, it all arose from a misunderstanding, which was soon cleared up. Galyon Hone would undoubtedly have behaved in just the same way.

Armed with a new understanding of the windows, James wrote a short guide to the chapel's glass in 1899, the first general handbook for seventy years. Lucid and accurate, it was an opportunity to expound his unrivalled knowledge of biblical literature and apocryphal writings, at a time when he was cataloguing all the medieval manuscripts in Cambridge. He was able to identify the precise literary source of every panel, and to distinguish the scriptural from the legendary.

In the autumn of 1893, the same year he started the window repairs, James performed the first public reading of a ghost story. This became an annual Christmas event. After dinner and Combination Room port, James took a chosen band up to his rooms, blew out all the candles but one, and began the tale, composed, he claimed, in haste but always delivered in a stylish manner: friends called him a born actor. The first collection of his stories was published in 1904, the year before James was appointed Provost of King's, a post he managed to combine with the directorship of the Fitzwilliam. It was typical of the contradictions of this proudly self-defined Victorian Anglican, whom no one would ever have described as flamboyant, that he sometimes walked around the college with a kitten perched on his cap, a surprising touch of *fin-de-siècle* affectation.

After leading the college through the dark days of the First World War, which cost 174 young Kingsmen their lives, James's career came full circle when he accepted the provostship of Eton in 1918 and returned to a place that held so many happy memories. The memoir he published in 1926 of his years at Eton and King's was full of gossip but generally benevolent. He did not once mention the name of another Kingsman, John Maynard Keynes, whom he disliked intensely, and he died in 1936 without the possibly dubious pleasure of knowing that Keynes had briefly become involved with the windows too.

Cambridge-born Keynes was, like James, a King's scholar at Eton. He came up to King's College as an undergraduate in 1902, when he refused to attend chapel regularly yet complained when the Dean would not let him read the lesson. He returned as a Fellow in Economics while James was Provost. There was a clash of generations and a clash of faith. The brilliant, self-confident Keynes was critical of what he perceived as the college's general inefficiency, and this turned into a major row in 1912, when Keynes forced through some radical financial reforms. A more fundamental division was between the old-fashioned, orthodox Christianity of James and his colleagues, and the agnosticism and dangerous Bloomsbury modernism of Keynes and his set. This was certainly one reason why James decided to leave King's for Eton in 1918, and only after his departure was Keynes appointed Bursar. When the latter stood for the contested provostship in 1926, James wrote to an old friend: 'An anxious question whom they will elect – as long as it is not one Maynard Keynes, I think all will be well.'

Keynes was dragged into reluctant contemplation of the chapel windows in the first year of the war, in the early summer of 1940, when people were unsure whether the Germans were going to bomb or invade Cambridge.

(There is still a local urban myth that Hitler intended to occupy St John's College, and planned to ride through the streets of Cambridge on a white horse.) Keynes was still Bursar, but lived mainly in London, working for the Treasury as special consultant to the Chancellor of the Exchequer. In charge of the windows was the Dean of Chapel, Eric Milner-White (he had inaugurated the Festival of Nine Lessons and Carols in December 1918), who had spent the last twenty years complementing the great windows by acquiring for the side chapels many other panels of glass of the period. As a precaution against bomb damage, the college agreed in principle that the glass should be taken out and put into safe storage. But the costs were daunting and there was no contingency fund in a time of more urgent priorities, when art came second to people.

The college had already decided to remove the East Window at the very outbreak of war, sending telegrams on 1 September 1939 to those Fellows who were out of Cambridge seeking their consent. In the strange lull that followed, undergraduates waited to be called up, the college housed students evacuated from Queen Mary College, London, and became the headquarters of the local Home Guard; Fellows took it in turns to firewatch from the chapel's roof. Meanwhile, Milner-White got estimates from the local firm of Rattee & Kett for the cost of removing all the windows, at around £50 per window.

After a panicky week in May 1940, when the Regional Commissioner for East Anglia announced to assembled college heads that the Germans might be on their doorsteps within the week, Milner-White had the inspired idea of asking Americans for the money, and specifically those associated with Berkeley College, Yale, which had special links with King's. Yale was already doing its bit for the war by welcoming as evacuees some 200 children of Oxford and Cambridge academics. On 2 June, Milner-White wrote to the Master of Berkeley College, Samuel Hemingway, to request financial aid to save the historic glass. Hemingway set to work targeting alumni and by August he had raised the necessary money.

However busy he was at the Treasury, Maynard Keynes in his role as Bursar learned of Milner-White's initiative and was shocked by its imprecision. For a start, the windows cost £60 each to remove, and not the £50 first estimated. Secondly, the terms of reference were not clear, because, as Milner-White defensively explained, he had not asked for the American money as a gift but as a loan. This thoroughly alarmed England's finest economist because, as he pointed out to Milner-White, gifts to charitable foundations were not liable to taxation while loans were. More seriously, receiving loans opened up the liability of future undefined obligations: 'the fact that it is between friends is far from making it better since, as all experience shows, nothing leads to more trouble in the end that undefined business arousing emotions between friends.' And Keynes unkindly added that 'connection with the chapel seems to breed so much financial irresponsibility', though grudgingly conceded that he was prepared to 'whitewash all that has happened'.

In a subsequent letter that demanded the names of all donors, proving that he was still struggling to clarify their status, Keynes suggested removing only the lower half of each window, on the grounds that this would diminish the effect of any blast: this was something that had apparently worked in the case of some London buildings. He ended by expressing pleasure that his recent broadcast had cheered people up.

The Master of Berkeley College wrote to Milner-White on 26 September enclosing the list of contributors to the windows, and asked anxiously about the 'extensive raid on Cambridge' reported by the Germans the previous day. Milner-White replied, three weeks later, that although a few bombs had occasionally been dropped, there was no damage to any university buildings or 'our ancient streets' although Fenner's hallowed turf had been hit. He was happy to report that 'all but three of our large windows are now removed and stored'.

This was a major feat of organisation – the relocation of a national treasure that was not one single priceless item but over 2,000 separate panels of glass from the great windows, together with the best pieces from two of the side chapels. Immaculate planning and record-keeping were essential. Rattee & Kett's men put most of the carefully numbered panels into the basements of the nearby Gibbs Building, those below H and G staircases, adjacent to the designated air-raid shelter in E staircase. Some, curiously and inconveniently, were carried all the way up the narrow spiral stone staircase in the north-west turret to the uneven space between the beautiful fan-vaults and the sloping roof above. The rest was farmed out all over Cambridge to anyone who had a solidly built cellar and some connection with the college. Maynard Keynes made available the basement of the Arts Theatre, the institution he had founded in 1936, Arthur Tilley, an ancient King's Fellow, offered the cellar of his house in Selwyn Gardens, and Allen Ramsay, current Master of Magdalene but former Kingsman, and old friend and holiday companion of M. R. James, took a number of panels into the cellars of the Magdalene Master's Lodge.

In the bleak chapel, the gaps were filled, in medieval style, by sheets of grey, heavy-duty paper soaked in tar to make them waterproof, with a layer of clear glass at the bottom to let some light in. Fellow L. P. Wilkinson described how 'the Chapel was colder than ever, and the tar-paper rattled thunderously in the wind'. He noted, however, that the West Window, which had not been taken out, was 'appreciated at last in the absence of unfair competition'. The Hedgeland window was also left to take its chance, so the two Victorian windows now provided the only patches of colour in the gloom and the cold.* Plans and diagrams of the numbered panels and their precise wartime location, dated December 1940, were discovered as recently as 2002.

In his letter thanking Berkeley College, Milner-White mentioned other glass that had been less fortunate, like many of the old windows of Westminster Abbey and some fine modern ones destroyed by bombing, including those in St Paul's Cathedral. He concluded: 'We are slowly plunging into winter and the trees on the backs are in their full autumnal dress of gold. What it will bring forth, we cannot tell; but no idea of defeat has crossed the minds of any of us yet.'

---

* Peterhouse similarly removed the seventeenth-century Crucifixion East Window from its chapel during the war but left the unloved nineteenth-century north and south windows *in situ.*

At least the King's glass was safe. It would emerge from the dark cellars after the war just as Jonah emerged from the belly of the whale, one of the most dramatic images in the chapel. The whale in Window 16 is a magnificent monster, its huge open mouth a black cavern fringed by jagged white teeth. Just one eye is visible, an angry red disc framing a white pupil, another of the glaziers' clever insertions. The writhing body and finned tail sweep halfway up the length of the window, the sinuous form and acid green of the glass making it clearly visible even though the scene is in the upper tier of the window. On the other side of the dividing mullion is Jonah, spewed out of this mouth of Hell, looking back at the whale in grave contemplation of the miraculous escape that God has granted him. The colours of his clothes – orange collar, blue robe and billowing ruby cloak – make him as prominent as the whale, and the glaziers have given him immediate pathos and humanity by painting his hair in untidy windblown strands, just like someone who has come out of the sea. His hands rest gratefully on terra firma which the glaziers have filled with the familiar tussocks of grass and pebbles. In the background at the very top are the usual wonderful details of the sea, Jonah's ship, trees and the city of Nineveh, all painted with exquisite care despite the great height of the setting.

Visiting the chapel today, watching groups of tourists march through the building, taking illicit flash photographs with their mobile phones, it is tempting to agree with M. R. James that few people properly notice the windows at all. The glass needs contemplation, the extended span of time available to a medieval scholar trained to meditate and to interpret complex strands of image and word. Yet, thanks to the glaziers' extraordinary skills, we can enjoy it in a completely different way, appreciating colour and line, and the effects of the changing light that shines through paint and stain, pot-metal and white glass. The King's glass has had a chequered history but it survives today as a glorious monument to the kings who commissioned it and the glaziers who made it.

Notes

Abbreviations for published and unpublished sources
BL: British Library
CPR: Calendar of Patent Rolls
JBSMGP: Journal of the British Society of Master Glass Painters
KA: King's College Archives
L&P: Letters & Papers, Foreign and Domestic, of the reign of Henry VIII
PCAS: Proceedings of the Cambridge Antiquarian Society
PRO: Public Record Office
RS: Rolls Series
Statutes: The Statutes of the Realm (1811–28), vol. II, *1377–1503/4;* vol. III, *1509–1545*
VCH: The Victoria History of the Counties of England

Astle: T. Astle (ed.), *The Will of King Henry VII* (1775)
Campbell: W. Campbell (ed.), *Materials for a History of the Reign of Henry VII* (*RS*, I & II, 1873)
Colvin: H. M. Colvin, *The History of the King's Works,* vols III and IV, *1485–1660* (1975, 1982)
Cooper: C. H. Cooper, *Annals of Cambridge,* vol. I (1892)
Dürer: A. Dürer, *Diary of his Journey to the Netherlands 1520–21,* ed. by J. Goris and G. Marlier (1971)
Gunn: S. J. Gunn and P. Lindley, *Cardinal Wolsey: Church, State and Culture* (1991)
Hamilton: W. D. Hamilton (ed.), *Chronicle of England during the Reigns of the*

Tudors from A.D. 1485 to 1559 (Camden Society, NS 11, 1875)

Harrison: K. Harrison, *The Windows of King's College Chapel, Cambridge: Notes on their History and Design* (1952)

Hymers: J. Hymers (ed.), *The Funeral Sermon of Lady Margaret Beaufort* (1860)

James: M. R. James, *Eton and King's* (1926)

Jones: M. K. Jones and M. G. Underwood, *Lady Margaret Beaufort* (1992)

Kirk: R. E. and E. F. Kirk, *Returns of Aliens dwelling in the City and Suburbs of London*, vol. I, *1523–1571* (Huguenot Society, X, 1900)

Law: E. Law, *The History of Hampton Court Palace*, vol. I (1890)

Oswald: A. Oswald, 'Barnard Flower, the King's Glazier', *JBSMGP* 11 (1951–5), pp. 8–21

Pollard: A. F. Pollard (ed.), *The Reign of Henry VII from Contemporary Sources*, vols. I–III (1913–14)

Ransome: D. R. Ransome, 'The Struggle of the Glaziers' Company with the Foreign Glaziers, 1500–1550', *Guildhall Miscellany* 2 (1960–8), pp. 12–20

Saltmarsh: J. Saltmarsh, 'A History of King's College', *VCH, Cambridgeshire and the Isle of Ely*, vol. III (1959), pp. 376–407

Skelton: *The Complete Poems of John Skelton, Laureate*, ed. P. Henderson (1931)

Sneyd: C. H. Sneyd (ed.), *A Relation of the Island of England about the year 1500* (Camden Society, XXXVII, 1847)

Vergil 1: *Three Books of Polydore Vergil's English History*, ed. H. Ellis (Camden Society, XXIX, 1844)

Vergil 2: Polydore Vergil, *Anglica Historica AD 1485–1537*, ed. D. Hay (Camden Society, LXXXIV, 1950)

Wayment: H. Wayment, *The Windows of King's College Chapel* (1972)

Willis: R. Willis and J. W. Clark, *The Architectural History of the University of Cambridge and of the Colleges of Cambridge and Eton*, vol. I (1886)

Prologue

2   'immense marshes': B. Colgrave (ed.), *Felix's Life of St Guthlac* (1956), 87.

4   'Cambridge, by reason': H. Porter (ed.), *Erasmus and Cambridge* (1963), 80.

4   'Englishmen never consider': *L&P* II:1 (1515–18), ccix.

Chapter One: The Warring Kings

8   'his two half-brothers': M. R. James (ed.), *Henry the Sixth: a reprint of John Blacman's Memoir* (1919), 30.

9   'kneeling on his knee': Willis, 322.

11   'for the great devotion': Saltmarsh, 378, note 32.

11   'considering their own numbers': ibid., 377.

12   'In the east end': ibid., 369ff. for the full text of Henry's Will and Intent.

12   'stuff with jewels': J. Nichols, *Collection of Royal Wills* (1780), 315.

13   'overchargefull and noyous': B. Wolffe, *Henry VI* (2001), 245.

15   'a stuffed woolsack': ibid., 344.

16   'devout intention': Cooper, 229.

16   'to take stone-cutters': Willis, 472.

16   'towards the building of the church': ibid., 473.

Chapter Two: 'My Beloved Mother'

20   'I should be as glad': J. O. Halliwell (ed.), *Letters of the Kings of England*, vol. I (1848), 1.

20   'My dearest': A. Crawford (ed.), *Letters of the Queens of England* (1994), 150–1.

22   'She ceased not': Jones, 188.

22   'your confessor': Hymers, 163.

23   'heir to all King Henry's godly intentions': H. Lloyd, *The Early History of Christ's College* (1934), 288.

Chapter Three: A Royal Visit

29 'of sanguine cloth': Campbell, 497ff.

30 'of body but lean and spare': Vergil, 2, 145.

Chapter Four: 'Your Blessed Uncle'

36 'the blessed prince': Campbell, 205.

36 'his uncle's great work': Saltmarsh, 389.

37 'towards the building': Willis, 476. See Henry's accounts for the years 1505–9 in *PRO* E 36/214. Those for the earlier period are published in S. Bentley, *Excerpta Historica* (1831).

38 'your most holy uncle': J. Lewis, *The Life of Dr John Fisher* (1855), 20–4 for Fisher's speech.

39 'uncle of blessed memory': Willis, 476.

Chapter Five: The Glaziers' Craft

43 'a night and a day': Theophilus, *On the Various Arts*, ed. C. R. Dodwell (1986), 40.

44 'in Queen Elizabeth's time': G. H. Kenyon, *The Glass Industry of the Weald* (1967), 7, note.

45 'paper or linen cloth': William Horman, cited by L. F. Salzman, *Building in England down to 1540* (1952), 173.

46 'who has returned of late': *CPR*, 3 April 1449, 27 Henry VI, pt 2.

Chapter Six: Rainbow Round the Throne

55 'paved, glazed and painted': Colvin (1982), 224.

56 'a great red rose': H. H. Drake (ed.), *Halsted's History of Kent*, Part 1, *The Hundred of Blackheath* (1886), 86.

57 'to give praise': Astle, 16.

58 'sumptuous and solemn chapel': ibid., 6.

58 'the walls, doors, windows, arches and vaults' and other quotations from the king's will: ibid., 8.

Chapter Seven: Beasts and Badges

62 'a gentleman of Wales': Vergil, 1, 62.

64 'a royal rich red rose': Campbell, 41.

66 'for the changing of the Antelope': Jones, 84.

Chapter Eight: Southwark and its Aliens

70 'as little openly known sin': *L&P*, IV: 2 (1526–8), 1697, no. 3815, 18 January 1528.

70 'These great riches': Sneyd, 43.

71 'a natural drink for a Dutchman': A. Borde, *A Dyetary of Health* (Early English Text Society, 1906), 256.

72 'glazed some Windows thereof': J. Stow, *A Survey of London*, ed. C. K. Kingsford (1908; reprinted 1971), 272ff.

73 'without sleight, fraud or deceit': C. H. Ashdown, *A History of the Worshipful Company of Glaziers* (1919), 19–20.

74 'the Flemings there': J. L. Bolton, *The Alien Communities of London in the Fifteenth Century* (1998), 1.

74 'in great number': *Statutes*, vol. II: 1 Ric III cap. 9, 1484.

75 'from beyond the Sea': *Statutes*, vol. II: 1 Ric III cap. 12, 1484.

76 'how many are suspected': Kirk, xiii.

77 'the King to all': W. Page (ed.), *Letters of Denization and Acts of Naturalisation for Aliens in England 1509–1603* (Huguenot Society, VIII, 1893), ii.

78 'they have an antipathy': Sneyd, 23.

78 'filthiness, infection and pestilence': L. B. Luu, 'Assimilation or Segregation: Colonies of Alien Craftsmen in Elizabethan London', *Proceedings of the Huguenot Society* 26 (1994–7), 163ff., and citing *PRO*, SP 12/81/34.

Chapter Nine: The King's Glazier

81 'well expert and cunning': Angela Smith, 'Henry VII and the Appointment of the King's Glazier', *Journal of Stained Glass* 18:3 (1988), 259–61.

82   'for keeping certain of the king's manors': Oswald, 13.

83   'both for glass and workmanship': A. Oswald, 'The Glazing of the Savoy Hospital', *JBSMGP* 11 (1951–5), 227.

84   'more like unto a paradise': Gunn, 35, citing *BL*, Harleian MS 2252.

84   'most sumptuously': *L&P*, IV:1 (1526–8), 1871, no. 4251, 11 May 1528.

Chapter Ten: 'Unperfected and Unfinished'

86   'for the remission': Astle, 8.

87   'a strong chest': Willis, 477.

87   'wit quick and ready': Hymers, 136.

87   'they had all their pleasure': J. W. Blench, *Preaching in England in the Late Fifteenth and Sixteenth Century* (1964), 229.

89   'the King wishes': Pollard, 239.

89   'King Henry VI': Jones, 237–39.

89   'within the chapel': ibid.

90   'when they saw so much power': Vergil 2, 231.

90   'superfluity of too great curious works': Willis, 372.

Chapter Eleven: The First Phase

92   'all the windows': Willis, 479.

92   'that prince': ibid., 482.

93   'received of Mr Robert Hacomblen': ibid., 498.

93   'imagery of the story of the old law and of the new law': Wayment, 124.

100   'accordingly and after such manner': ibid., 123–5 for the 1526 contracts.

103   'Master Dierick': Dürer, 66, 81.

Chapter Twelve: 'Cunning in the Art of Glazing'

110   'a costly canopy': G. Chainey, 'The East End of King's College Chapel', *PCAS* 83 (1994), 141.

112   'I, Barnard Flower': Oswald, 21.

Chapter Thirteen: The Evil May Day

114 'So many Easterlings': Skelton, 144.

115 'the strangers were so proud': *L&P* II:1 (1515–18), ccxvi, April 1516.

115 'to the great hurt': Ransome, 13.

116 'the merchant strangers': M. Holmes, 'Evil May Day, 1517', *History Today* 15 (1965), 642ff.

116 'You were born in London': *L&P* II:1 (1515–18), ccxvi, April 1517.

116 'the strangers compass': ibid.

116 'their industry and of the emoluments': *L&P* II: 2 (1517), 1031, no. 3204, 5 May 1517.

117 'they commenced threatening': ibid.

117 'some men, some lads': ibid, 1045, no. 3529, 19 May 1517.

118 'And when the Cardinal': ibid.

Chapter Fourteen: Cloth of Gold

119 'double red and white roses': D. Starkey (ed.), *The Inventory of King Henry VIII*, 1, *The Transcript* (1998) and M. Hayward, *The 1542 Inventory of Whitehall, the Palace and its Keeper* (2004), *passim*.

121 'it is very wonderful': Dürer, 94.

122 'this burnished summer palace': *L&P* III:1 (1519–23), 266ff. The bills are listed at 331ff.

124 'glittering garments': B. Bradshaw and E. Duffy (eds), *Humanism, Reform and the Reformation* (1989), 220.

Chapter Fifteen: Galyon Hone, King's Glazier

126 'The world is nought': *L&P* XI (1536), 74, no. 168, 27 July 1536.

127 'the king's arms': Colvin, 155.

128 'What a great charge': Law, 161.

128 '30 of the King's and the Queen's arms': ibid.

128 'scriptures with the King's': ibid.

128 'in the two great': ibid.

128 'in gilt letters': ibid., 349.

129 'With turrets and towers': Skelton, 311.

Chapter Sixteen: Wolsey to the Rescue

131 'With images embossed': cited by Gunn and Lindley: Gunn, 35.

132 'for drink and other expenses': Cooper, 303.

132 'which were right good': Lady Margaret was writing on 24 April 1497 to the Earl of Ormond. A. Crawford (ed.), *Letters of the Queens of England* (1994), 151.

133 'zeal and energy': *L&P* IV:2 (1526–8), 2065, no. 4765, 22 September 1528.

Chapter Seventeen: 'Surely, Cleanly, Workmanly'

135 'the right worshipful master': Wayment, 123–25.

136 'as good and hable': R. Marks, *Stained Glass in England during the Middle Ages* (1993), 22.

136 'for the mending': S. Sandars, *Historical and Architectural Notes on Great St Mary's* (1869), 35.

Chapter Eighteen: Glaziers at War

144 'good order and true workmanship': *Statutes*, vol. III, 14 & 15 Henry VIII, cap. 2, 1523.

145 'a lamentable bill of complaint': Ransome, 15.

145 'Act ratifying a decree': *Statutes*, vol. III, 21 Henry VIII, cap. 16, 1530.

147 'they wish to accustom the people': *L&P* IV:1 (1526–8), 2177, no. 5016, 9 December 1528.

147 'they convey themselves': *Statutes*, vol. III, 22 Henry VIII, cap. 8, 1531.

Chapter Nineteen: The King's Great Matter

150 'he in whom': *L&P* IV:11 (1526–8), 1745, no. 3918, 12 February 1528.

150 'in building and repairs': ibid., 2177, no. 5016, 9 December 1528.

151 'desirous to know': Cooper, 337.

151 'all the world': D. R. Leader, *A History of the University of Cambridge*, vol. I (1988), 127.

154 'arrogance, temerity': *L&P*, IV (1524–30), cccclxxx, 1529.

155 'the holy bishop': *L&P*, VII (1534), 127, no. 296, 7 March 1534.

156 'the king has caused': ibid.

157 'so that there shall be': Hamilton, 87.

Chapter Twenty-One: The Hand of Fox

167 'when I hear my Colet': F. M. Nichols, *The Epistles of Erasmus*, vol. I (1901), 226.

Chapter Twenty-Two: Dissolution

175 'the new church': Willis, 497; and see *L&P*, XIV:II (1539), 347, no. 788 for the college's petition concerning its poverty.

178 'the only patron': Harrison, 15.

178 'never saw the book': *L&P*, XIII:II (1538), 410, no. 972, 1 December 1538.

179 'the images of Our Lady': Hamilton, 83.

180 'two arms of the king's': Colvin, 235.

180 'for glazing and repairing': *L&P*, XVI (1540–1), 358, no. 745.

182 'to protect the glass': Willis, 509.

Chapter Twenty-Three: Wives and Windows

184 'set in the old garlands': H. Wayment, 'Wolsey and Stained Glass' in Gunn and Lindley; see Gunn, 123.

185 'item for the translating': ibid., 121.

186 'we be delivered': Cooper, 391.

187 'scriptures with the king's word', Colvin, 71.

188 'Moses, a most godly': J. N. King, *Rethinking the Henrician Era* (1994), 83.

Chapter Twenty-Four: Continuing Hostilities

189 'be so good, Lord': Wayment, 125.

190 'infinite number of strangers': *Statutes*, vol. III, 32 HVIII cap. 16, 1540/1.

191 'lawfully and quietly': Ransome, 16.

192 'six honest Englishmen': ibid., 17.

193 'he could not tell': ibid., 19.

193 'to practise the feat' and 'weighty affairs': Wayment, 126.

194 'doubtful and not suitable': Ransome, 19.

195 'the sacrament of the altar': Hamilton, 113.

Chapter Twenty-Five: The King is Dead

197 'monuments of feigned miracles': C. Woodforde, *English Stained and Painted Glass* (1954), 38.

198 'preserving nevertheless': ibid., 39.

198 'all images, shrines, tabernacles': ibid., 38, citing Harrison.

199 'two panes': Willis, 509.

200 'by virtue of a pretended commission': T. Cooper (ed.), *The Journal of William Dowsing* (2001), 53.

201 'King's College, Dec. 26': ibid., 179.

201 '51 foot of glass': Willis, 511.

201 'nor was it any whit strange': ibid.

202 'it was a wonder': Cooper, op. cit. above, 30.

202 'the popish pictures': Law, 131.

Chapter Twenty-Six: Enlightenment

203 'the painted glass': G. Miège, *The Present State of Great Britain and Ireland* (1750), 23.

204 'considerable painters': H. Walpole, *Anecdotes of Painting in England* (1761), 67.

204 'a rose impaling a pomegranate': H. Walpole, *Description of the Villa of Mr Horace Walpole at Strawberry Hill* (1784), 16ff.

205 'a numerous family': H. Malden, *An Account of King's College Chapel* (1769), iiff.

208 'Mr Pugin's Opinion': *KA*: KCC 61/1, 16 September 1843.

210 'work of destruction': ibid. for copious correspondence between March 1850 and March 1853.

211 'he then and there': W. Clarke, 'America's First Stained Glass: William J. Bolton's Windows', *American Art Journal* XI:4 (1979), 34.

212 'to equal if not exceed': D. Morgan, *Great West Window* (1979), 8. And see *KA*: KCC 61/2 for full details of the project.

Finale

215 'inevitably led': James, 65.

216 'all horses shield': ibid., 216.

216 'A Night in King's College Chapel': *Ghosts and Scholars* 7 (1985).

217 'intelligent members of the college': Anon. [M. R. James], *Cambridge Review* (May 1892), 331.

218 'from which every part': James, 227.

219 'this unfortunate question': *KA*: KCC 61/3, letter dated 13 May 1896.

220 'An anxious question': G. McBryde (ed.), *Montague Rhodes James: Letters to a Friend* (1958), 137, letter of 14 April 1926.

222 'the fact that it is between friends': *KA*: KCC/66, letter dated 3 September 1940.

223 'the Chapel was colder': L. P. Wilkinson, *A Century of King's, 1873–1972* (1980), 103; and see KA: KCC/352 for the diagrams of how the windows were stored.

223 'We are slowly plunging': KA: KCC/66, letter dated 19 September 1940.

Index

Index